# IF YOU CAN'T REACH THEM YOU CAN'T TEACH THEM

Building effective learning relationships

## Endorsements

*'... your book ... is fully in my scheme of teaching philosophy and will be useful to many young teachers who are wondering about how to navigate a successful and rewarding career ... it gets my full attention and backing.'*

**Keith Elms**
Headteacher (retired), North Kesteven School
Managing Director (retired), Headstrong Educational Leadership Consultation

*'Hewitson has distilled a vast range of literature on pupil engagement and his own teaching and management experience into a highly practical handbook for all professionals and senior students.... Relationships are at the heart of good teaching and learning. In a knowledge-based economy we all need to be active, engaged learners. Hewitson shows us how to do that and to support our colleagues and students. I would love to see every school and workplace creating total quality management circles... using this book as their guide'.*

**Charlotte Davies NPQH, FRSA**
Tomatis Consultant
Director
Fit 2 Learn CIC

Our titles are also available in a range of electronic formats. To order, or for details of our bulk discounts, please go to our website www.criticalpublishing.com or contact our distributor, NBN International, 10 Thornbury Road, Plymouth PL6 7PP, telephone 01752 202301 or email orders@nbninternational.com.

# IF YOU CAN'T REACH THEM YOU CAN'T TEACH THEM

## Building effective learning relationships

### Kevin Hewitson

First published in 2021 by Critical Publishing Ltd

British Library Cataloguing in Publication Data
A CIP record for this book is available from the British Library

ISBN: 978-1-913453-13-8

This book is also available in the following e-book formats:
MOBI ISBN: 978-1-913453-14-5
EPUB ISBN: 978-1-913453-15-2
Adobe e-book ISBN: 978-1-913453-16-9

The right of Kevin Hewitson to be identified as the Author of this work has been asserted by him in accordance with the Copyright, Design and Patents Act 1988.

**Cartoon illustrations by Élisabeth Eudes-Pascal represented by GCI and Kevin Hewitson**

Cover and text design by Out of House Limited
Project management by Newgen Publishing UK
Printed and bound in Great Britain by 4edge, Essex

Critical Publishing
3 Connaught Road
St Albans
AL3 5RX

www.criticalpublishing.com

Paper from responsible sources

# CONTENTS

MEET THE AUTHOR - page vi

INTRODUCTION - page 1

**1.** THE CHALLENGES TEACHERS FACE - page 5

APPENDIX A: REFLECTION PROMPTS - page 20

APPENDIX B: INTERVENTION MIC OVERVIEW: ANALYSING CAPACITY - page 22

**2.** THE LEARNING RELATIONSHIP RESPONSIBILITY - page 24

**3.** MEETING LEARNING NEEDS - page 45

**4.** THE FOUR LEARNING NEEDS - page 64

APPENDIX C: GETTING TO KNOW YOUR PUPILS - page 96

APPENDIX D: PUPIL LEARNING PASSPORTS - page 97

**5.** PLANNING TO MEET AND MANAGE LEARNING NEEDS - page 98

APPENDIX E: MY TEACHING STRATEGIES - page 131

APPENDIX F: THE COIN CHALLENGE - page 135

**6.** MINDFUL LEARNING AND TEACHING - page 139

**7.** THE INDEPENDENT LEARNER - page 157

**8.** THE DANGERS OF LABELLING LEARNERS - page 173

**9.** THE LEARNING MAP - page 181

**10.** TIME MANAGEMENT - page 188

**11.** JOHN'S 12 RULES - page 199

**12.** LEARNING INTELLIGENCE - page 208

INDEX - page 219

# MEET THE AUTHOR

## KEVIN HEWITSON

I have over 40 years of experience in teaching and have held pastoral and subject lead posts as well as being an assistant principal responsible for learning strategies and influencing teaching and learning. My aim has always been to support teachers and to engage and challenge both high-performing learners and those who see learning as a challenge. I have taken this forward independently into my current role as an educational consultant and keynote speaker working with educational organisations, schools and teachers. I am a practical, innovative, strategic thinker who enjoys finding beneficial and creative solutions for improving teaching and learning.

My life's work has been teaching and learning; even when I stopped being a professional teacher nearly ten years ago. I have never stopped discussing, writing about or researching education and helping teachers and pupils. This book is an outcome of my experience.

# INTRODUCTION

This text is written with the honest aim of helping you to become a better teacher. This is a bold ambition but it gets to the bottom of what teaching is essentially about – helping others on their learning journey. The text is a mix of my experience, research and insights that I believe provide an effective narrative to learning and teaching.

The education our children receive has been at the forefront of parental and political interest for some time. As a profession we have been asked to raise standards and focus on the basics. There has been a call to emphasise the three 'R's and a continuing debate about the nature and need for a curriculum suited to the twenty-first century. Within all of this noise, we work at establishing relationships based on trust and understanding while, at the same time, trying to meet the pressure for improved standards and achievement. In addition, we are placed under scrutiny in ways that sometimes hinder rather than help us.

My aim is to help refocus on what it is we know makes the greatest difference to learning outcomes: the pupil–teacher learning relationship. And I will help you build these within the constraints with which you work.

I also want this book to become your learning journal, a personal space for reflection, observation, comment, inspiration and ideas. It can function as your personal travelling companion, one that helps you to remember there is always another way.

I hope you will personalise the text by recording your own insights and ideas, so jot down your thoughts and underline as much as you want! This is your journey. There are spaces for you to complete the reflective tasks and at the end of each chapter is a section entitled 'Your notes' for you to record your personal musings and ideas. These sections provide you the opportunity to fully engage with the text.

## A reflection framework

Reading is one thing, planning to put ideas into action is another. I know how hard it is when faced with a blank page to write things down and sort your ideas out, so I have developed a framework that may help you. Part of that framework is something called the 'MIC model' and it will help you manage your workload (see Appendix B for an adaptable MIC model proforma).

MIC stands for monitor, improve, change. It is a method of approaching change in a systematic way but, importantly, it considers the capacity you have for change. Using MIC you should consider monitoring 80 per cent, making improvements to 15 per cent and changing only 5 per cent of what you do at any one time. Consideration of the capacity for change is a key factor in making successful changes. Reflecting on your ideas and inspirations using the MIC approach and the information in Chapter 10 on time management will help you identify your priorities (5 per cent) and manage your challenges (80 per cent + 15 per cent).

# feedback

Another aspect of reflection and change is feedback, a term with which you will be familiar. At times in the book, I use the term *feedforward*. This is not a misprint, I was sharing some of my ideas with a Dutch colleague and friend when she offered me feedforward. Having never heard the term, I thought it may be a mistranslation of 'feedback' from Dutch to English. As she explained during her feedforward to me, feedforward is a specific strategy and, as I later discovered, attributed to Dr Marshall Goldsmith.

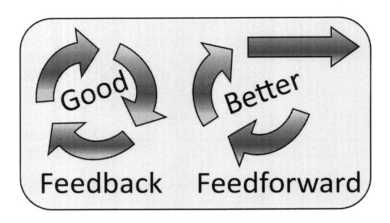

**Figure 0.1 Feedback and feedforward**

Figure 0.1 shows the principle of feedforward and how it compares with feedback. Feedback starts with what has been done or achieved. It is a review based in the past. There is an analysis of actions, strategies or the outcomes. Feedback is based on hindsight and can be accusatory because questions involving *why* often appear in the reviewing process. When we are asked *why* we naturally seek to defend what we have done. For example: '*Pupils' learning behaviour was not very good today. Why did you arrange for the class to sit in that way?*'

Here there are two defensive triggers. The first is a non-negotiated decision on the part of the observer with a negative accusation attached: '*behaviour was not very good*'. You can almost hear the inner dialogue on the part of the teacher who was observed; but defensive reactions stop us listening, stop us from engaging in the feedback process. The second trigger is the use of *why*. There is a suggestion that the decision by the teacher to arrange the pupils in that way was the cause of the poor behaviour. The decision or conclusion reached by the observer may not be shared by the teacher and so it will be countered, a defensive reaction once again. As for arranging the seating of pupils, I have known situations where the school sets a seating plan for all classes and had this been the case in this example, the teacher could have blamed the policy and not taken any responsibility for the outcome. The feedback overall would have achieved very little in terms of developing or improving practice and could have a negative effect on observer–teacher relationships and the level of respect held for the observer.

IF YOU CAN'T REACH THEM YOU CAN'T TEACH THEM

The defensive reactions we adopt to feedback limit our ability to listen, to embrace and to take in the comments or advice offered. Our memory of an event changes with the passing of time, so feedback needs to be timely to be most effective. Even if the feedback comes directly after a lesson observation, we may seek to protect ourselves from the comments by inwardly suggesting that the observer did not see everything and asking ourselves how a single observation can have any real merit. Where there are no strongly established relationships between those involved, feedback can result in a lack of respect or trust in those giving it as we seek ways to defend ourselves. This is in part due to the conclusive nature of feedback. Regardless of the person giving the feedback or their approach, you may feel on opposite sides. The feedback process can struggle to look forward because it means letting go of the past; something we are often reluctant to do.

## FEEDFORWARD

Feedforward is about moving forward, it is based on future actions or behaviours; what can be done next, working forward from where you are now. There needs to be recognition of what has gone before or has been produced. This needs to be agreed in the same way as in the feedback process. The difference is that this is a starting point not the end point. It is not about what has happened so much as what can be done. There is a different focus that affects any dialogue between the participants. It breaks the cycle of the feedback loop and strikes a forward path instead. The questions involved in feedforward are not so much about *why* but *how*. For instance: *'Looking back together at pupils' learning behaviours today, are there any changes you would make to bring about improvements?'*

This dialogue is reflected in the part played by the person offering the feedforward; they are on the journey with you. Feedforward involves both parties being creative, solving problems together. This personal investment is a key characteristic of feedforward and supports the building of relationships that can lead on to trust and mutual respect. Feedforward involves planning; there is a different clock at work from the one in feedback, driven by opportunity and enthusiasm about trying something new. Feedforward encourages objectivity. The 'Even better if' approach is more suited to feedforward since it builds on the past by requesting that we consider an alternative to our present situation and take from it only that which supports our learning.

## IN SUMMARY

Of course, feedback is an excellent way to support learning if done correctly but there is more opportunity to do it poorly than there is of providing poor feedforward. I would argue that putting yourself in the feedforward frame of mind can lead to a dialogue that involves greater objectivity and less defended ownership. The very nature of feedforward encourages you to think about the next step in the learning process. Consider these comments and see if you can see the influence of a feedforward thinking process.

- Measure what you achieved against what you set out to achieve. How successful were you and how will you take what you have learnt forward into your lesson planning?
- What message were you trying to get across today? OK, what I heard was... How can you close the gap next time between what it is you meant and what is heard?
- Now you have reached this point, where do you go from here? What resources or approach do you need to adopt in order to achieve the next step?
- What you are saying is important. How do you ensure others understand your message too?
- Knowing where you are now is important but how about where you need/want to be and how to get there?

I am not suggesting you replace all feedback with feedforward. What I am suggesting is that you can avoid some of the issues of poor feedback when you adopt a feedforward approach to the process of feeding back.

## Links within the book

To make accessing support material easy you will find a QR code at the end of each chapter. This can be scanned using your phone and will take you to a website featuring the links within this book as well as other resources.

Kevin Hewitson

PS: If you wish to send me a digital postcard or two as you progress through your learning journey then I am more than happy to receive them. You can contact me at:

Twitter: @4c3d

Email: kevin@ace-d.co.uk

## References and further reading

Education Technology and Mobile Learning (2015) *27 Reflective Strategies to Improve Your Teaching.* [online] Available at: www.educatorstechnology.com/2015/02/27-reflection-strategies-to-improve-your-teaching.html (accessed 1 November 2020).

Goldsmith, M (2015) *Try Feedforward Instead of Feedback.* [online] Available at: www.marshallgoldsmith.com/articles/try-feedforward-instead-feedback/ (accessed 1 November 2020).

Gonzalez, J (2018) *Moving from Feedback to Feedforward.* [online] Available at: www.cultofpedagogy.com/pod/episode-87/ (accessed 1 November 2020).

Hirsch, J (2017) *The Feedback Fix: Dump the Past, Embrace the Future, and Lead the Way to Change.* London: Rowman & Littlefield.

# I. THE CHALLENGES TEACHERS FACE

## Being a teacher

When I was studying to be a teacher in the mid-1970s, the three-year course had two components. The first was dedicated to subject knowledge and how to teach your subject. The second was named 'Education'. Each component carried equal weight, equal importance in assessing you as a teacher. 'Education' covered topics such as the history of education, child development and the theory and practice of learning. Along with teaching practice, this was our preparation for teaching. Looking back to the start of my career, I was prepared to teach but unprepared for the challenges of teaching. For example, why some classes were a pleasure to teach whereas others kept you on your toes; why even a change in the weather could result in unsettled behaviour; why a single pupil being 'off' meant a totally different classroom dynamic – these were more of a mystery to me. You learn to address such issues if you pay attention and work at your craft. As a teacher you realise that not all the challenges come from the classroom. Some are intrinsically linked to the nature and character of the school's environment and systems. It can be difficult for those outside the teaching profession to understand the full impact of the challenges teachers now face and how these can affect well-being, social life and relationships with the pupils. You can be reassured that, if you remain a learner throughout your teaching career, you will find the solutions to these challenges and continue to grow as a teacher.

### RELATIONSHIPS COUNT

There is a saying that, when buying a house, it is all about location, location, location. I would argue that in teaching, it is all about relationships, relationships, relationships. You cannot underestimate the importance of relationships in learning. Many adults talk of a favourite subject in school and, often, it has something to do with the relationship they had with the teacher who taught them. I have talked to trainee teachers and asked why they want to become a teacher. Frequently, they answer '*I was inspired by a teacher*'. I have also known a relationship with a teacher to continue into adulthood. If a teacher remains in a school for long enough, it is not unusual for that teacher to teach a generation of pupils' offspring. I have come to understand that building positive relationships with pupils is the first step to becoming an effective and respected teacher. I also know this is one of the most demanding aspects of teaching. A number of the challenges you face as a teacher, both inside and outside the classroom, can directly impact your ability to build and maintain effective learning relationships with your pupils. Put simply, if you can't reach your pupils you can't teach them. It is important for you to explore these challenges; the things that get in the way of teaching and yet are part of it. It is important you understand them fully and their impact on you as a teacher. In this way, you can build effective learning relationships no matter what the circumstances. My mentor would say '*in all weathers*' and if you have taught a class during a windy, rainy day you will know what he meant. (He claimed horses and pupils were a lot alike when it came to the weather; both would cause a fuss if it was unsettled!)

## SURVIVING OR THRIVING?

How you feel and how you act and react as a teacher say a lot about where you are, your relationships, state of mind, if you are still learning or just getting by. Recognising when you are struggling is important. As with many things in life, you can learn to cope with difficult situations. Coping strategies can lead to surviving, of just getting by, rather than thriving. Without doubt it is more fun, more enjoyable, and teaching becomes much easier, if you are thriving.

I have come across and worked with both categories of teacher: those who are thriving and those who are merely surviving. In each case, I find these teachers will display certain characteristics or behaviours. I have experienced times in my career when I was thriving and times I was merely surviving, so I know how to recognise the behaviours in myself, too. I accept we can move from one state to another and that we may express behaviours that are representative of both states at the same time. We do not live, work or teach in a vacuum and we each have a range of relationships, stresses and responsibilities that impact on our lives and the roles we have. Pressures at home can affect your behaviour in the classroom in the same way it can affect the behaviour of your pupils. Take a moment to reflect on the behaviours you may see in yourself or colleagues when surviving and when thriving.

### Surviving

Surviving teachers:

- are not always good at taking the stage, of being in control, when engaging with a class;
- do not take enough time for themselves;
- neglect to recognise and celebrate their achievements;
- fail to reach out and congratulate other teachers often enough, if at all;
- take work home or give up holidays to catch up but often bring it back untouched;
- appear as though they are always busy with the business of teaching and do not reflect enough in order to work smarter;
- have little or no capacity to take on change;
- stick to routine and stay within their comfort zone as much as possible;
- have muted relationships with their pupils and sometimes with colleagues;
- are not in a state of relaxed awareness (in Japanese martial arts this is called 'Zanshin').

IF YOU CAN'T REACH THEM YOU CAN'T TEACH THEM

*Thriving*

Thriving teachers:

- continue to be learners and share what they have learnt;
- motivate pupils through their enthusiasm and passion for teaching and learning;
- are able to be objective about their teaching and consider feedforward openly;
- look constantly for new ideas and are innovative;
- have a good work–life balance and maintain healthy relationships with those in their lives;
- engage actively in celebrating the achievement of their pupils and colleagues;
- are respected by their pupils and have good learning relationships;
- are fully aware of what is going on in every corner of the classroom.

## ❖ Reflective task

1. Are there any behaviours that you would add or disagree with? Perhaps you already recognise some in the ways you behave or in how other teachers are behaving around you. Take a moment to reflect and list those behaviours that best describe your present situation – remember there can be a mix.

2. Whichever way you see your present situation, either thriving or surviving, see if you can identify a colleague who, in your opinion, is in an opposite state to your own and list their behaviours.

## ❖ Reflective task review

In completing this exercise, you have begun to think about your teaching and the challenges you face in an objective manner. You have begun to explore what it means to be a teacher other than from a sense of pedagogy or subject knowledge.

Balance

While the negative impact of 'just surviving' on the quality of your teaching (and your health) is obvious, you need to be aware that thriving can have its negative aspects too. Perhaps *too much of a good thing* is another way of putting it. Teacher burnout is a recognised phenomenon these days and it can be brought on by surviving as well as by thriving. Taking on too much can be as harmful as not doing enough. Being in touch with, and being honest about, your feelings are important parts of getting the work-life balance right and of being an effective teacher.

# The dynamics of teaching

Dr Emma Kell (2018) analysed 3, 684 responses from teachers, former teachers and education professionals between March and July 2016 and expressed her findings under the format: '*If UK schools had 100 educators...*' There is a comprehensive list of responses but I have chosen a couple that relate to the dynamics of teaching. The statistics show:

- 57 would not recommend teaching to a close friend or relative;
- 88 would say they enjoy teaching in the classroom.

I find this almost contradictory. If you enjoyed something, you would recommend it to your friends or family. This not only shows the dynamics of teaching, the highs and lows and range of challenges, but also the need for you to have a good understanding of the many aspects of teaching and how they impact on you as a teacher. Since 88 enjoy teaching in the classroom, this indicates to me how much effective learning relationships add to the enjoyment and fulfilment of purpose we receive as teachers. The lack of recommendation of teaching as a profession points to other factors that add to the challenges of teaching from outside of the classroom. A key factor in this, the role of leadership, is examined in the next chapter.

One further statistic Dr Kell gives us is that:

- 82 would say they experience anxiety directly related to the job.

This underlines why it is important to understand how you behave and why. Anxiety does little to make something enjoyable. Of course, we may all experience a sinking feeling sometimes. Perhaps it's the anticipation just before a certain group on the last lesson of a Friday afternoon when they have just had PE and it is raining. You know you need to bring your best game to the session, but even then it will be challenging.

As teachers we are good at:

- shrugging off feeling low as soon as we take to the stage;
- taking on more and not making enough time for ourselves;
- failing to recognise or celebrate our achievements;

- forgetting to reach out and congratulate other teachers enough;
- taking work home, giving up holidays and arranging after-school catch-up activities.

It seems we are always busy with the business of teaching, but we love it when the lesson flows. There is a certain beat to it that you recognise as learning taking place and it's what motivates you. Your relationships, feelings and behaviours are all interlinked; one purpose of this book is to show you how to manage those links successfully.

## EXPLORING FEELINGS

I, like you, have asked people how they are many hundreds of times. We greet people all the time with '*How are you?*' and they reply '*Fine, and you?*' and we say '*Fine*'. It's a type of dance, a ritual of sorts, because we may not really want to know how people are but we go through the motions. When you are in teaching mode, however, it is different. You really do want to know because you acknowledge that how people feel is important to how you teach and to their ability to learn.

## Personal reflection

During a challenging time in my career as an assistant principal, I became very much aware of my feelings and those of the staff I was working with and the pupils we were teaching. I was being drained. In one of my weekly line management meetings, and with typical teacher reserve, I expressed how worn out and exhausted I felt. I said '*I am a very unhappy professional*'. This was a cry for help which was ignored by my line manager. I felt totally deflated, depressed even. I had opened up as best I could, and I felt let down. This was a turning point that later had significant impact on me and on my career. It could have been avoided had my words, my attempt to express my feelings, been questioned or even just acknowledged. Reflecting on this moment, I am aware how important it is to build an understanding relationship with colleagues too. Someone who knew me well would have recognised the significance of what I said and how difficult it was for me to express such feelings. A key skill of a teacher is to listen, to the words as well as the silences, of your colleagues and your pupils.

## ❖ Reflective task

Take a moment to reflect on your own feelings. How would you describe your feelings right now?

## UNDERSTANDING OUR BEHAVIOURS

Teachers, on the whole, are a dedicated bunch. Unless you unmask this dedication you will find it hard to understand what drives your behaviours and, in turn, to understand what drives the behaviours of your pupils. In many instances, behaviour is the result of a need we are trying to fulfil. It is only through understanding what drives your behaviours that you will go on to recognise your needs. For example, if you are feeling hungry your need is for food and you will go looking for something to eat. If you are feeling lonely, your need is to socialise and you will go looking for company. How we fulfil a need can be a complex process and is determined by agency, experience and past success rates. In his work on *Choice Theory*, William Glasser (1998, p 335) says '*All we can do from birth to death is behave*'. This is something I have come to understand in terms of teaching. I know that if I add my energy to a class that is just ticking over, then progress will accelerate. I also know if I add too much energy to an already excited class, the outcome can be far from desirable and I am better off adopting a calming energy. I know that if my pupils are feeling relaxed in my company, then my teaching behaviours are also relaxed and I can be myself. This is a situation that requires much less effort or energy on my part to maintain a positive learning environment. I can affect their behaviour through my own. What triggers the behaviour, what sits behind it, is what is interesting from a teaching perspective.

Your own behaviour as a teacher is not only driven by your needs but by those of your pupils. Once you recognise this, then you can start to see behaviour as a symptom of a set of learning needs and, where you are able to, address the need. Later chapters encourage you to see key learning needs within the teaching and learning context and then plan how these needs can be met in order to build effective learning relationships with your pupils.

# How are your Sundays?

The best way I find to explore challenges and their impact on feelings and behaviours, when working with teachers, is to delve into how you feel before Monday comes around. Apart from your behaviours, how you feel about the week or term ahead is a good indicator of how well you are managing the challenges of teaching, if you have good learning relationships with your classes, and whether you are surviving or thriving. Why Sunday? Well, Monday is the start of the formal teaching week. I say formal because, as you know, teaching never really stops. You never stop thinking, planning, ruminating, reflecting, editing, marking and resourcing. In short, you never stop the business of being a teacher. So, Sunday is most probably when high levels of anxiety can exist as you anticipate Monday morning.

How you feel as a teacher probably varies between exuberant and worn out. As a teacher, you will certainly experience the emotional highs and lows in life. You probably look forward to some lessons and find it harder to motivate yourself for others. However, nothing is predictable in teaching. It can take the slightest thing to change the character of a lesson. I am never quite sure why, on some days, groups are a joy to teach but, at other times, they are a struggle. It's as if I am being tested and, occasionally, they just want to know how far I will go along with them or to see if I am on top of my game. As I have reflected on the needs of pupils, I have begun to think that such challenges are also their way of being reassured that I still care about them. I like to think they are just checking all is still OK between us.

There are, however, signs I recognise in myself, and have seen in others, which point to more significant issues to be addressed. When we lose our perspective, when our own needs are not met, we struggle. Why this happens and what to do about it are two of the reasons behind this book. It is good that neither is as complicated or as difficult as you might think.

In November 2018, Ofsted (the Office for Standards in Education, Children's Services and Skills) presented their interim findings of the *Teacher Well-Being and Workload Survey*, in which they concluded that '*Concerns about the well-being of teachers are well founded*', and mentioned that '*teaching is one of the three professions with the highest reports of stress and anxiety*'. They listed a series of negative influences on staff well-being associated with '*the lack of*' certain things. I think that as you look through the list below, you will recognise a few. More importantly, four (in bold) out of the six are the focus of this book and I am confident you will find a way to address them using the knowledge and strategies presented within these pages.

- Lack of support to manage **behaviour**.
- Lack of **time**.
- Lack of money/budget/funding.
- Lack of resources.
- Lack of **communication**.
- Lack of a **work-life balance**.

## Personal reflection

A school asked that I coach a struggling teacher by helping her to build effective learning relationships. She had in the past been regarded as a good teacher but was now having problems with pupil behaviour, time management, communication and her work-life balance was causing her stress. Here is what she said when I asked her to evaluate our time together and after the school had reported a very successful outcome.

*I have a different approach to teaching. I work smarter, and when I started to believe in the strategies, and wanted them to work, they did, to my surprise. It felt good. All of a sudden, I got respect. I learnt that it was OK to say no; that I had a right to be heard and that not everything requires 100 per cent effort. Most importantly, I started to respect myself, and my own time. It is about balance. It is about 'What's best for me?' I have begun to change my work–life ratio, and am still working on it.*

You can access the coaching article and full evaluation via the link at the end of the chapter (Advocating Creativity, 2013).

# Monday morning

I am aware of well-being questionnaires that are significantly more sophisticated than asking how you feel before the week ahead, how you feel about Monday morning. However, simplicity can be an advantage at times. Figure 1.1 shows a grid I have used to start a conversation about the challenges teachers face and how well they are doing at managing them. Try the exercise and see if it gives you pause for thought.

## ❖ Reflective task

Using the grid in Figure 1.1, place a cross where your vocational drive, the motivation you feel for teaching, and the anxiety level you experience as you approach the week ahead coincide. There are no right or wrong answers to this exercise, only an honest representation of your feelings.

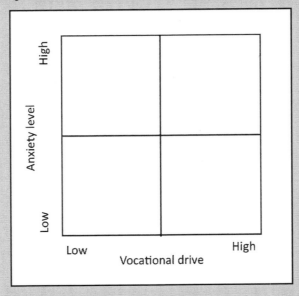

**Figure 1.1 Anxiety and drive**

Now use the space below to note down a few words or phrases that describe best how you feel about the week ahead.

Finally, look back at what you have written and the cross in Figure 1.1 and put a circle where you would like to be. Does the circle encompass the cross or are they in different positions? What does this suggest to you about how you are managing the challenges of teaching?

## ❖ Reflective task review

If your circle envelopes your cross and both are in the low anxiety zone then, depending on your vocational drive, the challenges may come from:

- refreshing your learning relationships in order to raise your vocational drive; or

- adjusting your work–life balance in order to have more time for yourself.

If your circle does not encompass your cross then, depending where they fall, you will face a different set of challenges. If you have registered your cross in the high anxiety zone, then you need to consider if you:

- could work at improving your learning relationship with your pupils;

- have the resources you need to teach;

- are doing too much for your pupils, perhaps due to taking too much responsibility for the learning outcomes (high anxiety and vocational drive);

- are receiving too little professional satisfaction for some reason (high anxiety and low vocational drive).

Whatever your response, I know from talking with teachers that it is easy to say you enjoy your teaching and it is also easy to dread your teaching, or at least some aspects of it. It is not always a straightforward case of love it or hate it. I also know that this exercise will cause you to think, to take stock and consider how to move forward. As you have seen in the '*lack of*' list from the *Teacher Well-Being and Workload Survey*, tensions do exist and you need to acknowledge and understand them if you are to maintain a healthy balance in your professional and personal lives.

You have to accept that teaching is a complex process, in part because learning is part of teaching too. If teaching was easy would you get so much from it when it all goes according to plan? Teaching is a full-on activity and will take as much time and energy as you are either willing or able to put into it. But when the teaching and your relationships with your classes go well you can get so much energy back that it can inspire and motivate you to do more. When it goes wrong and the pupils do not engage in the learning, then it is an uphill struggle. You may risk losing perspective or may find it hard to initiate those actions that will help you rise above the challenges. This is one of the reasons effective learning relationships are so important.

## RELATIONSHIPS AND FEELINGS

How you feel and how your pupils feel about meeting each other, or about a lesson, are connected. Pupils are adept at picking up on the small signals you may give off when you meet them. This is one of the reasons I always encourage teachers to welcome pupils to their lessons. If you look forward to the lesson and show it then, more than likely, your pupils will too.

## RESPONDING TO CHALLENGES

A key challenge you face as a teacher is to avoid confrontation and encourage willing engagement. Pupils will always test the boundaries; it is their nature and possibly should be yours too. How you respond to those challenges defines you as a teacher. I have found that if you have an effective learning relationship with the pupil, then you avoid confrontation, achieve willing engagement and even observe a stronger motivation to learn.

## SO WHY MIGHT YOU DREAD MONDAYS?

The reflective task above may give you some indication of the answer to this question. It could be the amount of work looming, the parent consultation sessions or any number of non-teaching tasks that form part of your role and responsibilities. In my experience, at the heart of it all is the relationship you have with your pupils. This relationship is a dynamic one and subject to a number of influences. Any relationship can, and will, affect what you do and why you do it. You also need to be mindful of the fact that any relationship is two-way; it involves another party and you cannot change what pupils are exposed to in other relationships or past experiences. All you can do is provide a consistently safe and regulated environment in which they know the rules, rituals and practices. It is an advantage if the whole school adopts the same rules, rituals and practices but you should also have sufficient flexibility to express your own character and be innovative.

IF YOU CAN'T REACH THEM YOU CAN'T TEACH THEM

# ON THE OTHER HAND, 'MONDAYS ARE OK'

It not as easy to analyse why you may not feel anxious about Monday but, once again, it is about the relationship you have with your pupils. You may question whether you should be concerned at all if you are not feeling any anxiety about the week ahead. The short answer is: it depends. Your feelings are very much linked to the nature of the relationships you have with your pupils. Although challenging relationships may bring anxiety, at least you are being challenged; it may be raw but it is out in the open and you know the situation you are facing. On the other hand, a lack of anxiety could suggest a very one-sided relationship where the pupils are passive, even compliant, and do not offer any challenge.

Some level of challenge in teaching is important. It adds energy to the process of learning and provides signposts that there is pupil engagement. Your relationship with your group will shape the nature of that challenge. Where you are meeting pupils' learning needs, the challenges will be those of clarification and extension to the learning. Meeting their learning needs will mean pupils will feel comfortable in the environment you create and confident to approach you, to ask questions and to offer their own ideas and insights. You are guiding the learning, but the pupils are experiencing it. Any anxiety you feel is born of the positive relationship you have with your pupils and is founded in a sense of responsibility. Where you are not meeting learning needs, it creates a sense of insecurity and an anxiety among pupils that is more intense.

If you do not experience a level of challenge in your teaching, then you have to ask yourself a question about your relationship with your pupils. Pupils may be compliant but learner compliance is not the same as learner engagement. You may not be challenged in the way I have described earlier and, instead, it may feel rather comfortable. Routine and familiarity may best describe the character of the week you face. You are in your comfort zone, but are probably not stretching your pupils or building learning relationships that will prepare them for when they do face challenges. It is easy to go along in your comfort zone and resist change but moving out of your comfort zone is where the magic happens (see Figure 1.2).

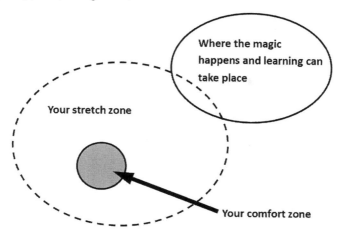

**Figure 1.2 Comfort zone**

I had the opportunity to ask Sir Ken Robinson (famed for his promotion of creativity in education) at a Festival of Education conference if compliance was a learning disability. He answered: '*No, but it is a disadvantage.*' It is a disadvantage, then, to both the teacher and the pupil – for teaching and learning go hand in hand.

Some pupils are quick to learn that compliance offers them a quiet life; they can pass through the day without challenge or commitment. Some also learn that if they wait long enough, the teacher will often fill the space with another question or move on to another pupil or offer the answer themselves. This does little to build learning relationships or to develop pupils' capacity to learn.

The learning relationship is based on meeting learning needs but it also offers you a vehicle to discuss the feelings that arise if those needs are not met. A teacher who understands this can both reach their pupils and teach them.

## Personal reflection

I started my teaching career in an ex-grammar school and over the road was the old secondary modern, both now comprehensives. Both schools had retained many of the same teachers and much of the character and local reputation of their earlier designations. My teaching focus at that time was very much subject-content based. Apart from a few, pupils were mainly quietly compliant and polite and those who were not were easily suppressed with a look or a word. My second school was a rural comprehensive and the nature of the pupils was laid back. I learnt that you could push but only so much at a time. As long as they liked and trusted me, then I could build a banter that allowed me to challenge them. My teaching was still very much subject-content focused although I had begun to understand the need to build relationships. It was in my third school where I began to embrace fully the need for building relationships first and delivering the curriculum later. This was an inner-town school in central England. On hearing that I was going for interview, a colleague who knew the school by reputation said to me: '*Don't go there Kev, you are too nice to go there!*' However, I am very glad I did for if I had not, I doubt I would have spent so much time learning to reach my pupils before I could teach them or embarked on this particular learning journey – a journey that has continued to this day.

## How could things be any better?

If you are taking everything in your stride, you may ask how could things be any better?

Consider how energised you feel after teaching a session or group of pupils. I find energy will undoubtedly carry me through the week no matter the hurdles or challenges ahead. You may be in a supportive school environment with compliant learners who suit your approach as a teacher. Or you may have, through experience and effort, managed to find a way to teach that works for you and your pupils.

The level of energy you have, reflected in your vocational drive engine (Figure 1.1), is a good way to determine what type of relationship you have with your pupils. A good teacher–pupil relationship will provide a positive energy that enhances your vocational drive, adding to your motivation. A poor relationship will provide negative energy that exhausts you and lessens your vocational drive, reducing your motivation.

There are always ways of improving how you teach, becoming more efficient and focused, and developing new ways and approaches. There are ways you can help pupils to become independent learners and ways you can make your teaching even better. As teachers, we should always see ourselves as learners. I would go as far as saying once we stop being learners, we stop being teachers.

## Time management

No chapter on the challenges teachers face can be complete without acknowledging how personally demanding teaching can be, how much time can be spent being a teacher. One area I often receive requests for from teachers is the challenge of time management, of finding more time. This includes *me time*, time to do things outside of school, time to relax, time to recharge the batteries. This can be as big a challenge to teaching as anything involved in preparing for Monday. It can certainly lead to many of the same outcomes, such as feeling tired, stressed or just worn out. Making time for you is as important as lesson planning and any other aspect of teaching. For this very reason, I have included a chapter specifically on time management and what I call the 'not enough time' equation. A hidden consequence of you feeling that you do not have enough time is the effect this has on the pupils you are teaching. Remember that not only are you teaching, you are also modelling learning behaviour.

## My reflections

Reflect on the points and issue raised in this chapter. In Appendix A you will find reflective prompts and a template which you can photocopy and fill in to use with any reflective tasks or in the *Your notes* section at the end of each chapter.

## What next?

The next chapter is about responsibility; responsibility for building learning relationships and responsibility for learning. We have talked about building learning relationships and about learning needs but not about how they work together and the ratio of responsibility each partner in the learning must take and when. You need to understand the teacher–learner relationship within the context of the school, with all of the demands and pressures that exist within that environment, if you are to manage learning relationships effectively.

## References and further reading

Advocating Creativity (2013) *How Can a Specialist Teaching Coach Help You?* [online] Available at: https://4c3d.wordpress.com/2013/12/26/how-can-a-specialist-teaching-coach-help-you/ (accessed 1 November 2020).

Glasser, W (1998) *Choice Theory.* London: HarperCollins.

Holt, J (1974) *How Children Fail.* London: Pelican Books.

Kell, E (2018) *How to Survive in Teaching without Imploding, Exploding or Walking Away.* London: Bloomsbury.

Ofsted (2018) *Teacher Well-Being and Workload Survey.* [online] Available at: https://educationinspection.blog.gov.uk/2018/11/30/teacher-well-being-and-workload-survey-interim-findings/ (accessed 1 November 2020).

Smith, N C (2012) *Choosing How to Teach and Teaching How to Choose.* Seattle, WA: Bennett & Hastings Publishing.

QR link

IF YOU CAN'T REACH THEM YOU CAN'T TEACH THEM

Your notes

# Appendix A
# REFLECTION PROMPTS

Reflection prompts include those that form tasks based on your reading and those that form questions requiring deeper reflection, for example.

- Chapter X caused me to think about how this links with what I have seen/experienced when...
- This is an area I need to...
- This reminds me of...
- My key learning points from this topic are...
- My key words or phrases linked to this topic are...
- Things I need to reflect on further...
- Things I need to research...
- Things to talk about to colleagues...
- In my experience...
- How might this affect my teaching?
- What is the situation in my own teaching now and what evidence do I have?
- Have I experienced anything similar to what is discussed in this chapter/section?
- Which points would I disagree/agree with?
- How would this improve my teaching?

## Change prompts

After saying why you are considering making a change the prompts form a series of questions.

- Why I am considering changing (describe the change then give your main reason)?
- What changes shall I make and why?
- Can I do this on my own or do I need to share this challenge/change?
- What resources do I need (time, equipment, access etc)?
- What will success look like (today, tomorrow, in a week or a month's time)?
- How shall I celebrate and share success?
- What might I have to give up by taking on change?
- What would motivate me to give this a try?

# Reflection template

MY REFLECTIONS ON SECTION/CHAPTER: _____

MY INITIAL THOUGHTS ON WHAT I HAVE READ ARE:




SOMETHING I MAY TELL A COLLEAGUE:




SOMETHING I MAY DO IN MY TEACHING:

# Appendix B
# INTERVENTION MIC OVERVIEW: ANALYSING CAPACITY

| TO WHAT EXTENT IS THE SCHOOL PREPARED TO INITIATE OR DEVELOP A CHANGE AIMED AT: |
| --- |
| STUDENT SELECTION |
| SUCCESS DESCRIPTORS |
| PARTICIPATION |
| CHARACTERISTICS OF INTERVENTION |
| INVOLVEMENT |
| MONITORING |
| RELATIONSHIP BUILDING<br>The time and effort given to building relationships with those involved in the intervention, before, during and after. |

→

IF YOU CAN'T REACH THEM YOU CAN'T TEACH THEM

**CO-ORDINATION WITH OTHER INTERVENTIONS**

**RESOURCES**

**REWARDS**

**FEEDBACK/FEEDFORWARD ARRANGEMENTS**

**PARENT INVOLVEMENT**

**TIMEFRAME**

**GROUP STATUS**
How the whole school views those involved in the intervention, the degree of regard they are held in.

**CONTINGENCY**

**LEGACY**

# 2. THE LEARNING RELATIONSHIP RESPONSIBILITY

## The context of relationships

As soon as two or more people are in the same space, there is a dynamic at play: a relationship. Even without a spoken word, we work at trying to understand the other person and to build a relationship of some form. Will we be friends or foes? Can we trust each other or not? The 'when, where, how and why' we meet all have an influence on how the initial relationship is formed, its character and how it develops. As I have found in teaching, even the most casual of meetings or interactions with a pupil, whether in or out of the classroom, can begin to establish a relationship. I have also found that the people involved may not see the relationship in the same terms or have the same understanding of it. There is not always a mutual understanding of the dynamic and the part each should play within that relationship. You will find that the space, the environment, can have a significant impact on a relationship. An initial confrontational encounter can define a relationship just as a harmonious one may. We are unable to come away from an encounter without forming an opinion, even if it is neutral. There is much that we do and, in some cases don't do, that helps to form an initial relationship. We can be influenced by a look or the way somebody moves. I have also found that after forming an initial relationship, it takes more effort to build a constructive one from an initially confrontational dynamic than it does to build on one based on mutual respect. First impressions count in the school environment as much as they do anywhere else, if not more so, since the relationship between the teacher and pupil is critical to an effective and positive learning experience.

### THE TEACHER-PUPIL RELATIONSHIP

No relationship exists within a vacuum and the teacher-pupil relationship must exist within the school community and its structures, rules and practices. The critical point at which the teacher-pupil relationship and learning come together is in the lesson. For learning to take place, each person must engage positively in the process. This is most easily demonstrated by the nature of the relationship between those involved.

Typically, in a school environment, we would find one teacher to a number of pupils and we would define this as the class. The classroom, however, can be defined not just by walls or buildings but by this very relationship. Classes can be as small as a few pupils or as large as hundreds. They may be the physical assembly of teacher and pupils, or virtual as with online learning situations. Schools exist in all shapes and sizes, each with its own character, mission or vision statement, set of values and expectations that sit as a mantle over the teacher-pupil learning relationship. They define the environment in which the school must function. The expectation and hope is that this environment benefits both teacher and pupil; that it provides for creating and maintaining effective learning relationships.

As a teacher, I know that my relationship with a class can be finely balanced, especially in the early days of a new term or year when we are getting to know each other. This is when class management, the setting of routines and expectations, plays an important part in helping to create the opportunity for positive relations to be formed. I also know that the balance can be disturbed easily by the addition of a new member to the class or the actions of a single pupil. It is not uncommon for a single pupil to affect the balance of an entire year group or for several pupils to have an impact on the entire school. How other pupils are brought into an existing relationship needs careful management if the balance is to be maintained. You should be mindful of this.

## Personal reflection

At one point in my career, I was involved in a town-wide reorganisation of the education system from three-tier to two-tier. Here I outline the situation I faced and how it helped me understand the complexity of the school environment and its impact on teacher–pupil relationships.

The change, which resulted in the loss of middle schools, was not universally popular and there was some parental and pupil reluctance to engage with the new system. Not all new school buildings were ready or built in time for the new term and ad hoc arrangements existed in some schools like my own. My own upper school, after being closed in July, opened as a new secondary school the following September. Demolition and building work carried on as we opened the new school on the site using a combination of the previous buildings, new, temporary and modified accommodation. It was not a smooth transition.

In terms of pupils and staff, the new school was approximately twice the size that any pupils had experienced in their upper or middle schools. This environment also presented challenges associated with teaching resources, staff and pupil movement, noise, pupil and parental anxiety and the management of the school day in general. Much of this work was carried out in an environment that was evolving on a daily basis.

The change alone would have been a challenge but the resulting additional turbulence had a negative impact on many of the basic aspects of the school community. Pupil absence and staff illness were two almost immediate consequences along with poor pupil behaviour and others that I would later associate with a breakdown in aspects of the teacher–pupil relationship.

The intensity of the challenges faced by staff and pupils demonstrated how important it is that we understand the teacher–pupil relationship. I learnt a great deal about how people behave when they do not feel part of something or cannot express their feelings or influence what is happening to them. Much of what I learnt through this intense period of change informed my professional development, my research and ultimately, through reflection and insights, this book.

The change came at a cost not dissimilar to challenges for teacher retention and recruitment in schools today. It is hard not to make the link between relationships and behaviours.

# Relationship co-dependence

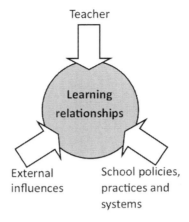

**Figure 2.1 Basic influences on the learning relationship**

What happens in the classroom is part of what happens in the school; one relationship affects the other. If you understand this you will be better placed to understand the drivers behind some of your pupils' behaviour.

The school and the teacher share a responsibility for building and maintaining learning relationships. One of the challenges you face is that you are not immune from any policies or practices dictated by your school's leadership and governing body. There are also external influences at work, for example imposed political or governmental policies and ideologies.

How the school responds to and manages these external influences determines many of the conditions under which you must build effective learning relationships. In addition, you must not forget the pupil and their parents (see Figure 2.2).

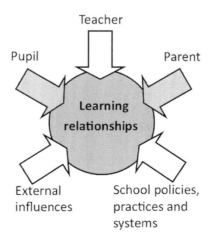

**Figure 2.2 Extended influences on the learning relationship**

IF YOU CAN'T REACH THEM YOU CAN'T TEACH THEM

How much responsibility should each party accept for building and supporting the learning relationship? In reality we must accept that the level of responsibility and, indeed, the timing of responsibility, in this relationship is a dynamic one; it changes according to the learning circumstances.

External influences such as standards or regulatory bodies will influence school policies and practices. Ideally, changes will be timed ahead of the academic year to give the school time to respond. Although planning is in place, at times you will need to react instantly to such challenges. The closer you get to the actual teaching, the fewer the players involved and the greater the responsibility each holds.

# Those involved in the learning relationship

Later in the chapter I describe a simple model to allow us to explore the learning relationship over time, but first let's look at the dynamics and responsibilities of those involved.

## THE PUPIL

We can place the pupil and the teacher within the circle that defines the learning relationship (Figure 2.1) for there is a direct and dynamic interplay between them. Others who hold responsibilities operate outside this direct interaction.

As for the pupil, I doubt any pupil would say they had any responsibility for the learning relationship other than perhaps doing as they are told or doing their classwork/homework. While teachers may wish for pupils to do as they are told, the learning relationship requires more than compliant behaviour, it requires engagement in learning. In order to engage in learning we have certain needs, beyond feeling safe, that must be satisfied. Meeting these needs is central to the learning relationship. There is much we can do in schools to promote pupil responsibility, including providing the opportunity to develop pupil agency (problem-solving skills) and the language to express needs in a way that avoids conflict.

## THE TEACHER

In addition to managing pupils, it is accepted that the teacher has the responsibility for lesson planning, delivery and for assessing the learning that takes place. They also have a key responsibility, that of building learning relationships.

In England, the Department for Education (2011) has set out a set of *Teachers' Standards*. Having the teacher's responsibility defined by a set of standards is helpful but we may ask who is actually responsible for learning? We can lead a pupil to knowledge, but can we make him or her learn? It is not just any behaviour the teacher has to promote or manage effectively; it is the learning behaviour and this requires an effective learning relationship.

## THE SCHOOL

Schools have leadership teams, those who are tasked to manage those who form the organisation's active elements. Typically, schools have a hierarchical structure for this purpose with a headteacher or principal directing a leadership team and in turn class or subject teachers. The actions of school leaders have a direct impact on the teacher–pupil relationship The policies, practices and systems the leadership team develop, implement and monitor all have an influence. A key aspect of the responsibility the leadership team hold comes from managing external influences and forces. External influences can have an origin in government or the local community and should be balanced against internal responsibilities and needs. Getting this balance right is a challenge. Schools are under pressure to perform and this is a key aspect when evaluating the leadership team. The outcome of this pressure can be a leadership team with a misdirected focus.

## GOVERNMENT

The educational ideology and policies of any government are a direct external influence on the school.

Changing the range of subjects taught in schools or placing an emphasis on some over others and the form of accreditation has a direct impact on teaching and therefore the learning relationship.

School standards are regarded as a responsibility of government and this is often delegated. In the UK, Ofsted holds this responsibility and assesses all aspects of the quality of education from behaviour to leadership and management. Any organisation whose function includes inspection or regulatory requirements also hold an element of responsibility for nature of the learning relationship.

## PARENTS OR CARERS

If you have taught for any length of time you will know what impact the pupil–parent relationship can have on the relationships a pupil is able to develop at school. It can also influence many of their behaviours in response to the situations in which they find themselves at school. The relationship the parent has with the school can be assessed by the degree of responsibility they take as a parent and how they express that responsibility. We also have to acknowledge that all parents have a view about school based on their own experiences as a pupil and that this helps to determine what they see as their responsibility in promoting a learning relationship with the teacher. Involving the parent in developing the learning relationship and giving them a clear role is something I believe many schools are yet to do. The traditional view of the parents' role is that of making sure homework is done, that their children get to school regularly and on time and that they show an interest (often by attending parents' consultation meetings at report time or they support other non-curricular activities).

## Personal reflection

As a young teacher I looked forward to my first parents' evening. I was going to enlist the parents' support in helping their children engage better in learning. After seeing a number of parents, I realised it was the parents rather than their children I needed in my class if I was to make progress in building the desired learning relationships. The children had learnt how to manage their parents and thought that they could manage their teacher in the same way!

## ❖ Reflective task

Take a moment to reflect and note down any policies or practices in your school that:

- enhance or support the development of learning relationships with your pupils;
- inhibit learning relationships.

## ❖ Reflective task review

I anticipate a number of your responses will fall into the category of behaviour; that is, how the pupils need to conduct themselves. Some will be associated with pastoral systems and some will come under the remit of achieving targets. I would expect a few to be associated with the pace of the school day.

I have tracked a pupil during a typical school day and found the expectations to be onerous, from arriving on time to completing tasks, eating, socialising, avoiding trouble and getting out on time. The factory analogy often applied to schools is not without some foundation if you consider some of the policies and practices put into place to manage the pupils and run the school.

No teacher or pupil is immune from what goes on in the rest of the school. In any school, there will be teachers who get on with their pupils and those for whom some pupils are a challenge. As long as those teachers who relate well to their pupils challenge them and do not allow them a free ride then there will be silos of effective learning relationships. These isolated pockets may cause a degree of conflict and/or chaos within the school as pupils will find it confusing when they move from teacher to teacher. Consistency and continuity are two persistent challenges for schools. This is particularly so where schools are organised into phases and are subject-based as in secondary education (ages 11–18 in the UK).

You need to understand how all these factors influence the teacher–pupil relationship, which in turn helps the pupil to meet their learning needs. It is in the meeting of those learning needs that the relationship is allowed to develop. It is clear that as a teacher you have to take the lead and have the greater responsibility for creating learning relationships and meeting the learning needs of the pupil. It is also clear that, at times, you may need to be creative in working within certain constraints.

## Personal reflection

On one occasion, when I was leading a project which involved teaching and monitoring a number of at-risk pupils, I asked for their evaluation at the end of the year. One wrote *'Mr Hewitson does not teach like other teachers'.* I was obviously doing something different and these pupils recognised it. It became clear early on in the project that I needed to give pupils the skills (agency) to manage themselves in order for them to avoid conflict when being taught by other teachers. I needed to explore their feelings with them and make them see a connection to their needs so that they understood at least some of their behaviours.

I am not claiming to have a magic wand or that there were not occasions when we fell out, too. After all, in any dance there are occasions when you may step on each other's toes.

## Towards developing a responsibility model

So now you have seen the players and their roles, what does that responsibility look like and how does it work? How can we model the learning relationship?

### THE LEARNING RELATIONSHIP

We know teaching and learning are at their best when the relationship is underpinned by respect and trust. We also know relationships are dynamic and change over time. Further, we recognise relationships often involve emotions and that communication of those emotions is often key to the health and well-being of those relationships. What does that relationship look like within the school context and how can we have a conversation about something that is often difficult to describe or is, in part, intangible? I found myself facing such a question some time ago when the school I was in had a professional development day. The problem we were facing was that too many teachers were *'doing it for their pupils'.* They were taking most of the responsibility for the learning outcomes and too many of the pupils had become disengaged in the learning, waiting for the teachers to do it for them. I find this is a common situation when schools are under pressure for results. This is somehow linked to the nature of teachers. I find they are, for the most part, a compliant and responsible group. This thinking led me to start sketching an idea during a coffee break. What started with this rough sketch has developed into a very useful tool. It is this tool we are now going to explore.

If you have an aversion to mathematics, particularly graphs, then please do not close the book or look away. The following graphs describe and explore the teacher–pupil responsibilities and show how they affect the teacher–pupil relationship. They also show how decisions at a whole-school level impact on this relationship and what the likely outcomes will be. The explanation takes three forms:

1. the ideal scenario;
2. the distorted scenario;
3. the impact of the decisions taken by the leadership of the school and their role in determining the nature of the relationship.

## INTRODUCING THE LEARNING RELATIONSHIP RESPONSIBILITY RATIO GRAPH (LRRRG)

We are going to start with a X-Y axis graph as in Figure 2.3. The Y axis represents the relationship responsibility percentage (ratio) between teacher and pupil; the X axis represents time.

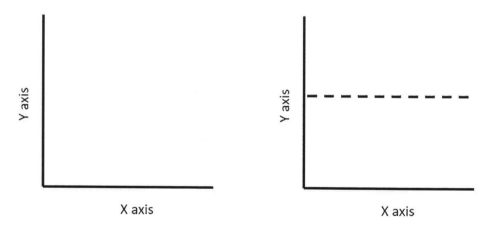

**Figures 2.3 and 2.4 Development of relationship responsibility ratio**

Starting with the Y axis, if we draw a horizontal line starting midway up the Y axis and the length of the X axis, this indicates that the teacher and pupil shared 50 per cent of the responsibility for learning, representing a responsibility ratio of equal proportions and unchanging over the length of the teacher–pupil relationship (Figure 2.4). The line we draw can represent the nature of the learning relationship between the teacher and pupil over time. The time period may be as short as a lesson or for as long as a term, year, key stage or phase of education.

The responsibility could be almost entirely that of the teacher or that of the pupil. The pace of change or transfer of responsibility can be indicated by the gradient and direction of the line. With the teacher handing over a percentage of responsibility to the pupil, the line would take a downward direction (Figure 2.5) and when taking back a percentage, an upward direction (Figure 2.6).

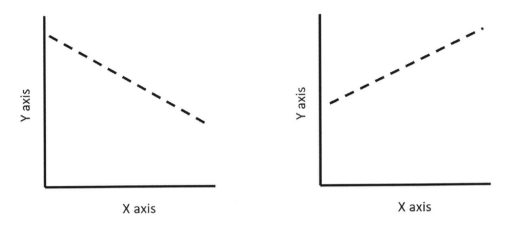

**Figures 2.5 and 2.6 Transfer of responsibility**

## ANALYSING LRRRG EXAMPLES

The power of this graph is not just in both the planning and analysis of learning relationships; it provides a means of discussing the impact of the relationship in emotional and resource terms. Once you become familiar with this way of representing the learning relationship, then it becomes a powerful tool in curriculum planning, resourcing and in building learning relationships as it allows you to see the impact of your decisions.

## ❖ Reflective task

Figures 2.7, 2.8 and 2.9 represent three planned learning relationship responsibility ratio graphs (LRRRGs). The graphs define the type of learning relationship the teacher has with the pupil by describing the learning responsibility for learning held by each.

See if you can offer an interpretation for each of them. You may suggest an approximate phase of education (primary, secondary or higher), the nature of the relationship over time and any issues you think may result from the relationship ratio.

IF YOU CAN'T REACH THEM YOU CAN'T TEACH THEM

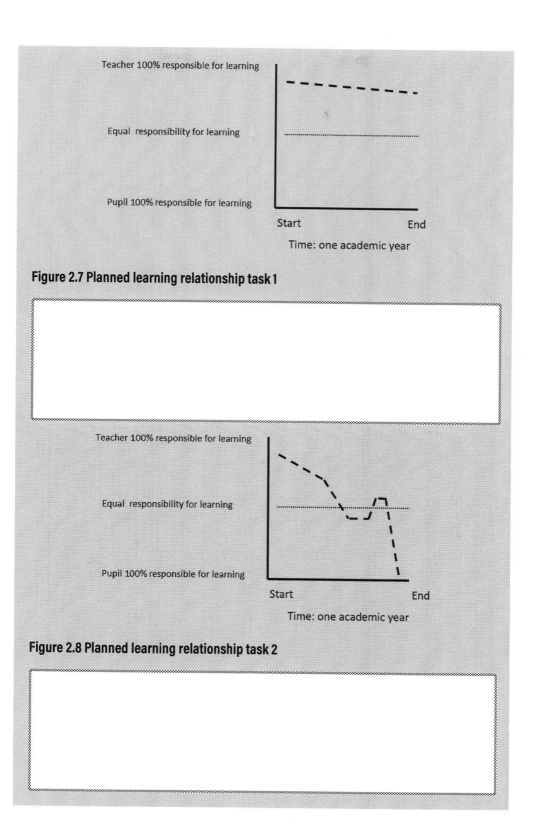

Teacher 100% responsible for learning

Equal responsibility for learning

Pupil 100% responsible for learning

Start      End

Time: one academic year

**Figure 2.7 Planned learning relationship task 1**

Teacher 100% responsible for learning

Equal responsibility for learning

Pupil 100% responsible for learning

Start      End

Time: one academic year

**Figure 2.8 Planned learning relationship task 2**

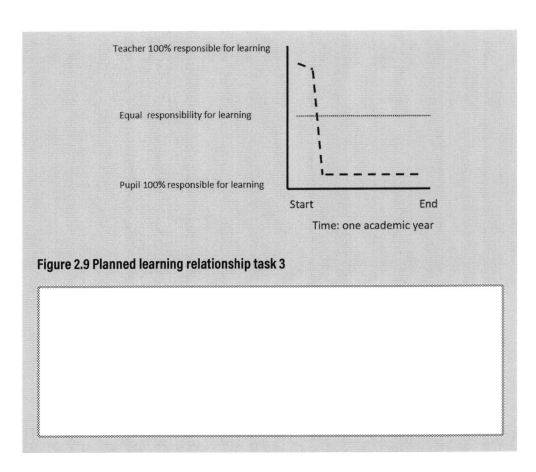

Teacher 100% responsible for learning

Equal responsibility for learning

Pupil 100% responsible for learning

Start    End

Time: one academic year

**Figure 2.9 Planned learning relationship task 3**

## ❖ Reflective task review

I do not suggest any of these three examples are how it actually is, that they represent a true learning relationship responsibility ratio. They are merely examples to get you thinking.

Figure 2.7 is a primary phase example, appropriate to pupils aged seven to ten years. As in all the examples, the teacher holds the major responsibility at the start. Although there is a transfer of responsibility, this is gradual, and the teacher maintains the greatest share. There is a great deal to do in this phase of education. Without the teacher taking a key role for learners who lack the self-direction skills, abilities and experience to take on greater responsibility there will be a lack of structure to the learning. There is also a high risk that learning will not take place as planned and effective learning relationships will not be established if too much responsibility is delegated to the pupil too soon.

Figure 2.8 is a secondary phase example, pupils in Years 10 and 11. You can imagine the teacher setting the structure and then guiding pupils through any coursework before perhaps structuring revision prior to examinations.

Figure 2.9 shows a higher education phase, possibly the first year of university. The teacher transfers responsibility quite quickly to the student who then takes responsibility for their own learning, having acquired the skills and abilities to do so effectively through prior learning experiences. There is less opportunity for the teacher to develop secure learning relationships with the students because of the rapid transfer of responsibility.

## Personal reflection

I have worked with students at this phase of their education and know first-hand the impact of not being prepared for this type of learning environment. The devastating outcome that can result when a student is not prepared for this form of relationship and responsibility was made clear to me at a higher education conference. Another speaker noted that they had experienced three unsuccessful suicide attempts that year. The transition was just too great for some students.

## The independent learner

We often hear in schools about preparing pupils to become independent learners. In my experience, this is often associated with skills and knowledge rather than learning needs or the relationship with the teacher.

## ❖ Reflective task

Having studied the graphs and read my explanation, what graph would you draw to represent the independent learner? Use the template below (Figure 2.10) to draw your graph.

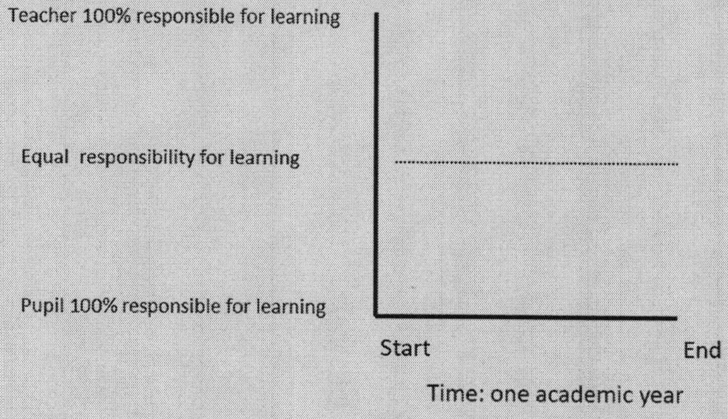

Teacher 100% responsible for learning

Equal responsibility for learning

Pupil 100% responsible for learning

Start      End

Time: one academic year

**Figure 2.10 The independent learner**

## POSSIBLE INTERDEPENDENT LEARNER OUTCOME

As the learner becomes increasingly responsible for directing and managing their own learning, then there is an opportunity for the teacher to become more of a learner too. I stated earlier that when a teacher stops being a learner they stop being a teacher. Another impact of no longer being a learner is that we retreat into routine and familiarity, our most comfortable of behaviours. I have seen this in schools facing significant challenges where the remedial course of action chosen has been more of what is not working. If anything, this behaviour further limits the amount of learning responsibility the teacher is able or willing to hand over to the learner. The graph can be drawn as almost a horizontal line high up the Y axis. Let us now look at how we may construct a more realistic and planned LRRRG model.

## A MORE REALISTIC AND PLANNED LRRRG

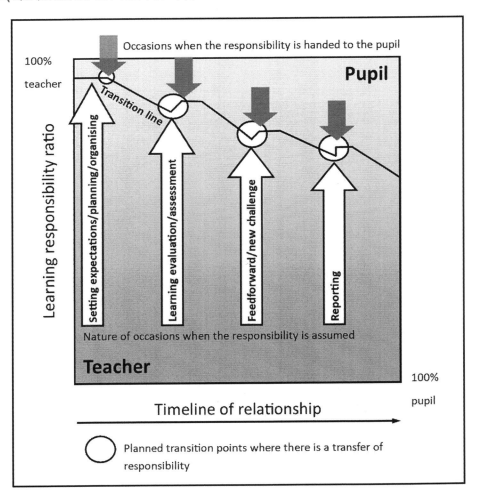

**Figure 2.11 Ideal relationship**

IF YOU CAN'T REACH THEM YOU CAN'T TEACH THEM

Figure 2.11 shows an example of a teacher who has planned to develop learning relationships over time; this is the ideal scenario. It is an *overlay* to the normal lesson or curriculum planning with which you are familiar. Its purpose is to build effective learning relationships and to highlight the need and timing of a dialogue with the pupil about their learning. This is only possible when learning needs are being met. As we shall see, there are times when specific learning needs become a focus for the teacher.

## LRRRG EXPLANATION

At the start of any course, year, module or activity, the teacher has the responsibility to plan and manage the learning; they are accountable for about 95 per cent of what is required in teaching and learning (Figure 2.11). The learner in turning up prepared to learn provides the remaining 5 per cent. In this model and at this stage everyone knows their part and the first couple of lessons normally go quite well. As the course progresses over time, the responsibility shifts and the learner has to take more responsibility for their own learning. In doing so, the learner requires certain skills, attitudes, attributes and behaviours in order to be successful. This is where difficulties can begin to arise for the teacher. If learning needs are not being met then any initial learner compliance can erode quickly once they begin to struggle.

If the learner is not focused in the learning or does not have the necessary skills, attitudes or attributes and does not display appropriate learning behaviour, they may not be able to engage in the learning and take their share of the responsibility. There are occasions where the teacher will need to regain, or assume once again, a little more responsibility. Nonetheless, this needs to be managed carefully if it is not to hinder the gradual progression and development of the learning behaviours that will ultimately result in effective lifelong learners.

Teachers who constantly give and take back responsibility for learning without good reason and explanation do nothing more than undermine the learner. In fact, the learner can be adept at allowing this to happen, even creating a scenario that will encourage it. In doing so, they are relieved of their responsibility for learning since the teacher assumes it for them. In such circumstances, at the end of the learning partnership timeline, we are left with a tired teacher and a learner who has learnt to allow others to do things for them. They are unlikely to have learnt the skills, attitudes and attributes or behaviours of an independent and engaged learner or to have understood their own learning needs and how these influence their behaviour. The result is a learner who is even more dependent on the teacher. This then requires more teacher time to be spent supporting them. A cycle of dependency can easily form.

Why should the teacher take back responsibility? There are genuine occasions during the time the learner and teacher spend together, such as assessment and reporting, when a teacher needs to manage the situation more directly and take responsibility for what is happening in the lesson or the course. There is a need to manage these occasions carefully in order not to make the learner a passive partner without responsibility. Done correctly it is a small and managed blip in the regulated and direct transfer of responsibility for learning and the relationship continues to meet the pupil's learning needs.

A deputy headteacher at my first school explained to me why new courses were always popular, especially with those pupils who had found it difficult to *engage* in learning in the standard curriculum subjects and had limited success in school. His explanation was simple and, looking back, insightful. He said: *'Pupils frequently opt for things they have not failed at yet.'* In some ways, this is encouraging and suggests at least they have not given up. In my own experience, pupils also opted for courses they saw as bringing them some form of rapid worldly success or status based on their value systems. For example, courses such as Business Studies. They saw these courses as meeting their need for a form of success measured in material terms rather than learning needs.

## EXTERNAL RELATIONSHIP PRESSURES

Earlier, we looked at who is involved in influencing the learning relationship and their responsibilities (Figure 2.2). There are times when pressure coming from outside the teacher–pupil relationship is applied – the occurrence of lesson observations or meeting new deadlines, for example – and the teacher will take more responsibility for the outcome than they planned to or should (even if it should be the responsibility of the learner). Significantly, this occurs when there is substantial pressure for pupils to meet targets. In such circumstances where the teacher takes back the responsibility there is an increase in learner complacency and a lack in the use of learning skills and strategy development.

Unfortunately, this situation does not only affect a single teacher–pupil relationship, as it can have implications across the school. Where the learner has multiple teachers, it becomes a strategy the pupil will use to avoid any form of learning challenge. This can cause conflict if the learner comes across a teacher who is unwilling to resume additional responsibility and allow the pupil to abdicate theirs.

Abdication of responsibility on the part of the learner can mean they fail to develop the skills, attributes, attitudes and behaviours needed to manage her/his own learning. I return to this in Chapter 12 on learning intelligence (LQ).

I believe there is a false truth used in addressing achievement: the more the teacher prepares subject content and resources for the lesson, the more pupils will achieve. If we return for a moment to Figure 2.11, the fallacy of this statement is clear. The more the teacher tries to do other than provide for the learner's needs, then the less the learner has to commit to the process of learning. The less they have to take responsibility for their learning. Here is an example from my own experience.

I had a Year 12 A level pupil join my class from another school, one acknowledged as very successful. His prior attainment was impressive. I welcomed him to the group and asked about his experience. A typical new pupil interview. As time went by he continually failed to live up to his claimed experience, wanting to spend time talking rather than working. When I asked him about this, expecting to hear a rational explanation, perhaps family problems or similar, I was amazed when he said to me: '*You do it for me, Sir; you know it will make you look good!*'

Be reassured, I did not do it for him and he did not make it to the end of the year, instead opting to leave my class.

## IMPACT ON LRRRG

Pupils who have no other strategies to use to meet a learning challenge fall back on what has worked for them before, as the pupil above did. They can learn to sit back and wait for the teacher to take on responsibility for their learning. This results in a distorted teaching and learning transition line as can be seen in Figure 2.12 below.

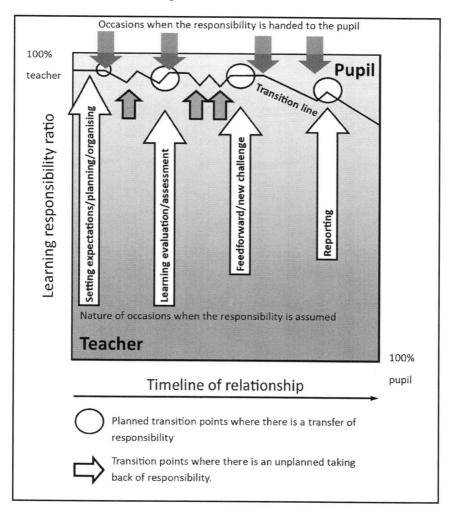

**Figure 2.12 Distorted relationship**

Such a relationship, as demonstrated by the distorted transition line in Figure 2.12 compared to that in Figure 2.11, shows several occasions when the teacher resumes responsibility as the direct consequence of unplanned, external influences. The shape of the transition line shows how irregular it has become, how the gradient of transfer becomes shallower and how much responsibility the pupil holds at the end of the period compared to the teacher and to what was planned (Figure 2.11). There can also be a slowing of pace and of covering less material as a consequence. As a result, an unsettled class and pupil behaviour issues are not uncommon. Ultimately, the pupil is not prepared to become an independent learner.

When we talk of unplanned occasions, we are talking in terms of curriculum planning and delivery. The teacher does not plan for learning walks (visits to the classroom by school leaders), inspections (Ofsted in England, who conduct short- or no-notice inspections) or a change in government or school policy or practice. It is a natural consequence of surprise that disorder occurs in the classroom. If we disturb any routine or relationship, the pupils will react in ways to seek security or reassurance. Of course, this may be the symptom driven by the behaviour; the actual behaviour will be as a result of past experiences and agency on the part of the pupils.

## Personal reflection

My position in school made me line manager to a faculty that I got to know over a period of about a year. I had visited lessons (learning walks) and discussed lessons with teachers and I had few concerns about relationships, behaviour or progress. We received notification of an Ofsted inspection and, due to the consequences of a poor inspection outcome, there were significant levels of pressure to do well. Teachers were notified of lesson observations involving an inspector. During one Ofsted-observed lesson, the teacher behaved differently, partially to stick to her lesson plan and partially due to feeling under pressure. The pupils did not recognise the change they saw in the teacher and reacted in a way that presented as a behaviour challenge to the teacher as they sought reassurance. All did not go well, and the outcome did not reflect the standard of teaching and learning that would have normally taken place with that teacher and group of pupils. This is an example of what can go wrong when the teacher–pupil relationship becomes unstable.

### THE RESPONSIBILITY OF LEADERSHIP

If a teacher repeatedly experiences unplanned disruption which is not managed correctly then it will result in the teacher's stress and tiredness, as there are significant demands on her/his energy. The responsibility for creating the environment for a managed and not a distorted learning transition line I believe rests with the teacher and with school leadership. It is here where a creative and critical mindset is most important in protecting the learning relationship.

Figure 2.13 below focuses on the role of leadership. It shows the role of the leadership team acting as a filter for those things that are outside the teacher–pupil relationship but which have a direct impact on it. I have not come across the role expressed in this way even during my leadership training but it is crucial in so many ways. Without a stable teacher–pupil relationship, little learning takes place and the school community can suffer.

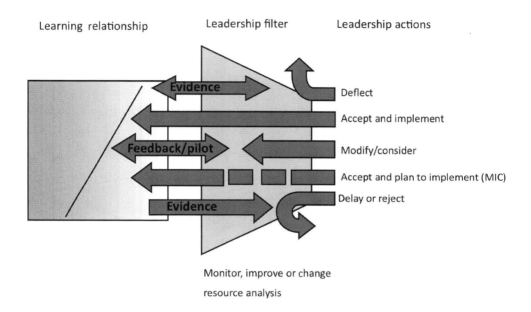

**Figure 2.13 The role of leadership in protecting and supporting the learning relationship**

The leadership role is to act as a filter, adopting one of several actions dependent on the mission statement of the school, MIC resources, anticipated impact on the learning relationship and any relevant learning and teaching evidence. This model fits in well with David Hughes' thinking in his book *Future-proof Your School*. Hughes (2019) mentions the concept of '*creative capacity*', which recognises the need to think and work within the constraints of time and effort available to us. This he links to the culture of the school and in turn its possible impact on the mission of the organisation. I strongly recommend reading Hughes' book if you want to explore how this model of responsibility of the school leadership team could make a positive impact on the culture of the school.

Many, if not all, schools have a mission statement and it is this statement that should act as the litmus test. If what is proposed moves you towards achieving the mission statement then do it. If it hinders or deflects you from achieving the mission statement do not do it, or at least resist or modify whatever it is in order to limit any damage. My personal mission for my work is '*To inspire and enable learners*'. If what I am doing or asked to do supports this mission, then I embrace it; if not I resist. Resisting may mean not doing it or may mean modifying or delaying. We have to be reasonable in our actions and we all have responsibilities. We can also be creative!

If the leadership team of a school adopts this approach and it translates into their roles then the pressure on teachers and their students to 'perform' is both limited and realistic. No teacher need take back more of the responsibility for learning or outcomes than is planned or appropriate in the managed teaching–learning relationship.

As a teacher you may feel as though you have no control over the actions or behaviours of the leadership of the school and the political interference we now see. You may perceive the targets you are given are unrealistic, that there are too many changes of direction and that change is too frequent. It may be that, in order to cope, you have to take more responsibility for learning than you may otherwise see as appropriate, in order to meet deadlines and achieve targets. So how can understanding the learning relationship help? How can it alleviate some of the pressure? Any relationship that works is an easier one to manage. Where there is misunderstanding, suspicion or lack of trust then it is not so easy to manage that relationship. We are unlikely to engage with anyone we do not trust, and this is the same in learning and teaching.

## ❖ Reflective task

Take a moment to go back to where you reflected on any policies or practices in your school that first enhance or support the development of learning relationships with your pupils and then those that you believe inhibit them. How many of them could have been affected by the leadership filter activities listed in Figure 2.13?

Your opportunity to reflect on the concept of a leadership filter role.

## THE IMPORTANCE OF THE LEARNING RELATIONSHIP

What if there was a way to make the job of teaching, that of having pupils engage in the learning, easier? As teachers, we know that engaged and focused pupils who are fully involved in the learning challenges are much easier to teach. They remain on task longer, produce better quality

IF YOU CAN'T REACH THEM YOU CAN'T TEACH THEM

of work, and are more amenable. You can focus on the teaching and not on managing disruptive behaviour or on having to apply pressure to complete tasks. Targets become outcomes of learning and not the focus for learning. This may sound fanciful when faced with a number of 'reluctant' learners who want you to do everything for them and moan loudly when you do not. There are, however, some basic learner needs you can address easily within your planning and time at school that will make a significant difference to your teaching.

The needs to which I refer influence learner behaviour. They are essential in bringing the learner to the start line. When we sit back and reflect on our teaching, what went right and what did not go so well, we can see the shadow of these needs. Where teaching and learning went well, the learners' needs were met in a natural and almost informal manner, they were part of the teaching. Where they were not met then our reflections contain the dark shadows of control, suppression, conflict and stress that spread across the teaching. They are represented by the 'saw tooth' profile of the distorted teaching and learning transition line in Figure 2.12.

## Learning needs

I have seen the best-planned lessons fail to engage learners just as I have seen off-the-cuff lessons, delivered with little or no notice or preparation, excite and motivate learners to the point they did not want the lesson to end. Why is this? Fundamentally, it is about building that bridge between you, the teacher, and the learners. It is about meeting their learning needs in order to help them learn, to help them engage with you in the teaching and learning process.

I hope you have begun to think about teaching and learning from a different perspective. Teaching is not just about subjects and pedagogy; it is about motivating and engaging pupils. It is about developing their understanding of how their learning environment impacts on them as learners. It is also about understanding how their learning needs influence their behaviour. Ultimately it is about creating independent learners. This quote is attributed to Alvin Toffler, American writer and futurist: '*The illiterate of the 21st century will not be those who cannot read and write, but those who cannot learn, unlearn and relearn.*'

This is a good point at which to begin to explore learners' needs.

## References and further reading

Advocating Creativity (2016) *How Parents Can Support Learning at Home.* [online] Available at: https://4c3d.wordpress.com/?s=parents (accessed 1 November 2020).

Advocating Creativity (2016) *My 13 Tips For When Starting University or College from ace-d.* [online] Available at: https://4c3d.wordpress.com/2014/09/16/my-13-tips-for-when-starting-university-or-college/ (accessed 1 November 2020).

Department for Education (2011) *Teachers' Standards*. [online] Available at: https://assets. publishing.service.gov.uk/government/uploads/system/uploads/attachment_data/file/ 665522/Teachers_standard_information.pdf (accessed 1 November 2020).

Department for Education (2019) *Guidance English Baccalaureate (EBacc)*. [online] Available at: www.gov.uk/government/publications/english-baccalaureate-ebacc/english-baccalaureate-ebacc (accessed 1 November 2020).

Gov.uk (nd) *Ofsted*. [online] Available at: www.gov.uk/government/organisations/ofsted (accessed 1 November 2020).

Hughes, D W (2019) *Future-proof Your School: Steering Culture, Driving School Improvement, Developing Excellence*. St Albans: Critical Publishing.

Peters, R S (1974) *Authority, Responsibility and Education*. London: George Allen & Unwin Ltd.

First published in 1959, this book may be from an age way before the computer or the internet but it has a wealth of philosophical and moral questions about education relevant to today. Relevant to exploring the role of the teacher and leadership is Chapter 4: 'Authority in Educational Institutions.'

QR link

Your notes

IF YOU CAN'T REACH THEM YOU CAN'T TEACH THEM

# 3. MEETING LEARNING NEEDS

*What kids believe about themselves is more important in determining their behaviour than any facts about them.*

**Dr Nicholas Long**

## Introduction

As teachers, we know that people need to be motivated to learn but there is more to successful learning than just being motivated, especially when we consider the reason/s for that motivation. Motivation can be associated with a desire to learn although motivation associated with aversion is also a part of learning. This section looks at what pupils need in order to be purposefully engaged and thus what supports their desire or motivation to learn. This chapter is not a review of motivation theory. Its focus is to root the experience of pupil motivation and engagement within the practice of teaching.

The chapter starts by signposting the various elements that come into play when we talk about pupils' engagement and motivation to learn. It introduces four learning needs I have found to be the key to reaching out to pupils and describes how as teachers we can plan to meet these needs without any meaningful increase to planning or preparation time. You will also find a number of reflective tasks. These encourage you to think mindfully about exploring and meeting learning needs. Following chapters will focus on each need and show how you can plan to meet these needs in a practical manner.

## Part 1: Engagement in learning

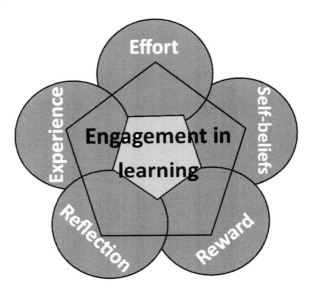

**Figure 3.1 Engagement in learning**

Take a moment to consider how you engage with the process of learning and what relationship you have with learning. You may dive in, observe before committing or perhaps need encouragement to overcome reluctance. You may be the type of person who cannot resist a learning trail, following one thing you have found out in order to discover another. Perhaps you are more of a sleuth, checking facts and wanting to find out more about a topic to satisfy your interest. You may adopt a problem-solving approach, needing to learn in order to complete a task you have set yourself. Consider if you engage differently with learning when you initiate the need or, for example, when undertaking a course of study when you are in a formal learning situation akin to the teacher–pupil relationship. Be mindful that how you engage with the process of learning may not be the same for your pupils.

How I characterise my engagement with the process of learning.

The character of our engagement changes according to the context in which we learn. Learning that is self-driven, if you are self-motivated to learn, is accompanied by significant levels of engagement from the start. Alternatively, if you are put into a learning situation not of your making, not driven by your own desire to learn, then there is a need to create a level of engagement that at least sparks your attention if not interest.

Advertisers are aware of this and successful campaigns will sell you the benefits before the product. There is a relationship between the level of interest, the level of engagement you have in learning and the level of effort you make in order to learn. It is easier to learn that in which you are interested (requiring less effort to be actively engaged) than that in which you are not.

## ENGAGEMENT AND EFFORT

In the formal educational context of the school, knowledge and skills are most often subject-based; some form of timetable is used to manage the process of learning multiple disciplines during a fixed period. This is far from a natural learning situation in which you engage in learning through need or interest. In such circumstances, you need to be encouraged to learn; there has to be some form of reward in order for you to engage. The nature of the reward can be very personal and can take many forms, from a relationship that is desired to a qualification or the acquisition of an item. Just giving a reward for something will produce false engagement and ultimately bargaining on the part of the pupil. Creating a desire and then providing the reward brings about true engagement. The key from a teaching perspective in relation to rewards is that they should be desired by the pupil and only awarded after being involved in a prior choice process where the conditions for receiving the reward are clearly described.

The degree of effort you make is influenced by your interest in the topic, how difficult you perceive the challenge of learning, whether the rewards that result are of direct and tangible benefit to you, as well as a number of other conditions such as previous successes or failures. I suggest that we can assess how truly engaged learners are in the learning by the effort they make to learn without external reward or coercion. I believe the eternal challenge and ultimate reward of teaching is to instil in pupils the pure joy of learning for its own sake.

As a teacher you must be mindful that, in the context of education, you can learn from your experiences, those things that happen to you or that you observe, but only if you process those experiences in a thoughtful way. I emphasise the term 'learn' and not just 'behave'. Your behaviour can be that of purely mimicking others, of doing what you hear or see somebody doing. As a teacher you may be fooled into thinking a pupil has learnt something by the way they behave when, in fact, they are just mimicking other learners.

## Personal reflection

During a lesson observation, I noted several enthusiastic pupils who were quick to put up their hands when the teacher asked the class a question. The teacher tended not to ask those who put up their hands but instead focused on those who did not. During the lesson I decided to stop by one or two of the rapid-fire 'hands-up' groups and check their understanding too. I discovered one pupil who admitted not knowing the answer but who was still quick to raise a hand. The pupil had observed the teacher and knew, by putting up a hand, they were unlikely to be asked. You may wonder why they risked putting up their hand when they did not know the answer. The reason was quite simple: the fear of looking stupid. The pupil knew, if asked by the teacher, they would not be able to give the answer and did not want to appear stupid. The pupil knew that the odds were in their favour if they put up their hand quickly. They adopted a behaviour that presented the least risk to their self-esteem as a learner. Afterwards, in conversation with me, the teacher acknowledged that they had recognised the rapid-fire 'hands-up' group and had assumed, because of the regularity of their response, that they were all capable of answering the question.

We will see later that there is a better approach when asking questions if you are going to ignore those pupils who are quick to put up their hands. The approach can be a positive one in that the teacher can rephrase the question or ask a sub-question of the pupil they chose. In doing so they build the confidence of the pupil and bring them back into the narrative of the lesson gently allowing them to engage further and build their self-belief as learners.

Pupils may also form an image of themselves as learners or set their level of effort and therefore engagement purely based on a previous learning experience, whether good or bad. Not all learning experiences are positive. Fear of failure can be very powerful and can have a significant impact on levels of engagement. One aspect of learning that is often overlooked in teaching is the emotional impact of learning, how we feel when we experience the highs and the lows, the successes and the failures, the easy and the challenging. I rarely find teachers who will discuss with their pupils how they feel during a learning experience or in preparation for the challenges they will face. As a result, many pupils when they experience a strong emotion make a link to the subject or even the teacher, often subconsciously. This can result in a lifelong aversion to a subject where the emotion is negative or love for a subject if it is positive. Through working with pupils, I know those who have never experienced failure or the inability to complete a challenge are poorly prepared emotionally for when the occasion does occur. They do not understand the emotions they experience and do not have the suitable tools to deal with them. The same is true for those who have not experienced success. The difference is those who hold a self-belief that they cannot learn rarely try without significant encouragement and, when they do, they find this hard to accept.

You can learn from the experience of others too. Their wisdom, knowledge and understanding are available to you if you are willing to listen. To learn through the teaching of others you need to engage with them and be motivated to learn. Respect is a key positive feeling when building learning relationships. In teaching, respect from the pupils will mitigate several issues that arise when pupils face challenges and do not know how to react.

Of course, we can learn not to do something because it is dangerous or harmful to us (emotionally as well as physically) but this is often an instinctive response and does not include any objective reflection or rationalisation of the experience. In an instinctive response you react without thinking and therefore without reflection. Without reflection and an objective rationalisation of what happens, you are prone to jumping to conclusions or taking from your experiences learning that later may prove to be inaccurate, misleading or false. The learning will be very much influenced by emotions or feelings. If you eat something and you are ill you may make a connection between eating whatever it was and being ill and you may reach the conclusion you are allergic to what you ate. While this may be true, it could also be that what you ate was bad or it was something else that made you ill, such as not washing your hands thoroughly before eating. Objective reflection on the experience may help you identify the true cause and therefore inform your future actions or behaviour; you will have truly understood something that you can apply to your learning in the future. What you take from an experience can colour what you think or believe, and you can hold onto those views and beliefs for a long time. You may hold onto them despite evidence to the contrary, even if that evidence is extremely powerful. In such circumstances several things will be influencing you, including the nature of your experience, relationships with others involved in the experience and past outcomes.

The pupils you teach may also be holding onto beliefs about themselves as learners. You need to be mindful of this for you create learning experiences every day in your classrooms and in your interactions with those pupils. No pupil comes to you as a blank canvas. You know and recognise that many carry preconceptions about their ability to learn, what they are good at and what they are poor at. A pupil's level of learning engagement and motivation to learn is influenced by prior learning experiences, both planned or unplanned. Often the challenge you will face in your classrooms, in your learning–teaching interactions where you seek engagement, is in dealing with your pupils' preconceptions about how clever or able they are, and what subjects they are good or poor at. In short, their self-belief as learners.

I have spoken to many learners of all ages about their self-beliefs. In many cases, limiting self-beliefs are associated with experiences that were not reflected upon or rationalised in any meaningful or objective way. The learning that was taken from the event was very much created from the emotions they experienced at the time. Limiting self-beliefs based on emotions can exclude us from future learning experiences; they prohibit or inhibit us from engaging in learning. As a teacher, you must acknowledge and cater for the emotional impact of a learning experience in your planning as much as you do for curriculum content. What emotions your pupils will experience will depend on the relationship you have with them and, in turn, on their relationship with their peers. Terms such as *belonging*, *trust* and *confidence* play a major part in those relationships.

The terms *growth mindset* and *fixed mindset* were introduced into the educational landscape by Carol Dweck. While the main concept behind this is that intelligence is something you can develop, it does open a dialogue around learning that has been absent since Barbara Prashnig considered learning styles in the 1990s. It may not focus directly on the emotions of learning, but it does involve the pupil in a discussion about learning and working at overcoming the challenges that are part of learning. Like all theories on how we learn that appear to offer a quick fix, growth mindset can succumb to adoption without understanding or adaption just like learning styles before it. In such cases where it does not produce the results promised within a short timescale, it can be discredited unfairly.

# Motivation to learn

It would be great if your mere presence in the classroom was enough to motivate your pupils to learn. It can happen. Just as with any audience you can prime them, suggest the benefits that will come their way and create an environment and relationship that stimulate and sustain their interest. In a school environment, the motivation to learn requires more than just compliance, doing as you are told. It requires a level of engagement, a willingness to take part in the learning. There is a saying that 'success = effort × talent'. There is a similar equation we can build for learning that involves replacing effort with motivation.

In a managed learning environment, such as a school, we need to be motivated to learn. Just being sent to school is not enough to motivate you to learn. Even when there is a desire to learn, there are other forces at work that influence your learning journey. Some of these influences can distract us, just as seeing a sign at the side of the road for free ice cream could cause you to interrupt a journey. The learning environment may not be critical to learning but it has a significant part to play when it comes to motivation. The teacher is tasked with not only managing the learning (planning, resourcing, presenting and assessing) but also motivating learners. You do not hold all of the motivation cards, but you can bring the key ones to the top.

# MOTIVATION THROUGH NEEDS

Learning through or as a result of a need is the type of learning we all recognise as being an effective learning driver. If overcoming a life-threatening challenge meant learning another language you would be motivated to learn the language. The need can be diverse and may not be obvious to others. The intensity of the need can vary too, from casual to imperative. Furthermore, the need can be very personal and not shared even within a very close group. Indeed, what brings a group together may be a number of very different needs, but ones that can be satisfied by the same experience. In complicated circumstances, pupils may be motivated to learn because their need is to be part of a group rather than what is being taught. The need to belong is a powerful driver, as you will see when we explore learning needs later.

## ❖ Reflective task

Think of a situation where a need has driven your own learning. How did you recognise the need, how would you describe it and how did you plan to satisfy it?

## ❖ Reflective task review

· In recognising your need, were any emotions involved and, if so, what were they?

· In describing the need did you say what the driver was as well as the benefits?

· Did you have a clear plan as to how to go about satisfying the need and were you successful?

## ❖ Reflective task

Ask your pupils what motivational needs they have. You may have to rephrase the question according to their age.

## ❖ Reflective task review

- Were you surprised by your pupils' responses?

- If any mentioned rewards, did they focus on short-, medium- or long-term rewards?

- Were any of the needs associated with their feelings or emotions?

Understanding pupils' needs within a learning context is essential in teaching and, as we shall see, a key motivational aspect. Not all needs are good in terms of learning though. It is recognised that we learn poorly in circumstances where we feel threatened or under stress. The flight or fight response tends to kick in when we feel threatened and there is a need to protect ourselves. When in this emotional state adrenaline is surging and your behaviour can become unregulated. Instinct or past success strategies will direct your response with little thought for rules, regulations or consequences. As a teacher I would safely bet you have seen such behaviour from pupils. There is a balance to be found when motivating pupils. You will often find that, in education, a reward replaces a threat. Both the carrot and stick are often present in schools. A key responsibility of teachers is to create or produce a learning environment that is of low stress for the pupil, an environment that meets their learning needs, those things that help them engage in learning and that get them to the start line of the learning journey.

IF YOU CAN'T REACH THEM YOU CAN'T TEACH THEM

## REWARDS

Rewards alone are often not enough to motivate pupils, especially if the rewards, the benefits for making the effort to learn, are deferred. The issue of rewarding pupils is one that will often divide opinion. For instance, people will disagree on the type of rewards and what the rewards should be given for. It is only natural that you should, as a teacher, create a need for learning. You can easily move to creating an environment that promotes learning through need rather than by reward by altering your approach. Let me explain.

Here are the two approaches based on how you may present a topic in order to motivate your pupils based on a reward strategy:

1.  You need to learn this in order to do or to have that (the outcome).
2.  In order to do or to have that (the outcome) you need to learn this.

Under the direction of the teacher, the two approaches are often regarded as 'push' or 'pull' motivation.

You may say there is no difference between the two or that the difference is so subtle as to make no difference in motivating learners. Putting the reward first, selling it, encouraging ownership, creating a reality is a technique that car salesmen have been using for decades. Once you buy into a future where you have something or the ability to do something, then you are more motivated to work to achieve the reward.

To promote learning through need you must change from approach 1 to approach 2, but you must first establish a value on what it is the pupil will gain. If you remain using approach 1 then you are focusing on a rewards-based system and if the reward is too distant then you end up replacing it with immediate rewards not connected to the learning. For example, the chocolate bar instant reward rather than the benefit of learning something that can be applied or that will lead to future understanding. Establishing what you will be able to do after and as a result of learning before you start the learning process leads to longer-lasting motivation. Many sporting coaches use a process of visualisation to embed motivation in their athletes. As a teacher, you must not only make desirable (and achievable) what it is you want your pupils to learn; you also have to model the benefits. This is more easily achieved if you have a sound learning relationship with your pupils. Attempts to motivate without a sound relationship, one that also involves respect, will only be partially successful as I have found out.

## Personal reflection

I found out the importance of a sound learning relationship when trying to motivate a pupil in my class who was quite capable of learning but reluctant to do so because she saw no benefit to her in making the effort. The pupil was from what is often referred to as a disadvantaged background. This is something I can relate to and empathise with having grown up in north-east England in the 1960s and 1970s. I tried using what I had achieved in life even though I had failed the eleven-plus (a form of UK education selection) to bridge the gap between us and encourage her to at least try, to show that with effort and belief many things are possible.

My achievements were thrown back at me. To the pupil I was bragging, for the want of a better word, about my job, my home and the things I was able to do. What I had achieved was still unobtainable to the pupil because she saw no common ground between us; the relationship at that time was not yet strong enough, I had not created that bridge. Essentially, I had not yet met the pupil's learning needs for engagement and motivation in my class. A lesson learnt, and one that underlined the importance of the learning relationship in motivating pupils.

## COMPLIANCE

You can also be motivated to learn only because others want you to do so.

This is not a true need in the learning sense but a form of compliance, not unlike that which results from threats or punishment. The outward sign of learning through need is self-driven engagement, a self-motivated learner. How you create the need to learn and the way in which you create it as well as how you satisfy the need is crucial if you want lifelong self-motivated learners. The alternative to a self-motivated learner is a learner who sees learning not as a reward in itself but only as a coerced action to be avoided as soon as possible.

The tradition in schools has been to create or stimulate the learning need through a process of encouragement. The form of this encouragement is often bound up in policies and practices. The school will expect to see, reward or insist upon a set of behaviours that are traditionally associated with being ready or able to learn. By complying, the learner outwardly expresses the motivation to learn but this is merely a set of behaviours that mimic true motivation. These learners sit quietly, they face the front and they obey all the school rules. They do this because they are told this is how you behave if you want to learn. As you will see when we explore learning needs, many of these behaviours can cause the stress or anxiety you hope to exclude from your teaching and your relationship with pupils. For ten false beliefs about learning and the effects on teachers see Prashnig (1994).

While absolute compliance may work for some of the pupils some of the time, it rarely gets the best from either the teacher or the learner. Nor does this approach match, in levels of determination or passion, the need that comes from within for learning. To ignite the internal motivation for learning is what we should aim for as teachers if we are to achieve true pupil engagement.

## ❖ Reflective task

Either search on the web for examples of behaviour policies or obtain your own school's behaviour policy and see if you can assess the tone of the document from the language and expectations. Highlight any guidance or advice that you would associate only with learning behaviours.

IF YOU CAN'T REACH THEM YOU CAN'T TEACH THEM

# RELUCTANCE

Although there may be a need within to learn sometimes there can also be overwhelming resistance to getting involved in learning too. This resistance to get involved, to participate at any level, or even to comply, can come from peer pressure or past learner experiences. It can also be linked to self-confidence or self-beliefs. As a teacher, overcoming a reluctance to learn may be your greatest challenge but it will also be your greatest reward. The first step is always recognising the missing need and not the behaviour.

## Peer pressure

Peer pressure can have a significant influence in terms of learner engagement. If the peer group association or relationship for the pupil is stronger than that which the pupil has with the teacher then the peer group will win every time. The time the pupil spends with an individual teacher is significantly less than that spent with their peer group. This is one of the reasons the peer group can exert a significant amount of influence over the behaviour of its members. Another is status within the group and the fear of losing face or position within the group. Belonging to the group can offer significant benefits and meet certain needs. The establishment of an effective teacher–pupil relationship is the only way of limiting peer pressure on an individual pupil and promoting their engagement in learning. This is another reason why leadership must protect the environment in which the teacher–pupil relationship is developed, and the teacher must work hard to establish a learning relationship.

While I have mentioned the nature of the influence of peer pressure and the strength of its influence, we can consider peer group pressure both in a negative and positive sense. The negatives are associated with behaviours or attitudes on the part of the peer group and adopted by the pupil that do not conform to teacher expectations nor support the building of effective learning relationships. It may not be cool to turn up to lessons on time or to complete homework or to even have a pen. There are positives too if the peer group behaviours are in line with learning behaviour expectations. This can promote engagement in learning. If the peer group has a strong association with learning it provides a positive form of peer pressure. While we may see this as a positive, it can also bring immense pressure on an individual, pressure to conform. The outcome could be the same disengaged learner outcome, especially if they feel they cannot cope or cannot access the learning. High stress levels can result from unregulated engagement and unrealistic expectations.

## Past experiences

You also know that learners can be influenced by past experiences of success and praise or failure and ridicule. The problem for the teacher is that you are not always aware of the impact your comments or actions may make on an individual. Some pupils express themselves openly while others bury their emotions. Past learning or relationship experiences within the teaching context can have a significant influence on pupil engagement. If the learner relationship with the school and the teacher is a strong and a positive one then much can be done to mitigate any negative past experiences. More on this later in Chapter 9 'The learning map'.

## The home

It is not all about school and I would be remiss if I did not mention the home when discussing engagement in learning. As a teacher, you have no control over home circumstances and the advantages or disadvantages that may result. Building effective relationships will help you understand the impact the home has on pupil engagement even if you can do little to mitigate any negative influence. Remember, not all parents will have had a good or rewarding educational experience nor may they have the skills to support learning at home. As a teacher you will know the importance of building good home–school relationships but one conversation that is often missing is how to help parents support their children at home. In discussing relationships with parents, David Hughes (2019) mentions some critical issues that are worth exploring as part of the school culture:

- recognising parents as learning partners;
- professionalising your relationship with parents – the parental view.

In essence, a well-developed structure has to be in place in order to ensure consistently high-quality relationships with your pupils' parents.

Offering to help can be a difficult and sometimes embarrassing situation for the parent if inadequacies are exposed. Parents who do not understand how to support their children's learning, however, can do a great deal of harm in terms of motivation to learn. Expecting their children to go to their room (if they have one and they do not share) to work and to work quietly can be toxic for some learners. If you want to read about how parents can support learning at home I have included an article in *Further reading*.

## The influence of needs

No matter how complex we think we are as people, many of our behaviours come about from satisfying some basic needs. As a teacher, I would remind you of this when we seek to create the learning need in our pupils. It is more effective to satisfy their learning needs before we seek engagement and motivation. An analogy would be preparing the ingredients of a meal before we start cooking. We also need to acknowledge there is a hierarchy to these needs and without satisfying some of the fundamental ones, the higher needs cannot be approached. Can you study effectively if you are cold, hungry or frightened? You would be unusual if you could; you may be able to carry out simple tasks but nothing that required the thought process, analysis or insight that learning requires.

One of the pioneering psychologists who explored human needs and their effect on behaviour was Abraham Maslow. Maslow is recognised for the development of the idea of a hierarchy of needs. It is presented in the form of a pyramid (Figure 3.2) with a broad base focusing on our physiological needs. The premise is that we cannot progress up to the top of the pyramid without satisfying the needs of each level. We will find it hard to develop a sense of belonging if we do not have friendships. Developing friendships is dependent on us feeling safe, and feeling safe and secure can only be achieved if our most basic needs are met, such as food, sleep and shelter.

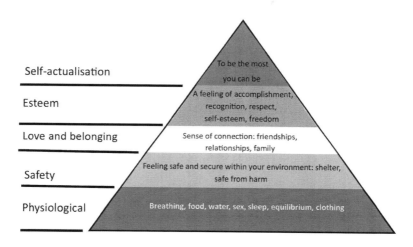

**Figure 3.2 Maslow's hierarchy of needs**

Maslow may not have identified learning as a need in its own right but we know it is essential for survival and is an inherent aspect of self-actualisation. We mentioned earlier about the impact the home can have on motivation to learn. If you look at Figure 3.2, at what level would you draw the line that would separate home and school influences when considering the five needs? Perhaps you would debate whether you could separate the influence of home or school. In some instances, schools certainly provide some of the physiological needs and certainly schools need to be safe places. The school can also be thought of as a family in many regards too; pastoral care programmes do much to nurture in the same way as a family does.

## PHYSICAL AND SENSORY NEEDS

In terms of pupil engagement, I believe problems arise when the home is not providing for the physiological and safety needs of the child. What you can do as a teacher to support your pupils in such circumstances can be both limited and time-consuming but is, in many ways, essential. Other agencies may need to be alerted to provide support, but it is important that any inadequacies are recognised when building your learning relationships with your pupils.

While we are discussing Maslow and the needs he identified, it is important that I mention physical and sensory development, for these can significantly impact learner engagement and behaviour. I have found that on many occasions a pupil's physical and sensory development may go unrecognised. As a profession, we are alert to such things as dyslexia, for the symptoms can be easily seen, but even then, a pupil can go through school without it being picked up early enough, if it is identified at all.

You must be mindful that pupils are very good at hiding learning disabilities. They learn strategies to disguise their challenges or even lower their expectations. I hid my problem with spelling for years by having scruffy handwriting or limiting my choice of vocabulary when writing. Not until the advent of word processors was I able to express my thoughts and ideas in the manner I wanted.

*Any consideration of education must be framed within the kinetic chain of children's development in all their senses and motor skills, both individually and holistically.*

**(Davies, personal communication, 18 May 2020)**

Much in the way of your approach in teaching relies on a level playing field, of pupils all being emotionally and physically ready to learn. This is not always the case and behaviours can signal deficiencies in development. A revolution in my thinking and awareness of the impact on learning and pupil engagement of early physical and sensory development came about when I discovered the work of Charlotte Davies. I think it is so important that you are aware of what Davies has contributed to the topic of needs that I have asked her to introduce her work and to provide links, which you will find at the end of this chapter under *Further reading*.

## THE LEARNING ZONE AND LEARNING NEEDS

While the needs identified by Maslow provide for the internal engine that gets pupils into the classroom and allows them to behave within social constraints, gets them to the starting line, nonetheless different needs exist if we are to engage with others in learning. My own experience and research recognises that there are four other needs that pupils must satisfy if they are to engage purposefully in learning. In fact, these needs apply to any co-operative learning or task where you wish to bring people together to function as a team. If pupils do not satisfy these needs they will rarely enter what I call a learning zone (Figure 3.3), a state where they are both co-operative and receptive to learning and you are able to build effective learning relationships. The addition of Wi-Fi and internet access as part of our basic needs is a little tongue-in-cheek but it highlights the inadequacies that can exist when addressing what is now part of our learning and communication landscape needs.

The good news is we do not need to meet all of the learner's needs within the learning zone all of the time. What we must do, however, and this is where rewards fail to work in stimulating internal

*IF YOU CAN'T REACH THEM YOU CAN'T TEACH THEM*

need, is to meet them in the now. A promise of a meal in two days' time does nothing to help your hunger now and a meal in the past will do little to fulfil your hunger in a week or month from now.

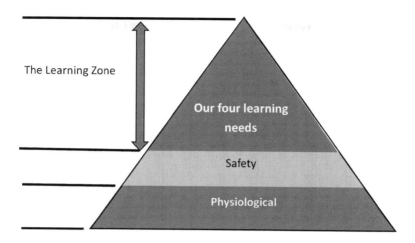

**Figure 3.3 Imposed learning zone**

The four needs that I believe directly relate to the learning zone in Figure 3.3 were identified by William Glasser (1988) in his book *Choice Theory in the Classroom*. Glasser identified needs that relate directly to the learner which, after satisfaction of the essential needs, are:

- belonging;
- power (voice);
- freedom (in a learning context I refer to this as 'choice');
- fun (associated with success or achievement).

Most teachers will recognise these needs but you may also recognise that, when there is focus on reaching targets, these needs are often ignored. This target-related pressure often distorts teachers' priorities, by putting outcomes before relationships (see distorted learning relationships in Chapter 2, Figure 2.12). This is a self-defeating action and ultimately leads to conflict and stress. Often it becomes a situation where there is more of the stick and less of the carrot – despite the pupils' lack of appetite for the carrot! In effect, you are not guiding or supporting learners but instead marching them along a certain route regardless of the process only to attempt to reach a specified outcome. If you pursue this course of action you can find a gulf opening up between you – the teacher – and the pupil. A gulf that will restrict your ability to satisfy the needs of pupils and, in most cases, will inhibit learning.

I have found that if you can satisfy, even in part, some or all of these needs most of the time then you can create the ideal conditions for the internal motivation to emerge from within the pupil and for them to engage in learning activities. If guided and supported appropriately you will achieve pupil engagement along with the benefits this brings to teaching and learning.

It is then up to you as the teacher to accept the responsibility and satisfy the desire to learn by guiding and supporting the pupil. You need to plan to meet these four learning needs, those that are part of the learning zone and lead to engagement. The nature of each need is discussed in Chapters 4 and 5, where I will show you how you can build meeting these needs into your teaching without any meaningful increase in planning or preparation time. First let us look at putting the four needs into a learning context.

## Part 2: Putting needs into a learning context

The context in which our needs arise is very important in terms of how we satisfy them. If we are thirsty and all there is to drink is lemonade, then we may or may not quench our thirst depending on whether we like or can tolerate lemonade. If there is a wider choice of beverages, then we are more likely to satisfy our thirst because there is more likelihood of finding something we actually like or prefer. So it is with our learning needs of belonging, power, choices (freedom) and fun. Note the change from *freedom* to *choice*; I have already said I refer to freedom as choice in the context of learning and there is a very good reason for this. You can imagine the chaos in a classroom if pupils were given freedom to choose what they did and when they did it! The context of learning in schools limits the freedom pupils have but, as we will see, there still needs to be choices.

The learning environment we find in many schools today is an artificial construct, one born out of historical and administrative requirements. It is directed by the timetable and exists to deliver and assess subject knowledge in the form of a curriculum. We could hardly imagine an environment more divorced from learning through personal need. This environment is camouflaged by creative and innovative teachers who carry their enthusiasm for teaching and learning with them into the classroom. I have seen primary classrooms turned into ocean liners or the cold landscape of the North Pole and the warm sands of Egypt. Teachers have gone out of their way to create a stimulating learning environment that is rich in resources and stimuli. We see less of this in secondary schools where the focus becomes more about examination grades and targets. This does not mean there are barren classrooms in all of our secondary schools, although I have come across a few more than I would like. You will still find the better examples of engaging and inviting learning environments in the creative subjects but there is opportunity in all subjects to say '*welcome to my world*' and to create interesting and focused environments for learning. Remember the need for you to model learning behaviours – awe and wonder are some of those behaviours. These are environments that address more than just the needs for the delivery of a subject or curriculum but also provide for learning needs.

The landscape our learners find themselves in recognises the need to learn but often fails to recognise other needs, those that help establish engagement, involvement, persistence, regulation of behaviour and co-operation. In other words we ask learners to learn but fail to recognise and address their learning needs. I am not talking about learning styles or multiple intelligences when I refer to learning needs, although these can generate individual specific learning needs. Instead, I am talking about needs learners have that must be addressed in order for them to engage in the learning process. We have established that to be fully engaged in learning, we must also recognise that the learner is required to have more than just enthusiasm for learning.

# Part 3: Addressing learning needs

I have tried to build a case for meeting learning needs, those that are part of our needs as humans and described by people such as Maslow and Glasser, but which also play a part in achieving learner engagement. The difference between a lesson where pupils are engaged in the work and one where they are not, even if only a few, can be significant. When we have to battle to control a lesson rather than guide the learning, we use more energy, suffer greater stresses and find it difficult to make learning fun. On the other hand, when the lesson flows and you are able to focus on the job of teaching, you often feel more energised and more relaxed. There is an almost tangible sense of mutual trust and respect. Lessons are more enjoyable and the time passes quickly.

# What next?

The next chapter is a practical exploration of the four learning needs within the teaching context. As stated in the introduction, I want this to be a practical guide to teaching and learning. I want it to be something you make notes on and in. I want it to guide your thinking and planning as well as your interaction with your pupils.

# References and further reading

Advocating Creativity (2016) *How Parents Can Support Learning at Home*. [online] Available at: https://4c3d.wordpress.com/2016/03/08/how-parents-can-support-learning-at-home/ (accessed 1 November 2020).

Creative Learning Company (nd) *History*. [online] Available at: www.my-learning-styles.com/about-us/history/ (accessed 1 November 2020).

Department for Education (2016) *Behaviour and Discipline in Schools: Advice for Headteachers and School Staff*. [online] Available at: https://assets.publishing.service.gov.uk/government/uploads/system/uploads/attachment_data/file/488034/Behaviour_and_Discipline_in_Schools_-_A_guide_for_headteachers_and_School_Staff.pdf (accessed 1 November 2020).

Davis, R D (1995) *The Gift of Dyslexia*. London: Souvenir Press.

**Davies, C, Healy, M and Smith, D (2018)** *The Maze of Learning: Developing Motor Skills*. Croydon, UK: Fit-2-Learn CIC.

As for the psychology behind motivation, there is much written by many authors on the topic of motivation. Here are some that were recommended to me with associated comments:

- *Vygotsky is worth looking at as he is theorising about extrinsic motivation within the environment (social learning).*

- *Bruner suggests movement from extrinsic towards intrinsic is desirable although still really in the context of rewards and sanctions*

- *Alfie Kohn is interesting on the intrinsic debate as is Carl Rogers.*

- *The work of Csikszentmihalyi on flow is also really interesting as is Barbara Freidrickson's Broaden and Build model.*

**Dawson, P and Guare, R (2009)** *Smart but Scattered*. London: Guilford Press.

**Dweck, C S (2008)** *Mindset: The New Psychology of Success*. New York: Ballantine.

**Hughes, D (2019)** *Future-proof Your School: Steering Culture, Driving School Improvement, Developing Excellence*. St Albans: Critical Publishing.

**Glasser, W (1988)** *Choice Theory in the Classroom*. London: HarperCollins.

**Prashnig, B M (1994)** *10 False Beliefs About Learning Causing High Stress and Burnout in Teachers*. [online] Available at: www.creativelearningcentre.com/downloads/10%20False%20Beliefs.pdf (accessed 1 November 2020).

**Prashnig, B (2004)** *The Power of Diversity: News Ways of Learning and Teaching through Learning Styles*. Stafford, UK: Network Educations Press Ltd.

**Selva, J (2020)** *Abraham Maslow, His Theory and Contribution to Psychology*. [online] Available at: https://positivepsychology.com/abraham-maslow/ (accessed 1 November 2020).

You can find more about Maslow and his background and contribution to positive psychology at this online source.

IF YOU CAN'T REACH THEM YOU CAN'T TEACH THEM

Your notes

# 4. THE FOUR LEARNING NEEDS

## Introduction

In Chapter 3, I listed four learning needs that I identified as being essential in building effective learning relationships with your pupils. I listed these as PBCF:

- power;
- belonging;
- choice;
- fun.

While they may appear obvious in their interpretation, they are susceptible to misunderstanding in the context of teaching. Before exploring each in turn, I will briefly describe each one so you are clear what they refer to when building learning relationships.

IF YOU CAN'T REACH THEM YOU CAN'T TEACH THEM

# Our four learning needs within an educational context

**Power:** to have a voice, to be listened to and to have a contribution to the learning experience.
**Belonging:** building relationships; being part of a learning community; affiliation to a class or group; having a common goal or purpose.
**Choice:** having more than one option but not without consequence; having the ability to decide upon an action or behaviour; understanding and accepting the potential outcomes.
**Fun:** celebrating achievement; enjoying a challenge; learning from mistakes without anxiety.

## ❖ Reflective task

A good way to understand these needs is to consider how you would feel if any were not being met. Take each in turn and note this down.

- Powerless, not having a voice.

- No sense of belonging.

- No choice in what you can do.

- Not having any fun in what you do or any sense of achievement.

There is no hierarchy to these learning needs; their impact on how we feel and behave can equally drive our engagement or lack of it. Within a learning situation, each can have its moment, a time when it is most important or of greater significance in building or maintaining a learning relationship. If you are observant and objective and recognise pupil behaviour as a symptom of a learning need then you can identify which are missing or which require immediate attention as part of your teaching. Therefore, the behaviours you witness and the interactions with your pupils offer a window into their learning needs. However, waiting until something goes wrong is never the best approach and I urge you to plan to meet all these needs during your teaching if you want to develop effective learning relationships with your pupils.

The essence of this book is based on the identification and the meeting of learning needs in your everyday teaching interactions and planning. To do so requires no special resources or additional time, only a mindful approach to your planning and teaching. Once you adopt PBCF as part of your way of thinking, then all the other elements of this book will come together.

You can remember the four learning needs with a mnemonic that uses the first letters of each need to form a phrase appropriate to your approach to teaching and building learning relationships.

**PBCF: please be child friendly**

I have developed this into a graphic that can be printed and used in numerous ways from a sticker in your planning book to a wall poster (see Figure 4.1).

**Figure 4.1 PBCF**

IF YOU CAN'T REACH THEM YOU CAN'T TEACH THEM

# Belonging

Although I said there is no hierarchy to the four learning needs from a teaching perspective, an argument could be made for making belonging your priority. Without welcoming pupils into our schools and classrooms, building any form of relationship is almost impossible. Belonging can also be the most powerful driver of our behaviours.

We all want to feel a sense of belonging in some way. This may be through our relationships, membership of groups or organisations or our jobs or professions. Some relationships are afforded to us (our family and possibly work colleagues) and some we seek out (our friends, hobbies, etc). Feeling a sense of belonging drives many of our social behaviours and decisions. We may dress or act in a particular way in order to fit in with a group to which we want to belong. Even if such behaviour challenges our existing sense of right and wrong we may still adopt the behaviour if the need to belong is strong enough. This is one of the reasons why, as a teacher, you must create a sense of belonging when welcoming pupils to your class or school.

Create a concept map or spider diagram that maps out your centres of belonging – the various groups or associations to which you feel you belong.

Imagine not belonging: how would this impact on your sense of identity and well-being?

Good teaching always fosters a sense of belonging. This is often easier to achieve and more consistent in primary schools where a single teacher has most of the contact with any one pupil or class. Secondary teachers face greater challenges developing a sense of belonging because a pupil may experience contact with several teachers in any one day or week. Pastoral systems in secondary schools have, in part, been successful in overcoming this challenge and helping to foster a sense of belonging. More recently, there has been pressure on this pastoral time as we chase targets and prioritise time for subjects within the curriculum. Nonetheless, I doubt if any teacher would argue against getting to know their pupils. We cannot, however, expect this to happen without making an effort. Knowing a name is not enough; you must go further. You must learn something of them as people. How can you do this? Take every opportunity to:

- meet up outside the classroom;
- chat in the playground;
- foster and take part in a school trip;
- organise and attend a school event or an after-school club;
- meet and greet in the corridor or in the lunch queue.

These things impact on your time, but balance that out against time spent dealing with pupils' lack of engagement or motivation, poor behaviour, a lack of work or work of a poor standard.

I encourage you not to ignore the pupil lingering after class has been dismissed or the one who appears uneasy for some reason. These may be signals they want to belong and you have an opportunity to make them feel that they do. You do not need to be their mate or act like a long-lost friend. Often a simple acknowledgement, a look in their direction at the right moment, is enough to develop that bond. Above all, learn to say through your actions, *'Welcome to my world, it is interesting and exciting, and I want you to be part of it'.* If you do, you will naturally create the sense of belonging that is essential to support pupils' engagement in learning. You will be sharing your enthusiasm for learning and, be of no doubt, this is infectious. You will be providing a reason for belonging, showing that there is something to be gained from this learning after all. Just ask yourself, would you want to attend a lesson taken by Mr or Ms Grumpy? Well, neither do learners.

Knowing even a little about a pupil beyond their name can have a significant advantage in challenging situations. Situations where the learner may not be compliant are often fraught and lead to direct challenges if allowed to escalate. They become a power struggle. Let me give you an example.

## Personal reflection

On passing a classroom where there was a disturbance to the lesson, I opened the door to see what the noise was all about. I saw a very animated teacher shouting at a boy running across the desks, encouraged by his classmates. Not an easy situation to resolve quickly. More shouting, more energy and it only fuels the situation. An audience is quick to assemble at such events and audience participation is not what is wanted in such cases. Luckily, I had come across this boy earlier in the term. I had found him outside another classroom; he was there because of his poor behaviour during the lesson. I took a little time to talk to him and find out why he was there. My approach had to be a measured one, he had that look! After getting his name and finding out why he was outside the classroom, I asked what he did when he was not at school. It turns out he was into fishing. I asked what would happen if he turned up at the riverbank without his bait or some other essential item. He told me he would not, that he always made sure he had everything because, if not, the day was wasted, and he had to go back home. I suggested school could be like that. Without the right equipment the day goes badly and it's wasted. Only that in the case of school there were rules and punishments too. I spent a few more minutes talking about where he liked to fish and the fish he caught before I asked the teacher if he could be accepted back into the room and rejoin the lesson.

Now back to this same boy running across the desks. I said nothing; I just stood in the doorway and looked at him. He looked at me and stopped running. I called him by name and asked that he follow me outside. He did as I asked. The look he had said it all; contrite and embarrassed. The lesson continued without further disturbance and we had a chat.

In talking to the teacher and pupil, the one thing that stood out was that the teacher knew nothing about this boy other than he often messed about in lessons. The only time she spoke to him was to give instructions or to reprimand him. Speaking to the boy, it was clear he felt anonymous and he had no sense of belonging. Does this explain why he responded to my presence and my request? There is no magic bullet or 'one way suits all' in teaching. I make no claims for the outcome being based solely on an earlier encounter but it was part of why things happened as they did in this case.

Taking the time and effort to get to know your pupils will pay off in the end. Some teachers have a knack for remembering pupils' names; others have to work at this. I also know some teachers teach far more pupils than others in any one given week. There are extremes in the number of pupils a teacher may come across in a typical week or even in a year. Primary teachers may only see one class of 30 or maybe 35 pupils each week and teach them throughout the day. Some secondary school teachers who teach a non-core subject may see as many as 20 classes in one week, each having 30 pupils. Appendix C lists some effective strategies for getting to know your pupils if you do not have the knack. There is also a very useful learner's tool, the 'Pupil learning passport', in Appendix D which will help in building their sense of belonging.

## THE BENEFITS OF BELONGING

In many situations the need for belonging can override the other three learning needs. We can tolerate not having fun if it means belonging to a group or sharing a common goal derived from a sense of belonging. As a result of belonging, we may sacrifice some or even all of our choices. This is a consequence of our decision to have our need to belong satisfied by a belief, ideal or action.

As for giving up power, our voice, we can easily accept our voice is that of the group to which we belong. We may decide or accept that the members of this group speak for us and this, in some ways, reinforces our sense of belonging.

Belonging is an important need in developing motivation and promoting engagement in learning. It is worth considering the benefits of belonging to a group or class.

- Creates a team, one of the most powerful combinations of human will.
- Able to relax – important for learning. We are able to let our guard down and are more likely to take risks.
- Able to give more of yourself – we are able to offer ideas and views without the concern of exclusion because of our views and we are more likely to be tolerated by the group.
- We learn and understand more quickly about social/group boundaries, customs and behaviours.
- We learn and gradually understand a common and possibly 'exclusive' language. Language is used a lot in developing our mental model, so understanding language used in a learning situation helps clarify the model and establish accuracy.
- Less bullying or victimisation, seen more as teasing within the group than possibly by outsiders.
- Benefits of shared experience for recall and establishing memory keys/anchors.
- Helps in building secure and long-term relationships that can survive challenges.
- More likely to listen to others and so have a better understanding of where they are coming from.

IF YOU CAN'T REACH THEM YOU CAN'T TEACH THEM

- Able to use shared humour, experiences and relationships in order to provide support during learning challenges.
- Shared understanding of drives and motives.
- Spontaneous support structures for members of the group.
- Less conflict between members of the team.
- Possibly subjugate own needs for the benefit of the group where a common goal is shared and believed in.
- Benefit of developing broader range of skills, attributes, attitudes and behaviours as a result of membership. Developing empathy, reading others, tolerating others.
- Belonging can bring out exceptional performance.
- Grit, determination and perseverance are all elements supported by the team and are all elements of overcoming learning challenges. These are encouraged in individuals by the sense of shared belonging.
- A sense of being cared for.
- Able to share.
- More readily willing to accept help.
- Identity – in fact several if you are a member of more than one group. This can cause problems if the behaviours associated with an identity are transferred to another group.

## Power

There is no doubt power can have a bad press. We all despise people who flaunt or misuse their power. Often, power is used to dominate others, to force contrition or requires compliance. The bully exerts power over those they bully. Interestingly, the Aboriginal word for a policeman is *'bullyman'*. We all need an element of power in our lives; to feel we have a voice. Not having a voice, believing no one is listening to us, being ignored, makes us feel powerless. In teaching, the need for the pupils' voice should not be seen as a power struggle.

William Glasser (2001) maintains that if pupils do not feel they have power in their classes, they will not work in school.

## ❖ Reflective task

Think of an occasion when you felt powerless and describe the circumstances that made you feel that way.

Pupils' responses to feeling powerless vary: some are contrite, and others try to reclaim some form of power or the feeling of having power. This can drive them to act in an aggressive manner towards others or to provoke and challenge those nearby, especially those seen as trying to control them in some way. In the school environment, the teacher is likely to be on the receiving end of such an outburst. There is also the passive demonstration of power. We can all recognise the pupil who refuses to move, to do as asked, who flaunts school uniform rules or who does not turn up to lessons or arranged meetings. I would suggest on many occasions these are acts symptomatic of the need to have a voice, that demonstrate a lack of more conventional ways of expressing need. Perhaps these pupils lack the language or the opportunity to express their needs in any other way.

Without co-operation and understanding, we strive to show our power by acting against what we see as the imposition of power by others. This may be a small symbolic gesture or a complete refusal to comply. Either way the gesture often attracts attention, an act that seeks to re-establish or emphasise some form of power. If your only focus in such situations is the challenge presented to you then you miss an opportunity to understand the struggle and to build belonging. Remember to see behaviour as a symptom of need and respond accordingly.

IF YOU CAN'T REACH THEM YOU CAN'T TEACH THEM

# FIRST STEPS IN EXPLORING POWER

The simplest and possibly earliest exhibition of the learning power struggle I can think of is the very young child who has yet to learn to walk or feed themselves and who, for the most part, has no power at all. Until they start to eat, that is. They then experiment, possibly through an internal drive, exploring the response they get to their behaviour. Perhaps they are trying to meet an internal need of which they have little or no comprehension. My example for this type of behaviour and need centres on getting the young child to eat something different. The child soon learns they can refuse to let the spoon into their mouths or that they can spit out the food. If you have the opportunity to watch this, then notice the effect it has both on the child and the parent and note also the eye contact.

The parent could see this as a challenge and want to end it by demonstrating the control or the power they have. You will recognise the facial expressions, tone of voice and other signals used. Perhaps you use similar ones with your pupils?

I believe that how we respond sets up many other condition/response behaviours further down the learning line. If alternatives are offered for each refusal, then we are teaching the young child that they can indeed control events around them. They have gained a small amount of power and they will flex and explore this power when they get the chance. Successful parents enter into a power-sharing agreement rather than a conflict situation. This does not mean the child and the parent will never challenge each other's power (wait until the teenage years!), but it does mean that rules and protocols are established that allow both to work successfully together. A win/win situation or compromise. What is essential, however, is consistency, for without it the power-sharing will be constantly renegotiated.

# CONSISTENCY IN THE SCHOOL CONTEXT

Schools are not isolated from the effects of families and how they bring up their children. If compromise and communication (listening and expressing) are the norms at home, then pupils will bring the same expectations (having a voice) and skills (negotiation and acceptance) to school. If, on the other hand, there is no compromise or only compromise (avoiding conflict and a lack of communication), then pupils may not be prepared to have a choice. This will certainly show up when there is a power struggle. A good example of when a power struggle can emerge is during the implementation of school rules.

Consistency in the application of school rules, from teacher to teacher and lesson to lesson, is a challenge. A lack of consistency could be the result of interpretation or of being new to a school and not yet fully conversant with how things are done. Whatever it is, a lack of consistency can result in a pupil renegotiating (challenging) rather than accepting the rules. These challenges can take up a great deal of time and resources and are a distraction from learning.

Let us look at the pupil who arrives without whatever is required for a lesson. You could say the pupil is not prepared to learn and you could go about enforcing whichever school rule applies. Enforcing a rule means initiating consequences, effectively a form of punishment. This is typical in such circumstances as we seek to discourage the breaking of rules. If all teachers are consistent in the application of this rule, then we hope the pupil gets the message and comes equipped to the lessons. If a teacher decides not to enforce the rule, then this lack of consistency opens the door for negotiation. In effect, they are initiating a power struggle by not being consistent (we are back to the baby and feeding ritual). The common strategy used by some pupils in the power struggle is an escalation of consequences, much the same as the teacher uses. If the pupil makes more of a fuss than the issue is worth (delayed lesson start, taking up teacher time, disruption, etc) then it is easier for the teacher to compromise and so the pupil gets their way. However, this is no solution and will ultimately encourage inconsistent behaviour. So how does this fit in with learning needs and power? The key question is: are you listening to the pupil?

Consider for a moment the pupil who has no voice, no involvement in the process of developing school rules. There may have been a pupil voice at the start of developing school rules but that could have been some time ago. It is my experience that present pupils may not have had the process, discussions and outcome rationale explained to them. Where I have done this, listened first then explained, there has been acceptance. We like to know why and we like to ask questions. This is a win/win situation and there is no reason to renegotiate a situation as there is common understanding of the reasons why and the benefits.

Finally, what of the pupil who forgets on purpose? This could be a symptom of not being heard and a desire to voice their needs.

Not all pupil actions are those of defiance or forgetfulness. For an excellent review of pupil voice in action I recommend reading David Hughes' (2019) chapter entitled 'Pupils: Passive or active participants in your school?' in his book *Future-proof Your School*.

## POWER IN TEACHING AND LEARNING

Power is not always about getting what you want or believe you need. Achieving power can take the form of mastering a subject or skill or acquiring a responsibility as a reward for an action or actions over time. In such examples, power is conferred by a sense of recognition, of having a voice, and is probably most closely linked to learning.

It is preferable that, in schools, pupils ultimately reach the understanding that knowledge and learning can bring a form of power that satisfies their need. It is up to the teacher to show they support and value this form of power and that it brings rewards with it. This is not the instant power, however, that pupils may crave. Learning that power has to be worked for and accepting the delay is helpful in sustaining effort when needs are not satisfied immediately. We may refer to this situation as deferred gratification. Saving up to buy a long-anticipated item or to go on holiday brings with it not only the reward of acquisition but the ability to maintain the necessary focus or effort over time.

If we consider being powerless, we think no one is listening to us. In a learning environment this is exactly what a lack of power means. How long would you go along with working in a voluntary manner if no one paid you any attention, did not listen to what you had to say, did not give you any responsibility or ignored your requests? If you have ever heard the argument from a pupil about you getting paid for coming to school and not them, then you will recognise the motive behind such arguments. Giving pupils a voice is part of meeting their need for power. It is also a way of developing their strategies for negotiation, compromise and sharing.

## Asking questions

Saying you do not understand something is a hard thing to do and, depending on the situation and environment, requires a degree of bravery. In a classroom, among peers, it is one of the bravest acts for a learner. As a teacher, you ignore such demonstrations at your peril. Remember, it is your job to help learners to understand and it is not their fault if they do not. If a pupil is comfortable enough with you to say '*I do not understand*', then listen and respond but not by simply repeating the same explanation or demonstration. If you do you are not listening; you are not empowering your pupils!

My advice is to first acknowledge and then question to determine what is understood. In doing so, you recognise and acknowledge the pupil's achievements and do not ignore them. Then tailor your response, your teaching, from this point using what they know to help them understand what they do not. In this way, you can help the learner build their confidence, while you have shown you have listened.

## EMPOWERING PUPILS IN YOUR CLASSROOM

Here is a list of common strategies you can use to empower your pupils.

- Allocate duties and responsibilities.
- Ask for feedback or suggestions as to any improvements that could be made regarding classroom or lesson organisation and behaviours.
- Encourage a managed voice. Discourage shouting out; this is not a voice but only noise. A managed voice involves considered questioning or opinion. Phrases such as '*Before I ask you to give me an answer I want you to think about...*' help to emphasise the value of a managed voice in terms of having power in the learning environment.
- Take time to ask opinions and discover views about what is being learnt.
- Involve them in future lesson planning and ask for ideas on delivery.
- Have a pupils' learning noticeboard in your classroom, one that they own and contribute to.

Remember with every question you ask a pupil, you can listen to them and have an opportunity to explain your side of things too.

# Choice

*May your choices reflect your hopes, not your fears.*

**Nelson Mandela**

Although William Glasser calls this need '*freedom*', within the context of learning I prefer the term '*choice*'. Why not freedom? The school environment is an artificial one, a construct, born out of a need to organise and manage learning through subjects. This environment cannot offer freedom to the individual (teacher or pupil), as they are contracted to operate within the organisational requirements such a system demands. We need to turn up at certain times, follow a timetable of some form, learn through subjects and demonstrate a level of understanding or knowledge specified as being appropriate to a specific age or stage in education. What is sought is compliance to whatever model is in place. Freedom in the school context is very hard to find, never mind choice.

## Choice in the classroom

Choice is a difficult need to manage because so much of the teaching and learning environment involves making choices. Choices are made in terms of topic, content, delivery, levels, pace,

IF YOU CAN'T REACH THEM YOU CAN'T TEACH THEM

assessment, seating, grouping and guidance to name a few! However, these are school or teachers' choices and not those of the learner.

As part of meeting learning needs and building learning relationships it is important that learners are offered a choice but within the terms set down by the teacher. Offering a true choice to pupils requires a confident teacher; not one who sees offering choice as giving away some element of control or power. Such a teacher is likely to withdraw choice when they believe they are losing control. Pupils can see through this type of teacher and soon recognise they have no choice at all. Offering choice should not be seen as a way of dealing with conflict either. Once again, this requires a committed and confident teacher willing to challenge those who have made a choice and not followed through. Making a choice and not sticking with it and then wanting another choice does nothing to generate a sense of responsibility. An important lesson to learn is that choice brings consequences and therefore a sense of responsibility for our actions.

## ❖ Reflective task

How do you behave and feel when presented with a challenge and you have:

1. no choice;

2. limited choice;

3. multiple choices?

If you have been honest with yourself, I believe you will see the same behaviours in your pupils.

## MAKING POOR CHOICES

Wanting to renegotiate a choice during an activity wastes a lot of time. This course of action may be the purpose of a learner who seeks a sense of belonging. By occupying your time, they are employing a strategy to meet their learning need for being acknowledged; they are in contact with you and they are your focus. This is not the type of relationship you, as a teacher, want, however, so it is best to find other ways of creating the sense of belonging as described earlier.

Wanting to change a choice that has already been made may also be the strategy or action of a learner who does not feel confident in tackling the learning challenge they face. By accepting or making an initial choice, they are merely avoiding conflict or hoping to delay actually undertaking the work at a later point. The choice they make may also be an act of bravado in front of peers and may be regretted later. Once faced with no other option but to face the learning challenge, they fall back on the choice change or renegotiate tactics. If this fails and there is a lack of sensitive support, conflict can erupt, especially with those pupils who have limited strategies in such circumstances.

Looking for the easy choice is also a strategy used by reluctant learners. Problems arise when they discover either there are no easy choices or the choice they made was a harder choice than they thought. Sometimes, the easy choice is best described as the one where the ratio between new learning and existing understanding or knowledge means less effort will be required by the pupil. This has its own problems too. Pupils who are not challenged can get bored easily and become a distraction to others or demanding of more teacher time. Explaining the choices and guiding the learner when there is a choice on offer is a significant part of teaching and in creating an environment where learning needs are met.

## MAKING A CHOICE

When faced with challenges, pupils tend to use strategies that have worked for them in the past. When choice is available we will all choose to react to any given situation in a way that best suits our needs. We are unlikely to opt for strategies that do not work for us. If, as learners, we are in a learning environment we find toxic (having a negative impact on our emotions, creating anxiety), we are faced with a choice about how to behave. The strategy chosen will depend on the success of earlier experiences as well as our inherent nature and the relationships we have with those around us. In my experience, there are two basic choices – flight or fight – the elements of any survival strategy.

The flight and fight extremes involve strategies that get learners out of the toxic learning environment in the quickest possible time. Non-compliance is often the favourite, a form of fight first and then flight, and knowing which buttons to press with the teacher to get sent out or excluded from the lesson is well practised. Flight may also mean doing nothing, withdrawing and avoiding any form of engagement. For those whose nature is compliant, this is the most frequently used strategy. Fight may mean being defiant or seeking attention in order to avoid facing the challenges. As a teacher, you have to decide what strategy the learner is using and for what purpose at any given time. The more you know your pupils, the more accurate your diagnosis will be.

## OFFERING A CHOICE

It is also important to reflect on the choices you offer your pupils. Are your pupils confident and able to deal with being given a choice? Are there choices within each learning occasion you create, do your pupils recognise them and are they practised in making a choice?

Some pupil responses or choices are traditional and well recognised. For example, raising the hand or calling out when a question is asked. Of course, you may not want these to be the primary choices for learners to demonstrate their understanding; you may want learners to consider other choices first, in some sort of hierarchy. Other choices may include the pupil writing the answer on a small whiteboard and holding it up (used to good effect in maths), explaining the answer to a learning partner or suggesting a question based on the correct answer. Anything other than a direct, hands-up approach is often used when trying to develop independent learning.

Not all choices are relevant to all groups of pupils. Much depends on the learning challenges, prior learning, resources and time. From the teaching perspective, the key is clear communication about what is available, when and why. The ability to make informed choices and find alternatives when faced with a learning challenge is very much what learning intelligence (LQ) is about (see Chapter 12).

## Case study

The teacher sets an extended task to research and present the historical events of a particular occasion. He has offered some choice as to how the report on the events can be presented. The pupils have four weeks to prepare and present their report and there is ample lesson time, access to historical resources and teacher support.

The three ways the report can present events are:

- a newspaper article, a type of front page reporting of events;
- a video interview with an eyewitness account;
- a traditional essay-style account of what happened.

Of the three choices, Jenna opts for the video interview. After a couple of weeks, she has done very little apart from become familiar with the video equipment. This was something she worked enthusiastically at mastering. The teacher is monitoring progress and challenges Jenna to account for her lack of progress since none of the historical research has been started. She is contrite and promises that now she is able to use the video equipment she will get on with the research. With only days left, there is no evidence to suggest that Jenna will finish the task on time or that she will have anything to present. She responds to a challenge about this saying no one would be an eyewitness and the video camera was playing up and anything she has done has been lost! The end result is that Jenna has nothing to show for her time spent on this task and does not pass the module.

## ❖ Reflective task

The case study is an example of where choice has not worked for the teacher or for the learner. Suggest what the reasoning is behind the strategy used by the pupil and why choice failed?

Reason for adopted pupil strategy:

Why the offering of choice failed on this occasion:

IF YOU CAN'T REACH THEM YOU CAN'T TEACH THEM

The offer of choice in this example could have been highly motivational. It could allow pupils with different strengths to tackle the same challenge but in different ways. I believe it failed for the following reasons.

- It was a free choice and not a guided choice. Free choice is not what should be available in a teaching and learning context. Somebody unskilled in using video equipment should have been discouraged from attempting the task in this way unless there was past evidence that they were capable of the challenge.

- Jenna probably saw the video task as a way of avoiding writing or as 'fun' (we come to that need next). She may dislike writing, or it is something she finds difficult. Once she realised a written script was still required, she avoided the task, finding excuses for not completing it. The consequences of making that choice had not been made clear to her.

There is more than one way to learn something or to demonstrate understanding. By scaffolding a research project and allowing different forms of expression and presentation we can offer choices in the way the task is completed. Each option has its own demands in terms of skills and abilities as well as time and interests. Whichever method is chosen by the learner, they still have the responsibility to finish on time and to show their understanding. We have a situation where the learner has made a choice but they must also accept the responsibility for their choice. Unfinished work is still unfinished work and the learner should be held accountable for this.

## BROADENING OUR APPROACH TO LEARNING THROUGH CHOICE

One response of educationalists to the challenge of learning has been to describe learners as having 'learning styles' and to suggest teaching them according to these styles. In effect, we are offering choices as to how to learn. This approach has received both support and derision. It is also one fraught with difficulties if we attempt to plan lessons to cater for each and every proposed style of learning and for multiple pupils. I am strongly of the belief that this is never what was intended and is an example of how education is susceptible to adoption of theories without fully understanding them. I happen to believe there is something in the concept of learning styles but see it as a way of describing our learning preferences, those approaches we favour and have therefore developed. If we are to fully prepare pupils we should, through managed choice, be encouraging them to develop other approaches and broaden their learning strategies. It is easy to allocate responsibility for failing to learn or having difficulty in learning to not having our preferred ways of learning open to us. This is one drawback of emphasising learning styles. Another is applying labels (see Chapter 8).

Reluctance to learn can be seen as symptoms of problems linked to learning and not the root cause. However, any approach that challenges us to look at the activity of learning in a new and objective way has some value. A preferred learning style suggests to me a dominating practical form of learning need outside of the four we are exploring here. Having a preference for something to do with learning does not mean we cannot learn without it being met, it may just mean it is harder for us learn when the preference is not accommodated. It may make us feel uncomfortable in that particular learning situation. For example, a pupil may enjoy and benefit from the opportunity to enter into a discussion about a topic in order to clarify and refine their understanding. If the teacher does not allow them to do this in class they may feel uncomfortable but still learn. Where motivation and drive to learn are limited, the result may be that the pupil switches off.

Staying with only one way of doing something is limiting; this is true in learning as in any other activity. Having the ability to throw or catch with only one hand can be a disadvantage if we hurt our dominant hand or arm. If through the absence of choice, we are not allowed or encouraged to explore other ways of learning, we may never extend our list of options, strategies or preferences. We may also never find a way that suits us and makes learning that little bit more enjoyable or easier.

Many teachers teach in the manner they were taught. When planning a lesson or breaking a concept down and deciding on how to approach teaching it, they make choices based on their own learning experiences and preferences. I do not have a problem with this. As teachers, our own understanding and confidence in what we are delivering and how are critical in our ability to inspire and motivate others. If you share the passion for your subject, this is infectious. Nevertheless, a consequence of this is that the teacher may not consider the choices their pupils need in order to meet their learning needs. By limiting choice, teachers may be disabling some learners, preventing them from either exercising choices that work for them or limiting the strategies they develop that may be of use in other situations or learning environments.

Let me give you an example of the above that draws on the use of homework.

Teacher A plans without pupil input, insists all key learning topics are covered in lesson time and controls the resources that are available for learning and the manner in which learning will take place. There is no time allocated to pupils who want to carry out independent study or research; neither is there any opportunity for group discussion or review during the lessons. Homework is mostly used to complete set tasks based on the lesson delivery.

Teacher B offers choices throughout the planning and delivery. Pupils are consulted on the focus for the topic, asked how they feel about their learning so far and how prepared they are for the challenges ahead, and if they can think of anything that could help or assist in their learning. Resources are controlled but the range and access offers some choice. At key points, pupils are given the opportunity to contribute to a review or summary of learning points and knowledge acquired. Homework is an opportunity for pupils to extend their work, prepare resources or complete classwork, depending on their progress.

A caveat here is there is nothing wrong with limiting choice, so long as there is some choice and there is support for developing agency, developing other learning approaches, when learning preferences are not available. The teacher must be confident they have planned and resourced their teaching to meet the needs of their pupils.

Finally on this point, as a teacher you must ensure you remain a learner and model learning behaviours to your pupils. Taking on something outside of your comfort zone, or learning something in a manner that does not meet your preferences is a sobering experience and reminds you how difficult learning can be; not because of ability but because perhaps the learning environment doesn't meet your learning needs. Since taking up tai chi, I am reminded of this every time a new move I am trying to learn ends up more like a pantomime than a graceful act of meditation through movement. Just watching does not help me learn; I like diagrams too, so I have made my tutor aware and we are working on developing a graphic language that I can use to support my learning.

There are emotional needs when we are faced with new challenges and learning is no different. A lack of choice can appear to mean no control or power over events, the outcome of which is stress. If as a teacher you offer choices that do not cater for existing pupil learning preferences then you should be aware of the additional challenges you are presenting to your pupils. You may have to provide additional emotional support or encouragement in order to help a pupil attempt new or different ways from those they prefer. Restricting choice has the same effect and so consider any rules you have for learners and how they may impact on their learning. For example, having a rule that prohibits doodling may remove an activity a learner associates with concentration and which helps them focus.

## THE IMPORTANCE OF CHOICE IN ASSESSING LEARNING

It is appropriate to mention the concept of mindful learning (see Chapter 6) briefly here because the choices you give during assessment impact on learning needs. Mindful teaching means you do not exclude learners from learning opportunities as a result of the limited choices you offer. Suggesting or insisting there is only one way to learn something or to demonstrate understanding excludes and demotivates those who are unsure. Excluding learners is one way of saying *'you do not belong'* and belonging is a need we have already discussed.

The choices you offer for assessment can significantly influence the demonstrated level of understanding (see Chapter 11, rule number 6 – Always work out what you want to know before you ask the question). It can also include or exclude pupils, affecting their level of engagement and motivation. Asking questions that only allow for a written answer can be an issue for those who do not like to write but prefer to discuss or verbalise their responses. Learners who exhibit a lack of confidence may not choose to join in a discussion but may have a thorough and insightful understanding of the topic. Without having an appropriate choice of how to demonstrate understanding, you may never know what has been learnt or understood. Mindful teaching offers better engagement and limits exclusion.

So choice is not necessarily a free ride to do as you like but to explore what works for you and then to apply this to learning. If pupils are encouraged to meet their learning needs and are given the freedom to discover for themselves what these are and how to satisfy them, then they will be engaged in learning. In many ways, they cannot do anything else but engage. Consider allowing pupils to doodle, to play with something (quietly without affecting the learning needs of others), or have time for self-talk when engaged in learning. Giving them these freedoms to choose their actions meets one of their needs and gets you one step closer to engagement.

What about learning teams? Can pupils be trusted to work as part of a team and how do you assess individual achievement or contributions? Please do not let these issues prevent you trying to establish learning teams for they can provide the freedoms that pupils need to become absorbed in learning. Teams also provide many of the other needs we have, a sense of belonging, of power and our next topic, fun.

The benefits of offering and having choice are as follows.

- Offering somebody a choice gives you an opportunity to present an alternative view or opinion about something.
- Having choice encourages us to be involved by providing an opportunity to ask questions.
- Making a choice carries with it a responsibility for your actions.
- Offering a choice makes you consider alternatives in either approach or outcome.
- Choice can provide a means of differentiation and access to a situation.
- Making choices offers an occasion to learn from the outcome and reflection.
- Choices can help you develop self-agency as you experience different options and build them into your learning map (what you believe we can and cannot learn).
- Choice helps you be creative if faced with choices that do not suit your needs.
- Defending the choices you make can help you gain an understanding of the impact they may have on others and therefore assist in developing empathy.
- Making your own choices helps you understand the process others go through in making their choices, offering a degree of insight.
- Being offered choice provides the opportunity to receive advice or guidance.
- Choice can help you learn to manage dilemma and conflict.
- Emotional states can be triggered by being offered a choice, helping you broaden your understanding of self.
- Learning to listen to and evaluate the choices you are offered develops your critical sense.
- Having made a choice, you may be more determined in your actions.
- Taking a choice you are offered may require you to be more courageous than you would otherwise be.
- Being involved in making a choice can encourage you to be more collaborative in your actions.
- Having to be more adaptable may be the outcome of having a choice.
- Making a choice may involve taking a risk; such actions are often required in learning something new.

IF YOU CAN'T REACH THEM YOU CAN'T TEACH THEM

# fun

*Never, ever underestimate the importance of having fun.*

**Randy Pausch**

Teachers are not stand-up comics and nor should they be, but in many ways lessons and learning are theatre. Imagination and creativity can expose the fun element of learning. Fun is often the best reason we have for doing something, so why leave it out of learning?

How many times have you said or been encouraged with the words, *'Come on, it will be fun'*? If you have said this or had it said to you then it was probably an effort in persuasion; we often use the lure of fun to spur somebody to do something, to encourage them to join in. Well that is what we want in our lessons, learners to join in, to engage. Accepting that fun should be part of a lesson is not a big ask. What is difficult when planning and delivering lessons is providing the appropriate structure that will manage the fun element. Fun does not mean being silly or losing control of the learning. One of the biggest challenges you will face as a teacher is to link fun to achievement but this is the key.

## ❖ Reflective task

Think about your own education and choose a subject you enjoyed. Now characterise the lessons and the teacher's approach, even their personality. Use as many adjectives as you like. Finally, underline any you would associate with fun, enjoyment or a sense of achievement. Once you have done this, contrast your response to one that you would make if you considered a subject you did not enjoy.

Having fun addresses our need to be engaged in something. Sir Ken Robinson (2010) refers to it as finding your element. The opposite of having fun, of being engaged, finding that times flies quickly, is being bored, and we know both the physical and mental impact that has on us. When you are bored time drags, you become lethargic; everything becomes a great effort.

We do not suffer boredom easily and we accept any diversion that takes us out of that state. Pupils will look for or notice anything that appears remotely interesting when they experience boredom. They may stare out of the window and allow their imagination to drift, count the ceiling tiles, doodle or play with anything to hand, provoke others to get a response (any response) and any number of other activities that will stave off the boredom. What they seek is a little fun to break the boredom. If you have ever had to invigilate an examination for an hour, you will know what this feels like.

Your challenge is to get the balance right between what can be considered work, pupils on task, and distractions. Fun can fall into the list of distractions but can also be what motivates pupils, keeping them on task. The lyrics 'a spoonful of sugar helps the medicine go down', from *Mary Poppins* reminds us how unpleasant tasks can be made more palatable with a little 'sugaring'. But be warned: too much sugar can make us ill too!

Creative teachers can meet the need for fun within the structured teaching and learning environment they generate but this requires careful planning and resourcing – and a sense of humour occasionally!

## THE CONSEQUENCES OF FORGOING FUN

Unless the learner is meeting their need for fun from within the lesson delivery and subject content, then there is the increased possibility that they search for it elsewhere. How any individual pupil will respond to a lack of fun will vary. Some pupils will attempt to distract other pupils, try to engage with you off topic or sit daydreaming.

Consider the example of the class clown. This character can be a major distraction in the lesson as they draw on their own need and that of others for fun. In addition, any pupil can be the nucleus from which a group can form. Such affiliations can be the beginnings of a sense of belonging, an allegiance you may not favour. What you do not want as a teacher is an alternative sense of belonging to the one you create. If you do not build an element of fun into the lesson and the class clown makes an appearance, you will find yourself facing behaviour that could be considered confrontational. This is also an example of how the four learning needs can work together in teaching, as the need for fun leads to the building of a sense of belonging. You need to be mindful of all four of the learning needs all of the time.

Things getting out of hand and a challenge to leadership of the lesson are of concern to any teacher but the element of fun within a lesson remains important. Without it you will be actively engaged in patrolling the class, trying to keep pupils on task. Whereas if the learner can discover or fulfil a sense of fun within the tasks then you can apply your energies to other aspects of teaching. I need to state here, however, that I am not advocating the telling of jokes, well maybe not constantly! The odd joke can help build up a rapport with individuals as you try to best each other for the most cringe-worthy joke perhaps or the one-liner with impact. Jokes are great ways of providing learning anchors; moments we remember most easily and to which learning points can be attached or associated with.

Fun can offer a platform for the other needs I have mentioned too. Sharing a joke or humorous event or set of circumstances can bring people together, creating a sense of belonging. People use humour to give themselves a voice. Making something fun can allow you to get a message across that may otherwise be censored. The phrase, '*I am only joking!*' helps you get away with whatever you did or said because you claim not to be serious. Fun can even make an undesirable choice a little more palatable. Finding the fun in an otherwise tedious task allows us to partake in the task without having the feelings associated with boredom. Activities such as singing, dancing, and clapping are useful additions to a learning activity – but only if associated with the learning objectives.

If you take a moment to consider what makes learning fun for you, what engages you, then you will begin to identify the fun you can have with your class. If you can convey your enthusiasm, your passion for your subject and the power of learning, then you are already halfway there in creating effective learning relationships. The problem I sometimes find when working with teachers is that they have lost their sense of awe and wonder and, as a result, their sense of fun in learning too. The focus of lesson planning and delivery for some has become subject knowledge and assessment. What can be missing is the passion for the subject that propelled them into being teachers in the first place. This is understandable for a few reasons.

## Why we forego fun

### I. A CONSEQUENCE OF A TARGET-DRIVEN CULTURE

The first reason we let go of fun as a learning need to be built into our teaching is that in a target-driven culture the focus is always the target. In such circumstances, we can become target fixated.

All we see, plan and do is based on achieving the target. We risk leaving out fun because we see it as having no direct relevance to achieving the target.

The issue, the problem of leaving fun out of learning, is that it is not an activity, it is more a state of mind, an attitude. It is what allows us to look at adversity and see the humour within in. It is what gives us the ability to not be overwhelmed by challenge and adversity but to rise above them. To leave fun out of the learning environment is to expect a car to run without refuelling; it will go along for a while but then everything comes to a standstill when the fuel runs out. Those of a more serious disposition (or who hold the overall responsibility for achieving targets) may see fun as a distraction, of being off task and as a reason for failing to reach a target. While this is understandable, it is wrong.

When we are looking for improvements, it is easier to do more of what does not work if it is considered a traditional way of achieving a target. It is often harder to do something unconventional, different from the norm, that may actually underpin achievement. The term 'tradition' is more often code for 'safe' and is a barrier to initiative and risk, both often associated with fun. Tradition also means it was somebody else's idea and so when targets are not reached, the responsibility for failure lies somewhere else.

Unfortunately, this can backfire too. If a traditional approach is accepted as a suitable approach but does not provide the required outcomes then it must be the person who is implementing the approach who is at fault. In a blame culture such as this, it is the teacher who is expected to work harder and we know what working harder means – there is little or no room for fun. Fun is the most variable of our learning needs and will need protection from misguided strategies for raising attainment and for reaching targets.

## 2. THE TEACHER AS A LEARNER

The second reason we may see fun wither in teaching is that the teacher becomes somebody who is no longer a learner. This can happen all too easily, especially when a teacher stops exploring their own interests and passions. The pressure of teaching, the demanding nature of the job, can become all-consuming if we let it. When we do, there is no time left for us to follow our own learning path and creative journey. We are also so familiar with our subject and the delivery that we no longer understand the difficulty of learning. We refer to this as mastery. To say we can end up going through the motions is probably unfair, but we can forget the difficulties we faced when we first encountered the learning challenges we now present as teachers. It does not matter what you learn, the taking on of a new challenge is a good way to reinvigorate your lessons and to rediscover the fun aspects of learning.

## 3. LINKING FUN TO ACHIEVEMENT

It easy to do the fun things when it comes to learning. We more often than not find easy things, things we have mastered, fun. It is the challenges we have yet to overcome that we find hardest to turn into fun. Some would say there is no fun in failure, in coming last or in struggling to get to grips with something while those around us appear to get it. It is easier to teach pupils while they are having fun. The challenge in teaching comes when pupils are experiencing a negative emotional state. When they want to give up, push away the task and say '*I can't do this*', you need a strategy.

If fun is always the easy things, the distraction or intermission in learning, then we shall constantly face a demand for fun over challenge in our teaching. The trick is to link fun to overcoming challenges, to seeing an element of achievement in everything we do as learners. You need to encourage your pupils to see achievement as fun in itself. Knowing something new, understanding a new concept or making a learning link, solving a problem as a result of what you have learnt, can all generate a great deal of fun if handled in the right way. I am talking about building a class culture of celebrating learning and achievement.

The caveat is that achievement is acknowledged for what it is and that we do not just see it as a target to tick off a list. Make and take the time to celebrate achievement and fun will no longer be a distraction to learning; instead, it will be a significant motivator.

## 4. DISCIPLINE AND FUN

One more reason for not having an element of fun (and remember that includes creating a sense of achievement) is that you are fighting a constant battle to engage the learners. In such a scenario you will naturally fall back on a strict set of routines or expected behaviours in order to establish discipline. In effect, you are trying to keep a lid on poor or disruptive behaviour in order to teach. In such an environment, having fun could be seen as a sign of weakness, a chink in your armour and something to be exploited by the pupils. I have fought such battles and know how draining they can be. If you were to look for a sense of priority in meeting learning needs, then you could ask the question: Can we have purposeful fun in a learning situation if we do not first have a sense of belonging? It is certainly much easier to have fun in a lesson when there is a sense of belonging. It is amazing what can be regarded as fun, and an element of fun together can be the start of forming a sense of belonging within a class or group. Fun activities can ease tension and disarm a conflict situation in the time it takes to smile.

## Personal reflection

Taking on what is regarded as a challenging group is something all teachers face at some point in their career. I learn a great deal about teaching from such groups; they certainly stretch me. This is a story about one of those groups that shows how important fun is as a learning need.

The group is made up of boys and girls aged 15 and 16 and of mixed ability. It is an option group, a subject they have chosen to study over the next two years for a GCSE-level examination but have not studied before. The members of the group are known to be challenging, opting for confrontation rather than compliance when faced with learning challenges. They were 'sold' a subject they had not failed at before and so took the offer, not really understanding what was involved.

They soon discovered the course was not what they expected and, in order to maintain a working level of behaviour, I responded by upping my level of control and authority. Learning tasks were tightly controlled although I maintained an element of choice. I refused to be negative about the group and always appeared happy to teach them. I looked for innovative ways to deliver a relatively theory- and textbook-based subject which did not interest them at all. I worked at getting to know each member of the class but was often met with suspicion.

In my judgement, I was not doing too well. Each lesson remained a challenge and progress was slow. I was not my usual relaxed self with this group and I was not having fun. The school had brought in a behaviour consultant to look at overall school behaviour in lessons and on visiting my lesson reported that this group behaved far better for me than for other teachers and that they liked me. Not a judgement I would have made but by then I had lost my perspective. This was followed by one pupil suggesting I '*lighten up*', as I was being too serious and strict all the time. Altering my perspective became my challenge. I began to relax a little in the class and take time to be mindful of the response I was getting from the pupils. The fact that I was not my normal relaxed self in the class meant they found it hard to relax too. I had to be careful not to go too far too soon, remember my behaviour was signalling a change to our learning relationship. I looked for opportunities to smile, the most easily recognised signal of having fun. After a while I was more my old self: firm, friendly and fair with a sense of fun that I was comfortable in showing.

This is just one lesson this group taught me. I had achieved more than I thought in terms of meeting their learning needs but in extreme or challenging situations it is important to cover all four learning needs, especially fun.

## FUN AND REWARDS

A warning I would give is not to link having fun to offering rewards. You can have fun rewarding pupils but please do not make the reward a fun activity in its own right; it has limited merit and is fraught with difficulties. Offering to watch a film or play games if the learning task is done only leads to the task being rushed and the learning aspects ignored. Offering fun before getting down to learning reinforces the idea that learning cannot be fun. Celebrating an achievement can be a fun activity, but only because the focus was the learning and not the activity of having fun.

## FUN CAN RELIEVE OR PREVENT STRESS

What happens when things are not fun or it is not shared? Well, I have already mentioned that learners will undoubtedly find their own ways of having fun but it is unlikely this will make it fun for you. You may find teaching less rewarding, so there is a chance you will make your lessons less rewarding, less engaging and so a downward spiral starts. I do not want to be alarming here but I do want to point out that when things do not go your way, when you feel you have lost control, when you have no power or freedoms, then you become disengaged just as the learner does. We are human after all and will seek the same gratification of our needs as any other human. In teaching, this can lead to a build-up of stress that is difficult to dissipate and this can have an impact on your physical and mental health. It can also lead to you having fun at the expense of the pupils. I am referring here to the use of sarcasm. Sarcasm is certainly not shared fun; in fact it is anything but. Sarcasm is often used to dominate, to put pupils in their place or to establish some element of superiority. In teaching, I see the use of sarcasm by the teacher as a sign of weakness, of laziness. Instead of working to meet and manage learning needs, some think they can achieve the same end through sarcasm.

From the pupil perspective, having a sense of fun, especially when facing a challenge, can go a long way to reducing anxiety and stress. If pupils look forward to having fun in your lesson then they will look forward to your lessons and we know we find it easier to learn if we are relaxed.

## THE BENEFITS OF MEETING THE NEED FOR FUN

Fun can come about through challenge, success, praise, collaboration, achievement, helping, recognition, feedback, insight and much more. With so many opportunities, it should not be difficult to have fun within any learning situation. Here is a summary of how fun influences learning and building learning relationships.

- Taking the opportunity to build celebration into recognising all forms of achievement can actively support our need for fun.
- It is better for the learning culture to celebrate achievement within a fun atmosphere or culture rather than isolating it and making the achievement the only outcome we focus on.
- Fun can help raise energy levels when faced with learning challenges and maintain a positive 'can do' outlook, despite setbacks.
- Fun can be the lens that helps us see our success and not linger on our failures.
- Fun can make feedback into feedforward, the act of using what we have learnt to improve future performance.
- Building fun into working towards celebrating success can be the spoonful of sugar rather a terminal reward that just distracts the learner from the task and prevents them from learning to enjoy it.
- Linking fun to achievement makes the acceptance of praise that much easier and can overcome peer pressures where these are working against achievement.
- The presence of fun is a great learning anchor, something we recall easily and which can associate learning with helping with recall.
- Fun is a good indicator of how stressful the learning environment is. The more relaxed, the better the learning environment and the easier it is to plan activities that are both fun and challenging. Sometimes, as in my example of the class I mentioned earlier, we have to work at implementing or building a fun environment in order to experience fun before we can link it to achievement.
- Fun can help build a level of empathy in the learner as well as helping them understand the impact of learning on their emotions. This is something I do not think we do enough in teaching. We allow learners to falsely make a link between feeling anxious and their ability to learn. This then becomes a self-belief.
- Fun helps in collaboration, working with others and overcoming barriers both in learning and in relationships.

## When elements of PBCF are missing

Here are some of the symptomatic behaviours you may recognise when PBCF learning needs are not being met.

# Powerless

**Power**

Nobody likes to feel powerless, to not have a voice. Please acknowledge me.

- Displays frustration at being told what to do
- Shows high levels of anxiety in learning situations
- Seeks alternative situations or environments
- Can be withdrawn and reluctant to engage, depressed even
- Adopts a 'victim' persona

**Figure 4.2 Lack of power**

# Lack of belonging

- Looks for attention
- Challenges instructions or requests
- The peer group relationship is more important than the learning relationship
- Does not accept responsibility for actions
- Can also be withdrawn, quiet and resigned to fate
- Shows little enthusiasm for task or activity
- Displays a 'so what' attitude when challenged
- Will form relationships where there is an offer of belonging despite consequences

**Belonging**

Get to know me and help me belong to your learning community.

**Figure 4.3 Lack of belonging**

IF YOU CAN'T REACH THEM YOU CAN'T TEACH THEM

# No choice

- Reluctant to make decisions, resigned to whatever occurs or happens to them
- Demonstrates impaired judging capacity
- When pushed will tend towards instinct and can offer no reason for actions
- Marginal participation in activities, little or no 'buy in'
- Fails to understand consequences of actions or behaviours
- Tends not to ask questions

**Figure 4.4 Lack of choice**

# No fun

- Sees learning as a chore, may refer to it as 'work'
- Seeks alternative fun gratification or possibly an audience for their actions
- Often distracted by what is going on with somebody else or elsewhere
- Tends towards mischief
- Reluctant to engage in learning activities, especially if they think them difficult
- Wants the reward before accomplishing the task

**Figure 4.5 Lack of fun**

## How to strengthen PBCF

When PBCF is being satisfied you can expect a double benefit, first for pupil learning and second for your teaching. Try adopting PBCF with your colleagues too – remember 'please be colleague friendly' (yes, it works). If you can achieve a whole-school culture of PBCF then it becomes easier to build effective learning relationships and raise achievement for all.

Here are some strategies you can adopt to ensure you include PBCF in your teaching.

- Respond to the symptoms and not to the behaviour.
- Plan your lessons to not only include content and resources but also to include how you will satisfy PBCF.
- Develop resources that target PBCF and remember to start with belonging by sharing the learning journey.
- Create a learning environment that reflects PBCF – displays, layout, etc.
- Celebrate success, remember fun.

If you are concerned that the PBCF approach will take more time or require more resources, fear not, Chapter 5 introduces you to practical ways you can plan to meet learning needs without any burdensome load or financial implications.

## References and further reading

Glasser, W (2001) *What Is Choice Theory?* [online] Available at: https://wglasser.com/what-is-choice-theory/ (accessed 1 November 2020).

Hughes, D (2019) *Future-proof Your School: Steering Culture, Driving School Improvement, Developing Excellence.* St Albans: Critical Publishing.

Robinson, K (2010) *The Element: How Finding Your Passion Changes Everything.* Harmondsworth: Penguin.

IF YOU CAN'T REACH THEM YOU CAN'T TEACH THEM

# Appendix C
# GETTING TO KNOW YOUR PUPILS

Below are strategies often used by teachers for remembering pupil names.

- Seating plans and asking and repeating names back to pupils.
- Meet and greet at the classroom door.
- Name badges. Including nicknames can be fun but be careful!
- Having a record book with pupil photographs alongside names (do not always rely on technology for this).
- Selecting names for tasks or questions during lessons (I have seen names on lollipop sticks in a jar on the teacher's desk used for randomly selecting pupils).
- Allotting tasks using a rota so you check who is doing what.
- Name association triggers (using significant individual features).
- Repeated use of a name in classroom interaction/activity ('John, here is your book' or 'Yes John, that is a good idea John, what else could you suggest John?').
- Pupil passports complete with photographs and some details about interests or hobbies that can also include achievement stamps (see Appendix D).
- A group photo with pupil names.

# Appendix D
# PUPIL LEARNING PASSPORTS

The idea of a passport is it allows you to access places, to make a journey safe in the knowledge that you have an identity. It carries stamps to show where you have been as well as visas that allow you to stay or work in a place. A learning passport is very similar, can physically resemble a real passport, and helps to promote a sense of pupil belonging.

A similar approach can be used when working with pupils facing challenges engaging in lessons. Rather than their sense of belonging meaning 'those who carry a report card' (a negative connotation), the 'passport' language conveys a positive approach.

The learning passport should contain the following sections.

- A cover that shows who issued it: this can easily be customised to be your class or course.
- Inside cover: in the UK passport it says the bearer is required to '*pass freely*', we can change this to '*learn freely*' and continue with the words '*without let or hindrance, and to afford the bearer such assistance and protection as may be necessary*'. This is a form of learning contract.
- Pages for stamps/visas of countries visited, etc. This can be used to record achievements, challenges, special agreements or benefits acquired.
- Identity page: a picture and some personal details. Apart from the obvious, you could allow a degree of personalisation here that speaks of the interests and character of the pupil.
- Emergencies: a useful page if we put this into the context of belonging and learning. '*Who could help me if I have a learning challenge that is concerning me?*' is one example of how this section could be used.

# 5. PLANNING TO MEET AND MANAGE LEARNING NEEDS

## Introduction

The second phase of this book looks at planning to meet and manage learning needs. Now you are familiar with the four learning needs, PBCF, let's look at how you can integrate PBCF into everything you do without adding additional demands on your time or requiring further resources.

Knowing about PBCF and then doing something about it may seem like another challenge, a further demand on you, but let me reassure you that once you are alert to the behaviour symptoms it is a most instinctive way of teaching. In working with teachers, I have found that changing established ways of thinking is often harder than learning new ones but once you recognise that learning relationships, pupil engagement and outcomes are improving then it becomes easier.

This chapter examines:

- lesson planning;
- approaches to learning involving PBCF;
- issues linked to learning;
- learner self-image;
- communication.

# Lesson planning

Some teachers naturally manage learning needs in their approach to teaching. They may not even be consciously aware of them, it is just part of their style of teaching. They don't necessarily plan for meeting them; they can react instinctively and amend their approach when needed. This has to do with recognising and interpreting the behaviours and emotions that sit behind learning needs (PBCF) and reacting accordingly. The term 'emotional intelligence' may be familiar to you through Daniel Goleman's book *Working with Emotional Intelligence* but the term goes back further and is credited to Peter Salovey and John D Mayer.

**(Practical EQ, nd)**

Goleman (1999) says that emotional intelligence is a skill that can be taught and cultivated. Within a learning and teaching environment, that process starts by recognising PBCF and then planning to meet learning needs within your teaching.

Teachers that display emotional intelligence are often successful in teaching a range of groups and can adapt quickly when faced with challenges. This is particularly evident when taking over a new class. Other teachers who are not so emotionally intelligent may have a style that suits the character of some groups better than others. These teachers are less likely to be managing learning needs effectively and are more likely to be successful working with compliant learners than they are those who present challenges. I was made aware of this as a head of department when timetabling teachers with classes. I am not referring to a pupil's level of ability; many more able learners can be found in the challenging or non-compliant category of pupils. All teachers benefit from recognising learning needs when it comes to building effective learning relationships as it allows them to adapt their planning and delivery quickly and effectively.

## PLANNING CONSIDERATIONS AND APPROACHES

The start of a new term or semester often means the start of a new module, new project, or chapter in learning for the pupils. It also means that a lot of lesson planning by you has already taken place and it is time to implement the material. There is a lot riding on how well the planning has been done, the resources that have been prepared and how it will all be introduced and delivered.

There is a false truth in teaching that having successful lessons is all down to the lesson planning paperwork. Get it right and you have engaged, interested and enthusiastic learners. Get it wrong and the consequences range from disinterest to conflict and behaviour issues. Planning is essential, yes, but you must put this into context. If something takes more time to plan than deliver you may have the balance wrong! If your planning does not allow you to respond to learning needs, to go off-piste, then it is not allowing you to reach your pupils. What are you planning for? Is it for you to deliver the lessons effectively or to show others what you are delivering?

While planning and preparation is essential, you need to focus on more than content and targets or completing some rubric. Being convinced of the four learning needs and how important these are in having engaged learners in your lessons, you should recognise the need to broaden your idea of planning to include PBCF too.

## CONSISTENCY

The challenge you face as a teacher is that once you are aware of the four learning needs and start to build them into your lesson planning and delivery you need to be consistent. When faced with demanding and stressful situations it is more than likely you will want to fall back to your old ways. You must resist this or you risk confusing the pupils, especially in their sense of belonging. I have seen great teachers fail to engage with a class because they are trying to deliver a lesson, sticking to a plan or teaching 'out of character' as it were. Don't expect overnight success; remember your audience has their expectations of you too and it may take some time to gain their trust and establish that all-important learning relationship. Be prepared for your pupils to seek reassurance, to probe and check as they build their confidence too.

## MANAGING LEARNING NEEDS

You cannot respond to learning needs if you do not consider them in your planning and this needs managing. In this section you will find common lesson planning headings that are often associated with good practice: those things that a teacher sets out in their planning over a period of perhaps a single lesson, one unit, a term or year. A search on the web will produce a great number of variants and ideas of how to plan a lesson. Your school may have a pro forma or set of templates that you are asked to use.

### ❖ Reflective task

No matter what system you use or how you approach and record your planning, take a moment to consider any headings that you would regard as specifically aimed at PBCF and make a note of them.

### ❖ Reflective task review

Did you find any? It is likely you did not, but you may have identified areas where you now recognise that PBCF plays a part. The following examples of lesson planning headings include headings that are specifically tailored to include the meeting of learners' needs, giving you a direct opportunity to include PBCF.

# EXAMPLE LESSON PLANNING HEADINGS

## What do I need to teach?

This is often the starting point in lesson planning. What is the unit about, what will it cover and what do you want the pupils to learn? Subject aims and objectives as well as ways of assessing progress can be written in response to this prompt. You can enhance this starting point by considering what it is about their learning needs you want your pupils to learn (PBCF) and how you will teach this. Look back at Figure 2.11 and consider how you can develop a sense of responsibility for learning through your planning.

## Where are my pupils?

This is a specific PBCF consideration. Reflect on each of the learning needs and ask yourself if there are any areas you need to develop before starting this topic. If you are teaching a new group with unfamiliar faces, then how you build a sense of belonging should be a key consideration in your planning. Reflecting on the four needs covered in Chapter 4 is essential at this point. Remember you are building learning relationships.

The set of questions below begins to address where your pupils are in relation to PBCF. A teacher that is in tune with their pupils knows that these questions and associated symptomatic behaviours will arise during the lesson. Including them in the planning helps you manage the learning much more effectively because you are focusing on the learning needs of pupils and not just content.

- How do my pupils feel about what they have learnt?
- How confident are they in taking on a new challenge or applying what they know already?
- Will they be able to find the courage to try, to face possible struggles and in some cases fail at the first, second or even third attempt?
- Have I established a sound learning relationship with my pupils, one that I can use to reassure and encourage reluctant learners?

## What do pupils know and what learning anchors can fix the new learning?

What is the extent of prior learning, what do my pupils know and how do I know what they know? Ideally you would be able to easily answer these questions; however, you may have to assume what the pupils know rather than establish it before planning begins. There may be reasons for this, such as limited time to get to know your pupils before the course begins or little or no past learning history (lack of records or record transfer issues). Experienced teachers know the pitfalls and outcomes of being in such a position and that poorly or inappropriately planned lessons can result in bored learners or learners who are unable to access the learning. Successful, experienced teachers are also very good at adapting lesson plans in response to the progress of the lesson. It is

IF YOU CAN'T REACH THEM YOU CAN'T TEACH THEM

no good making kites if there is no wind to fly them! If you fail to answer this set of questions before you start to plan then you are planning on poor foundations and need to be ready to adapt quickly if it is needed. Once again there is no departure from good lesson planning practice. Taking a moment to consider PBCF will make you aware that you also need to recognise and celebrate prior learning. It is also a way of helping establish what it is your pupils know and understand, giving you an opportunity to alter your planning if necessary. You have an excellent opportunity to build in fun and associate it with achievement too.

## What resources do I need to deliver lessons?

While there are physical resources you will need, there are emotional ones too. Being in the right frame of mind to take on a learning challenge is as important as having a pen or pencil to write with. Consider if you can build in a way for your pupils to communicate with you so they don't feel powerless. Can you provide an element of choice for your pupils and what are the consequences of those choices?

## What teaching approach should I adopt?

There is significant opportunity here to include PBCF in your planning. Differentiation considerations such as those for pupils with English as an additional language (EAL), those recognised as gifted and talented or having special educational needs or disabilities (SEND) will benefit from including PBCF in your planning.

## Other considerations

- What is the timeframe?
- What independent study or homework is required to support the learning?

## ❖ Reflective task

Look at an example of your own existing planning, perhaps a lesson or unit of work, and, using the letters for the four learning needs (PBCF), reference where opportunities could be developed for the benefit of building effective learning relationships and promoting the achievement of your pupils.

# Approaches to learning involving PBCF

Planning is one part of the learning equation, the other is the approach to learning. Ideally planning supports the approach. This section looks at two models I have adapted for approaching learning and highlights how PBCF can easily be integrated into each during the planning stages. They differ from traditional lesson or course planning models that you will be familiar with but are based on realistic learning experiences.

## LEARNING HEROES

I mentioned being a learning hero earlier and this is a good way of describing to pupils, especially younger ones, how they can face learning challenges. They can be a learning hero who will prevail in their quest for knowledge and understanding.

The idea of a hero is nothing new, *The Hero's Journey* by Joseph Campbell, an American professor of literature, is recognised as the structure behind many plots of famous fairy tales, stories and modern movies. From the call to adventure, through challenges, transformation and to the return, it charts the hero's ultimately successful journey despite adversity. You can find a link to a description of the hero's journey in the *Further reading* section of this chapter.

The concept of the learning hero translates nicely into a learning narrative involving PBCF. I have taken the original hero's journey and adapted it for the purpose of learning; see Figure 5.1. It is also

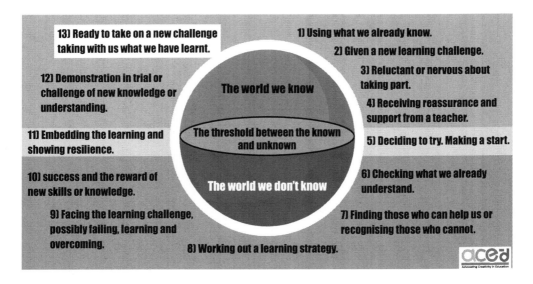

Figure 5.1 The learning hero's journey

IF YOU CAN'T REACH THEM YOU CAN'T TEACH THEM

a useful reminder that your planning needs to reflect the entire learning journey and account for the various emotional stages a pupil will experience. Each stage could be the focus of one element of your overall planning. Study it carefully and you will be able to see where PBCF also comes into play.

## THE LEARNING JOURNEY

### Step 1: Using what we already know

This is about being comfortable in our learning zone. You have mastered the earlier challenges and can use what you have learnt so far. As the teacher you can encounter reluctant learners in Step 1, those that may not yet have recovered from an earlier experience or challenge. You may find pupils who are comfortable here will make excuses not to move forward. At this point it is important to offer some form of choice; remember that this should not be free choice and that there are consequences. What happens if the learner refuses to engage in the challenge and what are the consequences? Staying still in learning is not really an option. Staying still can actually mean going backward as the world evolves and things change. We are prone to new experiences throughout our lives too. Being able to see the opportunities new challenges provide helps build lifelong learners. Having climbed one mountain does not mean you have seen the view from all the mountains around you. We also need to address the benefits of taking up the challenge, of moving forward in our planning.

### Step 2: Given a new learning challenge

This is the call to adventure, the start of a new learning experience. Learning should be seen as a rewarding adventure and teachers need to make it so. This stage is closely linked to the need for fun, fun in terms of challenge and achievement. There is also an element of the need for choice or options when given a new challenge. This helps build ownership of the learning and employs the pupil in the consideration of strategies that may be used in accomplishing the task.

### Step 3: Reluctant or nervous about taking part

Aren't we all? Is it not a natural part of a new challenge or learning journey? Some hide it better than others, so you need to be mindful of this. There are many symptoms that disguise a fear of trying something new. If you model learning behaviours then pupils are more likely to share their own fears or apprehension at taking on a new learning challenge. It is good for pupils to see this and it can help them to rationalise their own apprehension, especially once they recognise it as a natural part of learning. You need to make sure you listen to your pupils' concerns and acknowledge them. This element is linked to our need for power or having a voice as we discussed earlier.

## Step 4: Receive reassurance and support from a teacher

This is definitely part of a feeling of belonging, of not being alone in facing the challenge of learning something new. The building of effective learning relationships throughout the lesson is important and should not be left out of lesson planning, so include opportunities to reassure and support learners.

## Step 5: Deciding to try: making a start

This is the move from the known world into the world we don't know, from knowing and having confidence in our abilities into not knowing and possible doubt or uncertainty. In making this transition you need to have a voice (the need to feel a sense of power). You are making a declaration to yourself and your peers. Pupils are declaring to you, the teacher, that they are at least going to try to learn something about the new challenge, to give it a go. The pupil may be embarking on the journey but you should make sure they are prepared for it. Pupils are making a commitment and should be helped to recognise that much of the success will depend on their efforts and not just ability or skill. Making the pupil fully aware of the challenges that lie ahead is part of the lesson planning requirements. In this way they will be at least aware that they face challenges. In lesson planning and PBCF terms we can also use the need for fun to celebrate the start. After all, don't heroes get a good send off, or at least a hearty breakfast?

## Step 6: Checking what we already understand

This is part of making pupils ready, consisting of small challenges ahead of the main one. Lesson planning should include opportunities for the pupil to reaffirm what they already know or understand. This process helps build the pupil's confidence ahead of developing an approach to the challenge.

## Step 7: Finding those who can help us or recognising those who cannot

This involves all needs, those of power, belonging, choice and fun. In the original hero's journey, Step 7 is part of Step 6 (tests, allies and enemies). I made it a step on its own because of the challenges of managing learning. Learners often want to work with one another, especially in project-based learning approaches, but they do not always make the best choices as far as learning teams or partners are concerned. Friendship tends to trump effective learning partnerships. There needs to be an opportunity for learners to recognise who best supports them in their work and who does not. Once they do then some elements of conflict between them and the teacher can be avoided. A good way of demonstrating this is to set two tasks, one where the learners choose who to work with and one where they are directed to work with others as decided by the teacher.

Be sure to inform them how the tasks will be assessed. While the quality of the outcome can be judged, so too can the number of occasions where the group have to be directed back on task and how long the task takes to be completed or even if it gets completed at all. Of course, lesson planning will need to provide for such opportunities and even though it may place some pressures on time, more efficient and effective learning will save time and improve the standards of outcomes in the long run. Once the need for fun is demonstrated through achievement celebrations, learners are apt to want to work with those that give them the best chance of future success. It can also lead to more positive classroom behaviour and greater engagement if included in the lesson planning and learning strategies.

## Step 8: Working out a learning strategy

This involves ownership of the learning and it is a key component of managing our own learning. Having ownership of the learning is a recognised component of successful learning and a characteristic of lifelong learners. If we invest in something we feel more involved and gain greater sense of achievement from any success. We also learn from our mistakes, but only if we make or agree with the strategies in the first place. You can probably see the link with the need for choice in this aspect of the learner's journey but it also involves power through having a voice and being heard. Teachers who offer choice in how tasks can be completed or in which resources can be used are encouraging independence and self-reliance in their learners.

## Step 9: Facing the learning challenge, possibly failing, learning and overcoming

This is the point at which you need to stand back a little and allow the pupil to find their feet. Feeling secure does not happen by chance and the need for developing a sense of belonging is an important aspect of lesson planning if pupils are going to be willing to fail or at least see it as part of the learning journey. Taking the opportunity to establish how pupils feel about their challenges and progresses during the task needs to be built into the lesson planning. This is not difficult but does require a different form of assessment for learning or of progress. Figure 5.2 below is a simple strategy used for this purpose in a coaching model I was involved in writing for a literacy and numeracy project used in an independent learning centre for pupils aged 6–14. There was no teacher directing the learning; instead a learning coach supported the learner on their learning journey.

The key to this approach is the opportunity for the pupils to leave a comment about the entire task and about each sub-task within the pack by ringing a smiley face at the end of each one. The tasks are expected to take about 40 minutes to one hour and the pupils are expected to work independently. In reviewing the work, the coach has the ability to judge both the quality of the work as well as how the pupil feels about the task and their competence. A number of scenarios can result from interpreting the response of the pupils and these include the following.

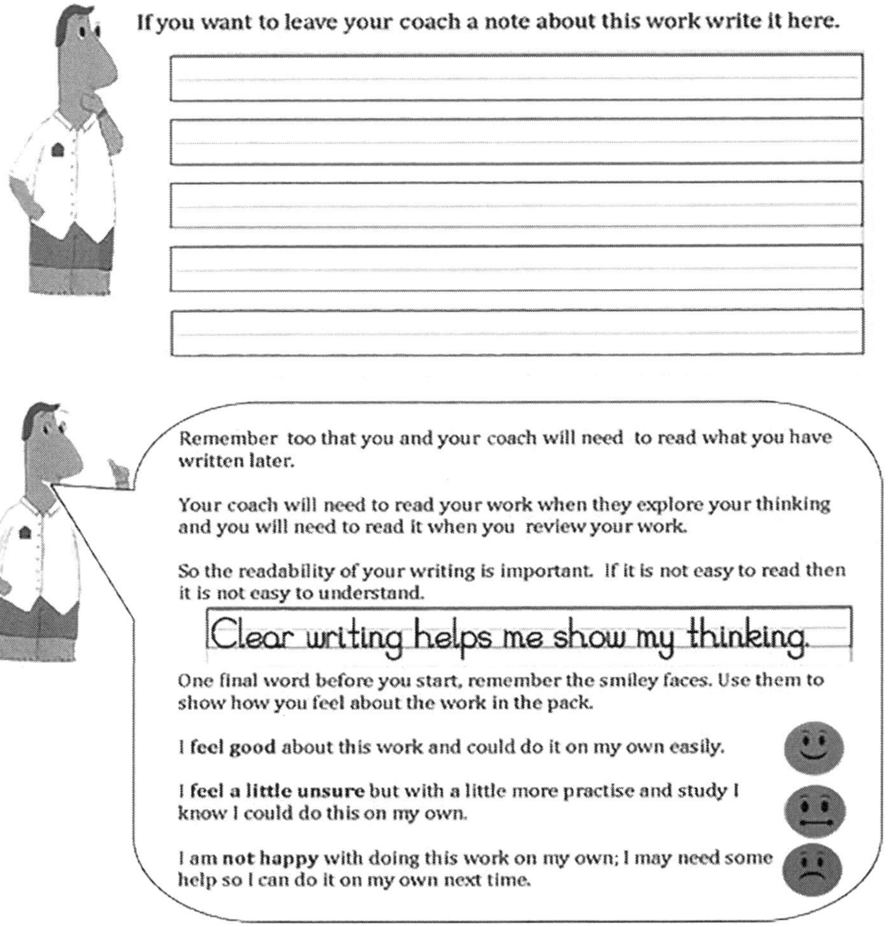

If you want to leave your coach a note about this work write it here.

Remember too that you and your coach will need to read what you have written later.

Your coach will need to read your work when they explore your thinking and you will need to read it when you review your work.

So the readability of your writing is important. If it is not easy to read then it is not easy to understand.

Clear writing helps me show my thinking.

One final word before you start, remember the smiley faces. Use them to show how you feel about the work in the pack.

I feel good about this work and could do it on my own easily.

I feel a little unsure but with a little more practise and study I know I could do this on my own.

I am not happy with doing this work on my own; I may need some help so I can do it on my own next time.

**Figure 5.2 Coaching model pupil voice (note: the three smiley faces are coloured, starting with feeling good, green, then amber and red)**

- The performance is much better than the pupil expresses through the smiley faces. This suggests a lack of confidence and something the coach can then address directly.
- The performance may be below that expected although the pupil expresses a feeling of being quite capable of doing the task. This raises the need to address the pupil's understanding of the task and what is expected of them.
- Combinations can prompt different responses both by the pupil and the coach. This approach also provides for other learning needs being met, those of power by providing a voice and of choice by providing options.

IF YOU CAN'T REACH THEM YOU CAN'T TEACH THEM

The impact of such an approach takes time to develop but avoids the high-stakes assessments and targets that can lead to perceptions of self and ability being negatively reinforced. High-stakes outcomes associated with learning, such as reaching targets, makes it difficult to develop a culture that supports this important step both in the pupil's learning journey and in lesson planning.

## Step 10: Success and the reward of new skills or knowledge

Having faced and overcome a learning challenge you need to plan time to both recognise and celebrate it. Remember you need to associate achievement with a sense of fun, and showing off can be good fun if done in the right way. Demonstrating what you have learnt also reinforces learning and understanding, part of the next steps in the learner's journey. In terms of lesson planning, giving time to this stage is important. We need to show the benefits of making an effort of facing and overcoming challenges and we need to meet the need for fun while doing it. Simply moving onto the next learning challenge is not part of the learner's journey, so we now need to ensure in our planning that there is an opportunity to complete all aspects of the learner's journey.

## Step 11: Embedding the learning and showing resilience

Please, please, not more tests! The worst example I can recall from my own education was the maths questions at the end of each chapter. Pages and pages of questions each with a slight variation or twist from the original in order to challenge you and show you can apply what you have learnt. While this approach works to some extent, it hardly meets any of our learning needs. What is needed is a limited challenge with structured support that will allow the learner to come at the topic from a different angle but not one too far removed from the challenge they have just faced. In planning terms we must be careful to construct opportunities that are not repetitive, too simple or contrived for the pupil to embed their learning and show resilience. If you are not meeting the need for fun through meeting and overcoming a challenge then you risk making things boring.

In terms of the learner's journey this is also the transition from the previously unknown world into the known world. It really means lifting a veil on the unknown world and a chance to look back and realise how far they have come, how what was once shrouded in mystery is now clear and understood. In terms of meeting learning needs it provides for further choice in future challenges, for the learner now has a greater set of skills, knowledge or understanding on which to draw. Having been with the pupil on this learning journey, the sense of belonging and the strength of the learning relationship you share is enhanced.

The use of the word 'resilience' is an important aspect of this part of the learner's journey. When what they know or can do does not appear to apply to the situation or challenge pupils face, they need to be able to maintain focus and sustain their efforts. There is great reward when they do but there is also great temptation for you to step in and provide help before it is necessary. Resist and think back to the responsibility ratio graph!

## Step 12: Demonstration in trial or challenge of new knowledge or understanding

This is a sort of 'You are on your own now' stage of learning. The challenge from a planning perspective comes when we have taught something in isolation from its context, a sort of 'no need to know why' approach. The pupil may not see a direct link or be able to make the cognitive leap that enables them to apply what they have learnt. This in no way means they have not learnt the topic or skill, just that we have taught it in a way that is so abstract from the context in which it applies that the pupil is too removed or remote to use what they have learnt without significant additional scaffolding. In schools where teaching is broken down into subjects, many pupils face the issue of not being able to transfer knowledge or understanding from one subject to another, from say mathematics to science. I accept it can be difficult to co-ordinate the teaching or use of knowledge or skills across subjects but that is one of the limitations imposed on us by delivering a curriculum through a subject-based model. There are other models available and they can be significantly better at transferable knowledge and skills used. Project based learning is one example of such an approach.

## PROBLEM-BASED LEARNING

*The real process of education should be the process of learning to think through the application of real problems.*

**John Dewey**

John Dewey, the American philosopher and psychologist and a significant influence in the field of education, advocated learning by doing. He also believed in a balance of collaboration between teachers and pupils, much as I have argued when looking at learning relationship in Chapter 2. The opportunities to develop PBCF are clear if you involve pupils in their own learning. You can present learning as a problem to solve through a planned structure much like the hero's journey I adapted for learning by taking a simple design process and applying it to your planning. Such an approach can be used by you through your planning to create the learning environment and resources and by the learner to solve the problems created for them within that learning environment. Throughout you can underpin the learning process by ensuring PBCF is part of your planning.

The design process, a way of problem-solving and seeing learning as a problem to solve, is a powerful way to look at the learning process. It's not just a process, however; it's a way of thinking. I cannot over-emphasise what a significant step forward seeing learning as a problem to solve is when planning learning, building learning relationships and meeting learning needs.

Seeing learning as a problem-based activity gives you a greater range of tools to apply to the learning process and it allows for a significant degree of creativity in managing learning and teaching. There are other examples you can explore with this concept at their heart, including project-based learning and flipped classrooms.

IF YOU CAN'T REACH THEM YOU CAN'T TEACH THEM

Although we may consider designing an intuitive activity, there is a certain logic that can be applied to it. In applying this logic, we can assist the process and improve the outcome. Designing is not a linear activity; it has many starting and dropping-off points and can even be cut short or involve loops both back and forward. This makes it very flexible in terms of learning and teaching. You can start a topic by looking at an existing situation or solution (evaluation) and reverse engineer it, working backwards and exploring the decision-making or knowledge that was needed (questioning and ideas) to reach the outcome (solution).

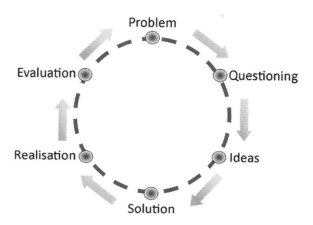

**Figure 5.3 Design thinking**

Figure 5.3 shows a simplified six-stage design process of developing a solution to a problem as applied to a learning scenario. There are more sophisticated design process examples you can explore but I would recommend starting with this.

Here is a brief description of each stage in the process and some suggestions of how you can include PBCF.

### The problem: identification/recognition/adoption/accepting a challenge

Presenting and sharing a problem can build a sense of belonging, a common challenge that you will both face together. You can show confidence in the pupil's abilities to take on the problem and find a solution.

### Questioning

This involves analysis/exploring in order to refine the problem and recognising and listing the needs involved in finding solutions.

You can develop a list of choices both in terms of knowledge and understanding as well as approach and discuss the consequences of each in terms of achieving a successful learning outcome. Listening to pupil concerns and ideas will empower pupils and show them that they have a voice.

## Ideas

This involves the generation of possible solutions or part solutions to the problem based on satisfying the need presented by the challenge. There is an ideal opportunity for pupils to understand the need for power (voice) as they share ideas and to see the consequence of choice as they decide a way forward. Experimenting with ideas can be a creative and a fun activity too. It is easy to link fun to achievement as the pupils overcome early challenges and build their confidence through this development stage. It also helps to reinforce that there is often no one way of doing something.

## Solution

Synthesis of a solution should meet learning needs as far as is possible. It requires enough detail to enable the solution (learning outcome) to be achieved independent of the designer (the teacher). The pupil will know how to approach the learning, what resources they need in order to learn and how they will record the process of learning. Choice and power are two aspects of PBCF involved in this stage.

## Realisation

This involves action to produce a solution to the problem. The activity of learning, either independently or as part of learning teams, can involve belonging and fun through achievement.

## Evaluation

This involves asking questions and comparing the outcome to the need, including testing, reporting and demonstrating understanding. All aspects of PBCF can be involved at this stage of learning.

## What this means for you

This approach to creating the learning environment requires an objective review of learning employing a mindful approach. In explaining mindful teaching and learning I find it easier to consider what is meant by a mindless approach.

IF YOU CAN'T REACH THEM YOU CAN'T TEACH THEM

Mindless learning often involves learning for no apparent reason or having no obvious application, knowing facts without understanding the context (like the wives of Henry VIII or dates of great battles). It often requires a grade or target to be achieved as the only proof of learning. The pupil is very much a passenger without a voice and little or no choice or fun through achievement exists.

Mindful teaching and learning moves beyond subject-based learning and uses elements of constructivism: a theory about how people learn. In effect they construct their own understanding and knowledge of the world through experiencing things and, importantly, reflecting (or evaluating) those experiences. I like to think of this as a learning map, a belief about what we think we can and cannot learn. Simply presenting the information to be learnt is not enough; you need to look at the problems associated with learning (barriers), context, resources or the environment, engagement or motivation and of course PBCF.

Being mindful gives a context, provides for inclusive learner options in answering, and excludes learning by rote. There is more about mindful learning in Chapter 6.

Questions need to be asked about the barriers and ideas generated and how they can be overcome. There is planning involved in achieving a solution and delivering it (realisation). Finally, there is the evaluation of the resources, process and outcomes of the solution used to achieve the learning. This should inform the development of future solutions and add to the teacher's professional development.

## What this means for the learner

A design approach to learning directly involves the learner; they have a responsibility for driving the process and keeping records. This process encourages the learner not only to see the subject as a learning activity but also as a study of how they learn. Learning is about understanding and is measured by breadth and depth rather than a single score. It also requires the learner to find ways to support their own learning and this has the advantage of broadening and deepening their understanding as well as encouraging independent learning.

## Summary of the design model approach

Another important point about the design process approach is that there is no single right solution to a problem. Rather, a solution involves providing ways to show understanding or of meeting learning needs. This revelation can be very empowering and break many self-beliefs about what can or cannot be learnt. Discovering that the learning environment has a significant impact on not being able to learn is the first step in rebuilding our learning map. Discovering that you can do something about the learning environment is an important realisation for both the teacher and learner.

By following a design-based model, questions arise along with processes that will challenge you to think about the broader aspects and implications of your planning. This includes building in opportunities to evaluate the lesson delivery as well as the learning. The outcome may be for you to invite a colleague to observe a lesson or part of it and provide feedforward.

## SHARING THE LEARNING JOURNEY

As a teacher wishing to manage learning needs you should be asking how you can begin sharing the learning challenges ahead. In planning terms you may refer to this as the introduction, but only if you focus on the content and not the process. Sharing the challenges and involving the learner in planning to meet them is part of developing independent learners. New topics can be approached in a number of ways and asking the learners to identify the most appropriate learning strategies can be helpful, even if this involves an element of guiding. This approach helps share the ownership and responsibility for learning. Sharing this aspect of planning is a little like offering a choice at meal times; it is difficult to push the plate away and say you don't like the food when you have chosen it! Remember that choice is one of the learning needs.

Here are more PBCF-focused planning questions and requirements for you to consider.

- How do I share my enthusiasm for this topic?
- How do I describe achievement and how will the pupils recognise it?
- What will my role be in the learning process and how do I signal this to the pupils?
- How will we celebrate achievement together and as individuals?
- How does the pupil go about reviewing their achievement against their learning map (what they believe they can and cannot learn) in order to redraw it to include new information about themselves?
- What resources will be required to support them emotionally through the learning challenges?

# Issues linked to learning

Ask anyone to learn something and past experiences will be part of the emotional response. How well PBCF was acknowledged and learning needs met during that process will be significant factors in that response. We can be excited to learn something new, especially if there is no history of trying or of failure. On the other hand, we can be anxious or even afraid if we had a poor experience or if there are similar factors at play within the learning environment. If PBCF has been ignored in past learning experiences, then we are likely to be fearful.

## OVERCOMING FEAR

One emotion that features a great deal at the start of something new is fear. Fear is often associated with rejection, of no longer being part of a group with which we want to be identified. Having a sense of belonging is one of our four basic needs as learners; without it we find learning much harder. We need to recognise that this emotional state is often the starting point for many learners when faced with a new challenge. If we fail to consider it in our planning then we are being rather cruel and possibly limiting the success of learners. Sharing the learning journey and considering how you will support pupils in their learning journey was one of the earlier suggestions to include in your planning.

## THE LEARNING ENVIRONMENT

You can support and develop PBCF through the learning environment you create. Creating the learning environment is the broadest description of lesson planning for it includes:

- timings;
- resources and access to them;
- teaching methods;
- physical appearance and atmosphere of the learning environment;
- the manner of assessments (establishing levels of knowledge and understanding);
- learning opportunities.

## ❖ Reflective task

Consider the learning environment that you are responsible for and list those features that support PBCF. You can use the learning environment headings above or use your own. Think about and record any simple changes that you could make to enhance or include PBCF within your teaching environment.

## MODELLING PBCF

Successful teachers are those who are still learners; they model learning behaviours. They often have a project in which they are involved (see Chapter 11, this is one of John's 12 rules), which can be anything in which you immerse yourself and broaden your knowledge or understanding in or in which you develop new skills. So you could decide to learn a new language, try your hand at archery or clay pigeon shooting. Whatever it is, you can use the experience to support your teaching. Take the time to register what it feels like to learn something for the first time, to be in a different learning environment with different people, to be a pupil again.

Being involved in learning is an emotional experience. The problem with teaching is that sometimes you have taught the same thing so many times since you learnt it you have forgotten how you felt on that initial journey. In going back, revisiting learning, you become more aware of the four learning needs. Perhaps before embarking on building the four learning needs into your teaching you should give learning something new a go! Having a project can also be a great source of energy and help reinvigorate your teaching. One further advantage is that it offers an opportunity to get out of the academic environment and provides contact with diverse groups of people.

The feelings you become aware of will find their way into the lesson planning and delivery cycle if you allow them. You will not be merely presenting stuff to learn; you will be able to guide pupils through the learning experience, demonstrating greater empathy for their journey, acknowledging their learning needs.

In being willing to discuss challenges you have faced, your setbacks and successes, your pupils will see learning as a journey; one that sometimes does not go to plan. You will help develop in your pupils the behaviours of successful learners; those that can manage their learning environment to meet their learning needs.

## HOW TO LEARN ANYTHING

Figure 5.4 is a guide on how to learn anything. This is a reminder of what is involved in learning and offers guidance on what you can put in place in your planning to make learning something new easier and meet learning needs. It is especially useful when discussing the act of learning with pupils. I have developed the idea from a blog by Krystian Aparta (2014) about an open translation project where translators shared their secrets to mastering a foreign language. I have taken each of the seven stages and described a learning action. They are not in any order; they are just a list of things that you need to include in your behaviour as you embark on learning something new.

# HOW TO LEARN ANYTHING

## Learn to actively manage your learning experience

**1 Get real**

Decide on a simple, attainable goal to start with so that you don't feel overwhelmed.

**2 Make a lifestyle change**

Make learning a lifestyle change. Put what you want to learn at the centre of what you do and why you do it.

**4 Use technology**

See if you can engage with people online that have the skills or knowledge you are trying to learn about. Look for different types of learning materials. Search YouTube, Khan Academy, blogs, Wiki, etc for relevant materials or resources.

**3 Dive in, get involved**

Find out more about what you want to learn. Find related, unusual or interesting facts about the topic. If possible visit places or find out about the people involved. This makes it more real for you and helps build learning pathways linked to images, sounds and emotions.

**5 See learning as a gateway**

Think about learning as a gateway to new experiences and opportunities that could open up for you. Recognising the benefits that could come your way through your efforts makes the goal real and therefore more achievable.

**6 Make new friends**

Interacting in the new learning is key to success. Surround yourself with people who are on the same learning journey. They may be ahead or behind you, it does not matter. What matters is you have the same learning objectives and therefore drives and possibly interests.

**7 Don't worry about mistakes**

One of the most common barriers to learning anything new is fear of making mistakes, of being a failure. Everyone makes mistakes but it is those that learn from them that learn the most of them. Failure is part of learning.

**Figure 5.4 How to learn anything**
Adapted from Aparta (2014).

## DIFFERENTIATION

Within any group of pupils you will face a range of levels of engagement, co-operation, interest, existing knowledge and understanding. To expect traditional lesson planning to accommodate all of these is fanciful, especially if it is the responsibility of you alone to meet those needs. It is much more productive if you focus on addressing pupil engagement, their learning needs (PBCF) and the why of learning. This will provide the foundations for engagement in the learning process and build a learning relationship that brings with it learner responsibility, tolerance and a degree of independence.

I believe the better model in terms of meeting individual needs is where the learner is responsible for recognising their needs and managing the learning environment to meet those needs (within limits of course – it is no good running outside shouting, '*I hate classrooms!*'). Not all learning environments suit all learners, in the same way that not all items on a menu suit all diners. At the restaurant it is the diners' responsibility to investigate the menu and determine their own way of satisfying their appetite. If we enable the learner by giving them a process, a set of tools or an approach like the design method, then they have the option to effectively manage their own learning environment within the constraints they face. The alternative is a dependent learner, one that requires you to provide the resources or create the opportunities to overcome learning challenges every time a problem or learning challenge is encountered. For such pupils, thinking for themselves, determining their own strategy, comes a distant second. While they wait for you they do little or nothing constructive and this only adds to the feeling of being powerless. There is no way our learning hero would complete their journey if they sat around waiting for others to do it for them.

## ❖ Reflective task

Select a topic you are about to deliver and consider the four needs. You should also consider some of the broader planning questions and approaches I have mentioned.

I find it useful to make this a personal exercise, as if I was the pupil. If you find this a difficult perspective then consider taking on a new learning challenge yourself. How would you like a teacher to make you feel you belong, have a voice, are able to make choices and to have fun in the learning challenge you face? Remember, 'please be child friendly' – PBCF.

You can either use Appendix E or create your own table. It is the four headings of PBCF that are important and not the amount of space you fill.

# Learner self-image

This section is about the importance of how you and your pupils see learning and how you see teaching. Take a moment to think about just what it is you want your pupils to be engaged in and try to define it in simple terms.

## ❖ Reflective task

Consider the options below and tick those you think should be included in your definition of learning and teaching.

Learning is....?

- ☐ Lifelong
- ☐ Personal
- ☐ Individual
- ☐ Challenging
- ☐ Of different forms
- ☐ Something we can all do
- ☐ Rewarding
- ☐ Empowering
- ☐ Fun
- ☐ A way to achieve what you need
- ☐ Discovery or insight
- ☐ About subjects
- ☐ About grades or qualifications

## ❖ Reflective task review

- · How many do you agree with?
- · Would you add any others?
- · How many of your pupils would agree with you if you gave them the same list?

Perhaps if you asked them to draw up a list of what learning is all about then their list may be a little different, possibly including:

→

- ☐ Boring
- ☐ A waste of time and of no use
- ☐ What we are made to do (work)
- ☐ All about assessments, targets or grades
- ☐ Going to school
- ☐ Doing homework

If your view about school and that of your pupils is different then you need to explore your learning relationship. It will be difficult to get your pupils to engage in the learning process if you do not share a common view. In order to modify such responses as these and build a view of learning that is supportive of PBCF there is a need to expose learners to a much more holistic view of learning (more than just subjects and assessments) and to meet their needs in accessing it.

Achieving a shared view has a lot to do with pupil self-image as well as the view your pupils hold of learning and of education broadly. Our views or the beliefs we hold have a great deal to do with our experiences and of the expectations placed on us. I return to this in Chapter 8, 'The dangers of labelling learners', and Chapter 9, 'The learning map'.

## WHAT INFLUENCES US AS LEARNERS

Our view of learning and how successful we are at it can be influenced by a number of factors. These include our parents, past learning experiences, key people in our lives and our past success. How easy it is to change our views on learning and our sense of self as a learner depends on the strength of influence of these factors either individually or in combination.

This is different from motivation to learn but strongly linked to it. It is about how we perceive ourselves as learners. You may hear people say '*I am no good at maths*' or '*I cannot hold a tune*'. These people are declaring a self-belief, what they believe they can or cannot do or learn. Often, if challenged, they will tell a tale of an occasion that helped them create this self-image. They may have gone through their lives reinforcing this image time and time again so that eventually it is a truth to them. Unfortunately for the teacher, a self-image, a self-truth, can be formed in an instant and it may have no truth in it at all. This is one reason why you should be careful when talking to pupils; always focus on the behaviour as distinct from the person.

As managers of learners (I include parents in this category) we have to be very careful what we say and how we act when engaged with someone with the focus on learning, and especially with those who are susceptible to being influenced by others. It is all too easy to affect the self-image of learners. I once sat and made a list of the limiting phrases people use, especially those directed at young learners. These statements can often appear innocuous but can impact self-beliefs in a damaging way without us even realising it at the time.

Here are a few from my list.

- Get down from there, you will hurt yourself.
- Leave it alone, you will break it.
- You have never been any good at that sort of thing.
- I have told you hundreds of times, you must know by now.
- Don't be stupid and come away from there.

## WHAT WE FOCUS ON

If you ever ask anyone what was said to them during an assessment, review or feedback session they will more than likely tell you the negative things first. We appear to be programmed to remember the negative more than the positive. We instinctively look for the danger, a possible survival trait. This is one of the reasons I favour feedforward. Focusing on the negative may be a survival trait but it is also bound up in self-belief. We are even inclined to believe the negative over the positive when presented with two conflicting assessments or comments. Far worse is the conclusion we can draw when we receive no praise, no attention or no comment at all, interpreting this as criticism.

There is research that suggests it takes five praise comments to balance one negative one. April Stevenson (2017) in her *Kidblog* tells of her approach to overcoming what she recognised as a lot of negative self-talk among her students. I find that the situation is compounded by the culture that can exist in the learning environment which is anti-success or anti-praise. In such cultures, praise is not a cause of celebration but a cause of embarrassment.

The good thing is people can alter their self-belief. Albert Bandura (1989) argues that people can change and that the more confident they are, the better their problem-solving capabilities and analytical thinking, the better they perform. Many sports coaches would agree, as they would with the suggestion that where individuals visualise success, they achieve better performances. Motivation is very much linked to self-belief and problem-solving is very much a part of effective learning. Knowing you can change and by doing so learn to manage your learning environment to meet your learning needs is the belief that sits behind learning intelligence too.

Self-belief also plays a part in resilience; getting back on the horse after falling off. Passion and a strong belief in what you are doing enables people to overcome many of life's problems: '*It takes a resilient sense of efficacy to override the numerous dissuading impediments to significant accomplishments*' (Bandura, 1989, p 1177).

People who believe in their ability to cope and overcome challenges tend not to dwell on their inabilities but instead look for ways of moving forward. This is important when we consider what I call our learning map. Effectively our learning map is a composite of what we believe we can and cannot learn, what we are good at and what we will fail at. The learning map landscape is often defined by school-based experiences and what is said to us by significant people in our lives.

Being able to redefine our learning map has a beneficial, long-term impact on our ability to learn: '*After perceived coping efficacy is strengthened to the max level, coping with previously intimidating tasks no longer elicits differential psychobiological reactions*' (Bandura, 1989, p 1177). We become imbibed with the belief that we can cope with what were possibly considered too risky or too demanding situations. This makes it more likely we will develop adaptive strategies. Believing you can do nothing about your situation is debilitating. Being aware of PBCF, of learning needs, helps you do something about the self-belief of your pupils.

Everything you do as a teacher will have an impact on learning needs, whether you are aware of it or not. There will be occasions where you missed opportunities to add to a sense of belonging because you were in a hurry. There will be occasions when you felt as though you were losing control and so removed choice. The problem you have is that your pupils readily remember these occasions and they absorb them into their self-belief models. In my experience, schools function more on a control model, one where compliance is expected but often not rewarded. On the other hand, non-compliance is seen as an act of defiance rather than a result of learning needs not being met, and is met with actions that undermine PBCF as well as limiting the positive self-belief of the learner.

## ❖ Reflective task

In one of your lessons, keep a record of the number of praise-related comments you make to your pupils and also the number of times you criticise them or miss an opportunity to offer them praise. How close to a recommended 5:1 positive to negative ratio were you?

If a pupil is late to a lesson and you decide to rebuke them then you need to find four points or features within the lesson to provide praise just to balance your opening remark. Remember to praise the effort and strategy, not the person. Seeing learning as a problem-solving process makes this much easier as the strategies become apparent at the ideas stage and are acted upon at the solution stage. Assessment involves how a pupil deals with the learning challenge as well as what they have learnt.

# HOW WE SEE OURSELVES IN TERMS OF BEING ABLE TO ACHIEVE

As a result of different influences, we form various opinions about ourselves. I have mentioned limiting phrases and the work of Albert Bandura earlier but we can go further and consider where we get our views of self from.

What is the biggest influence on your ability to learn; what do you attribute your success or learning difficulties to? You, like your pupils, will have a history of learning experiences and of those who influenced those experiences either through teaching you or being present during the learning journey. You may have experienced an act of encouragement, praise, criticism, rebuke or of being mocked. Each action has an emotional impact which we register, whether we recognise it or not at the time. If we are mocked by a group, we can feel as though we don't belong. If we are given encouragement then we can feel part of the same team. How we react, how we register the impact, either positively or negatively in terms of our self-image, also depends a great deal on the relationships we share. It is for this reason that the importance of sound learning relationships with your pupils cannot be overemphasised. The people around you and your own internalisation of the learning experience influences your self-belief. As a teacher you need to be aware that you will have to contend with the influence of significant people in the life of your pupils. Your pupils' views on their abilities can and will be influenced by those around them and may not be based on any factual base at all. PBCF is an effective tool when challenging false self-beliefs.

Within this section I can only offer a brief tour of the various theories and ways of thinking about how learners see themselves. There is much written about how we can improve or change self-image and beliefs and I encourage you to explore those I mention here.

Bernard Weiner, a social psychologist, proposed his attribution theory, which considers the effect of internal and external factors on an individual's opinion about learning and hence motivation and engagement. Weiner describes four attributes in learning, given here.

1. **Ability:** This is fixed and the learner can do little about it.
2. **Task difficulty:** This is beyond the learner's control and they can do nothing about it.
3. **Effort:** An internal factor that the learner can exercise a great deal of control over.
4. **Luck:** The outcome is down to chance and not related to ability or effort or the task.

You can see the difficulty you will have as a teacher if a pupil attributes their likelihood of success in learning down to luck or if they believe something will be forever beyond them.

Carol Dweck's theory on mindset proposes that a pupil's belief is one of two types, a fixed versus a growth mindset.

1. Their ability is fixed and if things are difficult they should give up because it is beyond their ability.
2. They have untapped potential and if they try harder or find a different way they will succeed.

The challenge for the teacher is to move pupils' beliefs about their learning and outcome success from one state to another. Of course you may need to teach the skills needed to approach difficult tasks (and they may only be difficult because of the way they are presented) and provide enough evidence through experience to demonstrate that luck has very little to do with learning outcomes. In doing so you will also show that ability is not fixed or of one type and that with the right strategies (remember the benefits of seeing learning as a problem-solving activity) pupils can be successful learners.

In order to change mindset, Dweck suggested moving from person-oriented praise to process-oriented praise. So from '*You are good at this*' to '*That was a good way to do it*'. We can return to the learning journey, approaching learning as a problem-solving activity, to see how easy it is for you to adapt to this way of thinking. It is also true that while we can all learn, we will learn more if we work to our strengths and are able to meet our learning needs as we do so.

If you are successful in facilitating the transition from one state to another, motivation and engagement will be that much easier to achieve. What is more, you will have improved your learning relationship with the pupil.

We have probably all experienced pupils taken out of one lesson and given extra time in another in which it is decided they need to improve. While on the surface this may sound a good strategy, if we think for a moment we will realise it begins to deny the pupil a number of their learning needs. If we think about PBCF, we will see that this strategy needs careful management. Taking a pupil from one group where they are established risks undermining their sense of belonging. You also risk undermining their self-belief and with it their sense of fun. Further, since the decision was made for the pupil, with the likelihood being they were not consulted, you are likely to diminish their sense of power and choice. You can still adopt this strategy as a way of raising achievement but you need to involve the learner and focus on deploying strengths rather than making up for weaknesses: you do this through PBCF and by focusing on strengths.

Pupils who learn that they can be successful in one area can use this success to motivate themselves in others. A pupil who constantly faces and is unsuccessful in challenges will not find it as easy to motivate themselves or to try other things. In fact this may go some way to convincing them that they may never learn; a Type 1 according to Dweck. Tom Rath (2007) also demonstrated the impact of effort in his formula for strength. It is a clear example of how a lack of natural talent can be made up for through effort:

Talent (a natural way of thinking, feeling or behaving) × effort (time spent practising, developing your skills, and building your knowledge base) = strength (the ability to consistently achieve near-perfect performance)

$$T \times E = S$$

You can see from the example below how two people can achieve the same score if one lacks effort (E) and one lacks talent (T).

$$T (2) \times E (4) = S (8) \text{ achieves the same outcome as } T (4) \times E (2) = S (8)$$

You may see investment (effort) in success as the driver behind the school strategy of extracting pupils from lessons but this is not the case if it only includes doing more of what has not worked. For investment to work you need to change what happens during that time. You need to do something different and that may involve building self-belief, developing a subset of skills or understanding, promoting LQ or helping learners to understand and satisfy their learning needs.

This section has dealt with a number of issues related to the learner and, by association, the teacher. The key is to make learners aware of the process of learning. Certain myths need to be dispelled and care taken when presenting learning challenges in order to improve engagement and promote motivation. One of the easiest ways of doing this is to share your learning challenges. Remember, you appear as an expert to the learner and if you think how easy experts often make things appear you will understand how some learners feel in your classes. So talk about your learning journeys, show how you used your strengths in one area to overcome challenges in another and find occasions to become the learner once again. In this way you will remain grounded and close to the needs of the young learner.

## ❖ Reflective task

Think of a learning challenge you have faced where you were out of your comfort zone or anxious.

- Describe how confident you were of being successful at the start.

- What aspects of your self-belief were involved in the learning challenge?

- Did you change any aspects of your self-belief as a result of the outcome of the challenge?

- Did you reinforce any self-beliefs as a result of the outcome of the challenge?

# WHAT IT FEELS LIKE TO BE A LEARNER

Our emotional state and associated feelings have an impact on us as learners. Feeling confident and positive about a learning challenge helps us to focus on the learning aspect but may not help when we are faced with a challenge to demonstrate understanding or apply what we have learnt. In other words, confidence may help us learn but can also trip us up if we are overconfident when we are asked to demonstrate knowledge or understanding. Conversely, excessive anxiety or stress may not help us in the learning situation, but milder levels may improve our concentration or degree of awareness.

Getting the balance right and knowing how to manage the learning environment is easier if as teachers we can remember what it is like to be a learner.

## How does it feel to be put on the spot?

Teachers rarely experience the pressure of demonstrating understanding, of applying knowledge and of being right, yet we frequently ask this of our pupils. Are you truly mindful of the situation you create, and do you acknowledge this in your planning and teaching?

Honest answers please!

When I am working with teachers I like to create a situation where they need to demonstrate understanding, apply knowledge and get the answer right. I am in fact duplicating the very situation they often create; I am putting them under pressure. The stakes, and as a result the pressure, are raised by expecting a correct answer. How this is presented and managed is important too for it has the opportunity to create a great deal of emotional impact on the learner. I find that this is best done when I have the confidence of the group and have built a positive relationship with them, not unlike a teacher in a class.

To help you experience being under pressure I have included a challenge I use on my training courses in Appendix F. When presenting the challenge I ask teachers to record their stress level, their confidence and how much they are enjoying the challenge. This is repeated during and at the end of the challenge and forms part of the review. The whole thing is stage-managed and includes things I have seen teachers do and say during their teaching, things that I know will cause a reaction.

My experience of using this exercise with teachers has resulted in them displaying the types of behaviour we would call uncooperative or non-compliant from pupils. I have seen arms folded across the chest, pens slammed down, doubting and undermining self-talk, chairs pushed back, increased verbalisation. To me these are all signs of stress brought on by a challenge they are unfamiliar with but also the conditions under which they were expected to solve the exercise. I was purposefully denying them access to some of their learning needs. Try undertaking the challenge and see if you can you identify which learning needs are easily excluded.

Earlier I mentioned how we can build our opinions and picture of self from what we experience and what is said to us. We are, however, often unaware of how subtle this influence is. If you are interested in this aspect of self-talk then I recommend a book by Shad Helmstetter (1991), *What to Say When You Talk to Your Self.*

IF YOU CAN'T REACH THEM YOU CAN'T TEACH THEM

# Communication

Do what you say and say as you do. Obviously!

Teaching is all about communication, in all forms from what you put on your classroom walls, the way you talk, what you say (or don't), how you look, your expressions and your interactions with pupils and colleagues. Whatever happens to you, however you feel, once you meet your class or walk into a classroom you must be on top of your game. You need to exude calmness and somehow communicate the principles of PBCF. Saying one thing and doing something different confuses pupils. They try to read you and can't, which causes anxiety and in turn impacts behaviour. But it is not enough to say and do the same thing if you want to embed PBCF in your planning and teaching; you must also share your thinking in a way that builds the learning relationship and supports PBCF.

## Personal reflection

I attended a course on communication during which I had to answer questions from a panel. I listened to each question and gave my answer clearly and succinctly. The debrief was enlightening and directly related to PBCF. Although the panel were happy with my answers we did not bond; it was them and me and not us. Getting to the bottom of why I had failed to create a common sense of belonging revealed a key element in the way I answered the questions. I did not share my thinking with the panel on the way I had arrived at my answer. Communication is not just what you say; it is also saying what you are thinking as you build up to saying what it is you want to say, especially if you want to promote PBCF.

In promoting PBCF in your teaching, explore all aspects of your communication and ask yourself what it is you are actually saying. Are you explaining yourself clearly? The poster you put on the wall or the display you create will communicate aspects of PBCF (or not) to your pupils, as will the tone of your voice, the words you choose and how much time you spend answering questions. Remember listening is a significant part of communication too.

## ❖ Reflective task

For each of the following, which aspects of PBCF could be promoted by your communications and how?

- Wall displays.
- Reminder notices (school rules, classroom expectations etc).
- Outside your classroom.
- Marking work.
- Giving feedforward.
- Welcoming or dismissing the class.

# What next?

At the start of this chapter I set out to show you how you can integrate PBCF into everything you do without adding additional demands on your time or requiring further resources. To do this we have looked at a range of issues related to learning and teaching, those everyday aspects of building learning relationships and understanding the learner perspective. These are the things you need to be mindful of in your approach to teaching if you are to integrate PBCF. This is a key point to make: those initiatives or ideas about teaching that as an educator I have had to accommodate, that are effectively bolt-on (almost parasitic of my time and effort), are soon abandoned and leave little lasting impact or change. In the next chapter I will raise your level of awareness of PBCF in your teaching with the aim of making a lasting change.

## References and further reading

**Advocating Creativity (2016)** *How to Learn Anything*. [online] Available at: https://4c3d. wordpress.com/2016/03/18/how-to-learn-anything-2/ (accessed 1 November 2020).

This site features a colour, printable version of the 'How to Learn Anything' poster as well as a more in-depth article about its conception and use.

**Advocating Creativity (2017)** *Why Creativity?* [online] Available at: https://4c3d.wordpress.com/ 2017/01/31/why-creativity/ (accessed 1 November 2020).

**Aparta, A (2014)** *How to Learn a New Language: 7 Secrets from TED Translators*. [online] Available at: https://blog.ted.com/how-to-learn-a-new-language-7-secrets-from-ted-translators/ comment-page-5/ (accessed 1 November 2020).

**Bandura, A (1989) Human Agency in Social Cognitive Theory.** *American Psychologist*. [online] Available at: www.uky.edu/~eushe2/Bandura/Bandura1989AP.pdf (accessed 1 November 2020).

**David, L (2007)** *Attribution Theory (Weiner)*. [online] Available at: www.learning-theories.com/ weiners-attribution-theory.html (accessed 1 November 2020).

Bernard Weiner (born 1935) is a social psychologist who is known for developing a form of attribution theory that explains the emotional and motivational entailments of academic success and failure.

**David, L (2014)** *Emotional Intelligence (Goleman)*. [online] Available at: www.learning-theories. com/emotional-intelligence-goleman.html (accessed 1 November 2020).

**Goleman, D (1999)** *Working with Emotional Intelligence*. London: Bloomsbury.

**Helmstetter, S (1991)** *What to Say When You Talk to Your Self*. London: HarperCollins.

**McLeod, S (2019)** *Constructivism as a Theory for Teaching and Learning*. [online] Available at: www.simplypsychology.org/constructivism.html (accessed 1 November 2020).

**McLeod, S (2019)** *The Zone of Proximal Development and Scaffolding*. [online] Available at: www. simplypsychology.org/Zone-of-Proximal-Development.html (accessed 1 November 2020).

**PBL Works (nd)** *What is PBL?* [online] Available at: www.pblworks.org/what-is-pbl (accessed 1 November 2020).

A description of and support for project-based learning can be found here.

**Practical EQ (nd)** *A Brief History of Emotional Intelligence.* [online] Available at: www.emotionalintelligencecourse.com/history-of-eq/ (accessed 1 November 2020).

**Rath, T (2007)** *Strengths Finder 2.0.* New York: Gallup Press.

**Stanford Encyclopedia of Philosophy (2018)** *John Dewey: Bibliography.* [online] Available at: https://plato.stanford.edu/entries/dewey/#Bib (accessed 1 November 2020).

**Stevenson, A (2017)** *The Power of Words: Positive vs Negative.* [online] Available at: https://kidblog.org/home/the-power-of-words-positive-vs-negative/ (accessed 1 November 2020).

**Study.com (nd)** *Resources to Flip Your Classroom.* [online] Available at: https://study.com/teach/flipped-classroom.html (accessed 1 November 2020).

**Teachers Toolbox (nd)** *Dweck's Theory of Motivation.* [online] Available at: www.teacherstoolbox.co.uk/dwecks-theory-of-motivation/ (accessed 1 November 2020).

Carol Dweck is Professor of Psychology at Columbia University. She is a leader in the field of pupil motivation.

**Teacher Toolkit (2018)** *The 5 Minute Lesson Plan.* [online] Available at: www.teachertoolkit.co.uk/5minplan/ (accessed 1 November 2020).

**Tes (2019)** *Pedagogy Focus: John Dewey.* [online] Available at: www.tes.com/news/pedagogy-focus-john-dewey (accessed 1 November 2020).

**Wikipedia (nd)** *Hero's Journey.* [online] Available at: https://en.wikipedia.org/wiki/Hero's_journey (accessed 1 November 2020).

The Hero's Journey is a pattern of narrative identified by the American scholar Joseph Campbell that appears in drama, storytelling, myth, religious ritual, and psychological development.

QR link

Your notes

IF YOU CAN'T REACH THEM YOU CAN'T TEACH THEM

# Appendix E
# MY TEACHING STRATEGIES

## Considering PBCF in planning

Here is how I go about such an exercise when reviewing my teaching and planning. In design teaching I used a process called a user trip. It is a way of visualising an event or process as if you were the user, in this case the pupil. Imagine a bell ringing to signal the start of a lesson change. Imagine waiting by your classroom door for your pupils to arrive. It involves a lot of visualisation and empathy so you will need to clear your mind and find a quiet place before embarking on such a trip.

---

### ❖ Reflective task

Once in your quiet place, put yourself in a pupil's shoes as they make their way from one lesson to another or make their way into school for the day with you.

- **What are they feeling?**

- **What expectations did you set last time you were together?**

---

- **What will they experience on their way to you?**

[ ]

All these things have an effect and so you need to plan for them. The pupil behaviour you will encounter as they join you for the lesson will give you some idea about what needs have not been met and those that will need to be a priority if the lesson is to get underway without a great deal of turbulence.

## PROVIDING FOR PBCF

Your lesson may start as pupils arrive but you must consider events even before you start teaching. So long as the pupil has access to you it is important you think about 'please be child friendly'. I have listed belonging as the first need to consider but that is only because on arrival it is the most appropriate to implement. You can start anywhere – P, B, C or F – and move back and forth.

## How I provide for the four learning needs of pupils

**BELONGING**

[ ]

IF YOU CAN'T REACH THEM YOU CAN'T TEACH THEM

**POWER**

**CHOICE**

**FUN**

IF YOU CAN'T REACH THEM YOU CAN'T TEACH THEM

# Appendix F
# THE COIN CHALLENGE

## What you need and setting the scene

Before you start you need a baseline. There are three things I would like you to consider and rate them regarding your emotional state at the moment. Use a simple low to high scale with 1 being low and 5 being high.

- **Stress level:** This is your reaction to the situation you find yourself in. This will vary from very relaxed to feeling anxious and will depend on how much control over the situation you have.
- **Confidence level:** This is how you feel about your ability to deal with any aspect of the challenges that lay ahead. This may range from 'bring it on' to a feeling of being pushed outside your comfort zone.
- **Enjoyment level:** Enjoyment is linked to being successful, understanding or feeling comfortable. It may range from boredom to excitement about what comes next.

## HOW I FEEL BEFORE I KNOW WHAT THE CHALLENGE IS:

### Emotion score 1

Stress level ☐   Confidence level ☐   Enjoyment level ☐

You will score your emotions twice more, once when you know what the challenge is and again at the end of the challenge.

This is a logic challenge. I have chosen a logic challenge in order to avoid giving anyone a distinct advantage in terms of subject knowledge.

- Most people can complete the challenge in under three minutes.
- Ten year-olds have no difficulty at all in getting it right.
- Obviously you are not allowed to ask anyone else for help. You are on your own.
- You will need something to write with.
- You will need something to time yourself with (a mobile phone or watch will do).
- Where you do this challenge is up to you. You may like to find a quiet place where you are on your own so others don't ask what you are doing or see you possibly struggling!

# HOW I FEEL BEFORE I BEGIN THE CHALLENGE:

## Emotion score 2

Stress level [          ]     Confidence level [          ]     Enjoyment level [          ]

## THE LOGIC CHALLENGE

Set your timer: you have five minutes to solve this problem.

### The task

You have 15 one penny coins and four envelopes. Place the coins in the envelopes in such a way that you can pay any amount from 1 to 15 pence by handing over one or more envelopes. Every envelope has to contain at least one penny and you may not have any coins left over.

### Working-out space

### Your answer

Envelope 1 will contain _____

Envelope 2 will contain _____

Envelope 3 will contain _____

Envelope 4 will contain _____

If you run out of time you may continue with the task but you have failed!

IF YOU CAN'T REACH THEM YOU CAN'T TEACH THEM

## HOW I FELT AT THE END OF THE CHALLENGE:

Emotion score 3

Stress level [ ]        Confidence level [ ]        Enjoyment level [ ]

## MY EMOTIONS AND FEELINGS

Compare your three emotional scores.

1. Before knowing what the challenge was:


2. Before starting the challenge:


3. At the end of the exercise:


Ask yourself what changed and why?

## EXPLAINING THE CHALLENGE

When I have used this exercise with groups of people there is a definite and almost tangible sense of stress and anxiety in the room. This starts to build as the exercise is introduced, mainly because it is something new, a new challenge or experience.

You have to be aware of how you introduce the exercise and the impact that has on people and their emotional state. For example in my introduction I said '*Most people can do it in under three minutes and ten year-olds have no difficulty at all!*' I was purposefully trying to build the level of anxiety by providing you with a comparative measure for your own performance. To make you even more nervous I presented you with the opportunity to be shown up by a ten year-old, something few adults are comfortable with. So I raised the stakes, turning a fun challenge into something that could embarrass you.

If you felt under pressure, stressed or anxious during the exercise, even though you were not doing it in front of others, this was done purposefully.

- How you would rate the experience? Would you like to repeat it?

I would bet that the answers would depend a great deal on how successful you were in meeting the challenge. How successful you were will influence your willingness to try again or try a new challenge. This simple exercise highlights how important our emotions and learning needs are.

- What have you learnt as a result of the exercise in terms of your teaching?
- Take a moment to reflect on your answers and to put them into the context of the learners in your classroom. Think about the learning needs, power, belonging, choice and fun. Think about how your view of self influenced your approach.

I am sure you want to know if you got it right so here is the answer to the challenge.

> Envelope 1 should contain one penny.
> Envelope 2 should contain two pennies.
> Envelope 3 should contain four pennies.
> Envelope 4 should contain eight pennies.

Using a combination of one or more of the four envelopes can make up any number from one to 15. For example envelope 1 and 4 will give you a total of nine pence and envelope two, three and four a total of 14 pence.

- Now try the coin challenge on a colleague and remember to purposefully build the level of anxiety.

IF YOU CAN'T REACH THEM YOU CAN'T TEACH THEM

# 6. MINDFUL LEARNING AND TEACHING

*Things don't change unless there is a change of mind.*

## Being mindful

Mindfulness is being in the moment, an awareness, of paying attention to thoughts, sounds and sensations. There is a similar state in teaching, something akin to Zanshin in Japanese martial arts where you are relaxed and alert.

In teaching, being mindful is a way of ensuring you embed changes to your approach to learning and teaching, taking every opportunity to build effective learning relationships and meet the four learning needs. It means you do not wear yourself out and you do not limit your pupils' potential; instead you foster creativity and raise standards. Essentially you are mindful of your own needs and those of your pupils. Being mindful in learning and teaching is about being present, being aware of your own presence in the classroom and the interplay of the various elements within it. When you have an effective learning relationship with your pupils you will be able to experience this state and teach in such a way that you can observe and finesse what is happening in your lessons.

# Mindless learning and teaching explained

Mindless learning and teaching is a state you need to avoid. A quick look at a thesaurus provides ample synonyms: tedious, unnecessary and foolish are just a few examples. Now consider the disengaged pupil's opinion of school. You could expect to hear that school is '*a waste of time*' or perhaps '*boring*'. The language pupils use to describe school indicates their experiences and views about learning, if they believe what they are learning is a mindless exercise or not.

The coin and envelope challenge I set in Appendix F was conducted in a mindless way since it ignored learning needs. However, if a pupil is prepared and the debrief for exercises such as this are conducted in a constructive way, you can make all learning challenges mindful experiences.

## MINDLESS LEARNING

If a pupil asks '*Why am I learning this?*' it is possibly because either the pupil thinks the work is irrelevant or too difficult. Ignoring learning needs and learning by rote and without a context that involves understanding or application is mindless learning. If a pupil indicates that they think it is a mindless learning experience they will give little effort unless you change their mind.

## Personal reflection

I was coaching a pupil in basic mathematics for their GCSE examination. A stumbling block was number pattern recognition, a key building block in mathematics. For example, recognising that the number 72 can be arrived at in a number of ways ($6 \times 12$, $144 \div 2$, $3 \times 4 \times 6$ etc). Multiplication tables were not seen by the pupil as an important part of developing their mathematical language, of becoming fluent in numbers. They had given little effort to understanding it although it had been learnt to a point where the pupil could recite it. When I compared this to how much effort and time they had put into learning to read, the penny dropped. We explored the table together and the pupil developed a new understanding of its value and place in mathematics. He was also successful in developing a better understanding of mathematics and ultimately in his examination at the end of the year.

## MINDLESS TEACHING

Your natural response to the pupil question '*Why am I learning this?*' will be to motivate them. You may use the phrase '*It's needed for the exam*'. This is an example of a mindless response. You have failed to address the issues raised by the pupil's question. If they trust you they may accept your reasons and if not they are likely to challenge you further or decide to not make any more effort than they are already doing. This latter response I call 'compliant disobedience'. Mindless teaching is behaving the same, regardless of the feedback you receive from your pupils.

My recommendation in circumstances where a pupil challenges why they are doing something is not to focus on the question itself but instead to be mindful of it. Pupils will often give us signals in the form of a challenge when a need or combination of needs are not being met. I find if you do not recognise the signals then the challenges are likely to escalate.

# Mindful learning and teaching explained

In mindful teaching you use all of your senses to take note of the learning environment, your relationship with your pupils and their behaviour. What you hear, what you see, are equally important as what you don't. You use this information to make informed decisions and take actions that will support learners in meeting their needs and in building effective learning relationships.

When a pupil's needs are being met they are more likely to engage with the challenge.

Consider each need (PBCF) and each element of a learning challenge.

- Having something explained allows pupils to express their needs and develop understanding.
- Being asked to take part in an activity willingly empowers pupils and offers them choice.
- Being part of a collaborative or team activity promotes a sense of belonging.
- Being engaged results in the pupils enjoying themselves; there is a sense of achievement. Making the link between fun and achievement is a key responsibility in teaching.

Time spent being mindful in your approach with pupils is time well spent for it will help you take your pupils with you on the learning journey and result in a much more rewarding experience for you both.

## MINDFUL LEARNING

In mindful learning you encourage pupils to also be mindful. You want them to be aware during the learning experience of how they feel, not just about what they are learning.

- Do they feel comfortable about what they are learning?
- Are they confident in their understanding?
- Are they anxious about what comes next (perhaps a test or working independently)?
- Is their attention wandering?

This mindfulness helps break some of the bonds that tie their self-belief to their ability to learn and to what subjects they favour. You want them to recognise how they feel and its impact on their learning; you want them to look for solutions where emotions are not supporting their learning. You also want them to recognise and celebrate success and positive emotions.

## MINDFUL TEACHING

As a way of introducing the idea of mindful teaching, read the following scenario and complete the reflective task.

### Case study

You have planned, resourced and delivered a successful lesson. The questions you asked about the topic were answered succinctly and accurately. You begin to think it was a job well done.

The bell is about to go and the pupils start to collect their things together. As they do, a pupil says to you '*I didn't get it!*'

### ❖ Reflective task

With only a couple of minutes left of the lesson what do you say and do?

As teachers we have all been here. The temptation is to repeat, question, repeat, question, rephrase, question and so on. There is a significant chance that the learner will leave the lesson feeling negative and carry this into the next lesson you have with them. They will have added to what I call their learning map (more of this in Chapter 9), a belief about what they can and cannot learn, and it is unlikely that it is a positive addition. Tackling the problem in this way, the teacher may know that the pupil does not get it but they are no nearer getting the pupil to understand. This is not a mindful approach.

Suggest a key question you could ask the pupil if you were to think mindfully at this point in the lesson.

You want to know the foundation of understanding on which to build. You can also reassure the pupil that you will think about how to better explain it for the start of the next lesson. The mindful teaching question would be '*Tell me what you do understand?*'

This simple change of approach has significant consequences for the pupil and you. Here are some I want you to consider and in doing so remember PBCF.

- The focus is not on a failure to understand. It is instead on what has been understood.
- The pupil is not lectured to, a strategy that builds pupil confidence.
- Because the response is personalised, the learner is treated as an individual with their own needs.
- There is an opportunity for the teacher to actively take some responsibility for the learning too, helping learners see learning as a journey you are both on.
- You are not trying to rerun the lesson in two minutes, possibly further confusing the pupil.

Ellen Langer lists characteristics of mindfulness. One of these is an implicit awareness of more than one perspective (Langer, 1997). Since teachers should also be learners these two perspectives come together to form a mindful approach. As teachers we need to ask questions to discover what our pupils' perspective is regarding their learning and how they feel (PBCF) rather than just what they have learnt.

## BEING MINDFUL OF LEARNERS' NEEDS IMPACTS TEACHING

Where there is pressure in classrooms for pupils to make progress and for lessons to demonstrate pace there can be a tendency to have very closed and limiting questioning sessions. This is not a mindful approach; a situation made even more ineffective when the teacher waits for the shortest of times before either giving the answer or rephrasing the question. In such circumstances pupils often learn to wait rather than offer an answer they are unsure of. See *Further reading* at the end of this chapter for a link to Mary Budd Rowe's work on questioning.

You need to be mindful that the question and answer technique can limit creative engagement in the lesson and therefore the learning. You can so easily enter the world of mindless learning where there are only right and wrong answers, only those answers that satisfy the assessment criteria, of memorised facts without understanding the context. To ensure you support PBCF and promote mindful learning requires only a small change to both your manner of questioning and how you respond to the answers you are given. Consider the responses of two teachers involved in teaching science and a Q&A session.

## Case study

### TEACHER A

**Question:** *What are the three states matter can exist in?*

**Analysis:** The focus is not on understanding or the context but purely on recall. It excludes creative thought and can exclude pupils. In my experience, where learning is not secure, silence will often greet such questions. An analysis of the question itself tells us a number of things about the learning and teaching. In this example there is a right or wrong learning atmosphere, a high-stakes situation. The pupils in the class are being told there are only three states matter can exist in and that only a complete answer (all three states) is required. Thinking mindfully about how this question is phrased:

- if a pupil can think of only one or two, should they attempt an answer?
- if a pupil thinks they can suggest more than three states for matter, how do they answer the question?

### TEACHER B

**Question:** *In what states, that we know of, can matter exist?* or *In what states do you think matter exists?*

**Analysis:** As before, an analysis of the question itself tells us several things about the learning and teaching. The pupils in the class are being asked to contribute what they know or believe to be part of, or all of the answer. Thinking mindfully about how this question is phrased compared to Teacher A above:

- There is no right or wrong, no limiting number and all contributions are openly encouraged.
- Pupils that can think of one or four states can contribute and the resulting discussion, if managed mindfully, can help to reinforce the learning.

How close to Teacher A or Teacher B is your questioning technique? Are you being mindful? Depending on how the teacher phrases the questions they ask and responds to the answers they are given, they can encourage an inclusive discussion and avoid a high-stakes, 'right/wrong' scenario. Teacher B will learn more about how the class are responding to their teaching and the degree of understanding of the material. Mindful follow-up questions can be easily added in by Teacher B, such as:

- why do you think that?
- who agrees/disagrees with the list we have so far?

Instead of silence I have found pupils are eager to contribute what they know when questioning is managed in a mindful way.

There are a number of other areas in your teaching where you can employ a mindful approach. Consider:

- the request to 'pay attention';
- defining work and play;
- drawing distinction (see Figure 6.1);
- a learning hierarchy (see Figure 6.2).

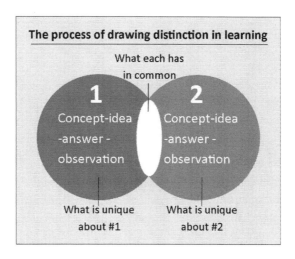

**Figure 6.1 Drawing distinction**

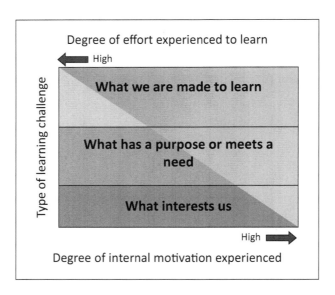

**Figure 6.2 A possible learning hierarchy**

# Improving the way you teach

You can bring about significant improvements in learning and teaching through the adoption of a mindful approach in many aspects of your teaching. Being mindful in your teaching is not a major shift in what you teach, more how you teach it and how you explore and respond to your pupil's needs. When you are teaching be mindful of your behaviour and that of your pupils. Take a moment to reflect on what messages you are giving your pupils and what messages they are sending you. I believe you will identify three key learning groups within your classes.

## THREE KEY LEARNING GROUPS

These groups are especially evident at reporting time. These are not hard and fast groups and membership can vary according to teacher, subject and the learning environment. Some classes may exhibit the behaviours of only one group depending on such strategies within the school as streaming or indeed the character or nature of the school and its catchment. In many ways the three groups of pupils reflect your relationship with them. Not all pupils in a class have the same needs. You need to react mindfully as each group places different demands on your time in the lesson and in your planning.

### Group 1

There are those pupils that do well, are active participants in the learning, those who ask questions and who are confident. You know them well and find it easy to say something about their progress, attitudes and behaviours. At reporting time you may use phrases such as 'Well done' or 'Keep it up'. I find that many pupils in this group may be labelled gifted or talented.

## Group 2

There are those pupils who have presented challenges, often of behavioural or relating to engagement in nature. Once again you know them well and you do not struggle to offer advice on how to do better next year. Typical reporting comments include 'Learn to focus and avoid distractions'. In a mild form these are the cheeky group but behaviour can escalate to a disruptive level if not managed carefully. They normally do well when not in school. For example, when on work experience or placement outside of the school setting.

## Group 3

The last group are not so well known to you. They are often quiet and do as they are told and take up little of your time. I would term them compliant learners. When it comes to writing reports, this group provide the biggest challenge; often you will be left wondering what to write. This group may represent the most untapped learning potential.

## ANALYSING THE THREE GROUPS

Confident learners, those in Group 1, will also take up your time as they require additional resources but only if they have a dependent relationship with you. Helping this group become responsible for extending their own learning is part of the learning relationship we looked at in Chapter 2 and exemplifies a mindful teaching approach.

Disengaged learners, those in Group 2, are the most demanding of your time; they are often characterised by impatient and challenging behaviours. They adopt strategies they have learnt and developed to get your attention. There is much at risk in terms of disruptive behaviour if you fail to respond to their needs. These behaviours are symptoms of learning needs not being met and you need to be mindful of it. Using sanctions or controlling strategies may suppress the behaviour but it does little to build a positive learning relationship with these pupils. Nor does it help them understand why they behave as they do and to learn other strategies that enable them to engage in the learning. It is this group with which you will have the most immediate impact in terms of learning relationships if you adopt a mindful PBCF approach in your teaching.

Group 3, the compliant learners, will do little to disturb the flow of the lesson or make demands on your time. If you are not mindful of this group they can receive little attention as you are drawn to Group 1 or Group 2 in order to keep the lesson flowing. You may not be aware of their learning needs or their specific learning challenges unless you engage with them.

# What if you are not mindful of learning needs?

It is not easy to ignore learning needs; you are driven to satisfy them. Sheer determination or significant motivational factors such as fear or threat could subdue them, but they do not go away. Significantly, understanding the emotional impact in an educational context of unfulfilled needs will determine your success with pupils. Without being mindful and recognising how your emotions influence your thinking, you are more likely to think and act instinctively rather than reflect on learning.

## Personal reflection

I entered an ICT lesson and picked up on a certain atmosphere in the room. It was the one that often precedes an incident; something felt uneasy. I was scanning the room for the source when an incident erupted between two boys and a fist flew. I took the boys out of the lesson and into the nearest empty room where I sat them down. I sat quietly with them for a little while to give time for the adrenaline to subside before talking with them. I did not go into the whys and wherefores of the situation but instead asked if they understood why they behaved in the way they did. I explained about our reptile or lizard brain function (see *Further reading* for details of a great book about our amazing brain by Andrew Curran) and how it can dominate our behaviour if we let it. I also explained that if we pause then the thinking brain will cut in and allow us to make rational decisions rather than instinctive ones. This delay is easily achieved if we slowly count to two before responding. The two pupils I took out of the lesson shook hands and apologised to each other and to me. Notably their calm entry back into the lesson also had the effect of extinguishing their peers' interest and hopes for a further fight after school.

### THE PEER GROUP INFLUENCE

Peer groups can develop quickly and can offer the need for choice if none is forthcoming from the existing situation and, most importantly, they promote a sense of belonging. Their purpose can also become fun, not the recognition of achievement in terms of learning but other less desirable outcomes such as disturbance or mischief. By being mindful to all situations in teaching you can work towards developing a sense of belonging with your pupils, which has the effect of limiting challenging peer group pressure. You can use PBCF to get the pupils on your side and build effective learning relationships.

# Behaviour and mindful learning and teaching

All schools have a behaviour policy that describes expected pupil behaviours. These behaviours require compliance from the pupils. Behaviours that are essential in a safe and well-ordered classroom are promoted. We cannot teach in chaos and in practical terms where you must manage a class, a year group and a school some common elements of behaviour are essential. Mindful teaching asks us to see any behaviour as a symptom of need (or possibly acknowledgement of the need being met) rather than an action on the part of the pupils to antagonise or challenge. Mindful teaching also asks you to consider the behaviours you are creating, supporting or fuelling by your behaviours. So, out with the behaviour policy and in with the learning relationship policy?

Well, not quite. The behaviour policy is a legal requirement of schools in the UK and so cannot be omitted from the list of policies schools must have and follow. Any policy can be designed solely in terms of discipline and the consequences for the pupil for not behaving appropriately. But you can and should question the purpose of a behaviour policy, or rather what it means in your schools in terms of learning and teaching.

## MINDFULLY LINKING BEHAVIOUR TO LEARNING

While you need to have a behaviour policy, I recommend that you supplement it with a policy that aims to promote learning, a learning relationship policy. Such a policy is not just a change of name, but a change in emphasis from behaving to avoid chaos to behaving to promote learning. In writing and adopting a policy you accept responsibility for the content and direction and therefore you are accountable. Policies that are developed through consultation are also a way of informing and educating people with a greater success rate in terms of accepting and carrying out the policy requirements. As in any community, you expect people to follow a collectively agreed policy. A school with a learning relationship policy places learning needs at the centre of the learning approach.

## Language and mindful learning

As a teacher you must be careful about what you say and the message you convey to pupils about learning. The most common issue in this respect is what behaviours you refer to as work or as play. Think how many times you have heard a teacher say *'Get on with your work', 'Have you come ready to work?'* Referring to learning as work can promote a set of pre-programmed emotions and attitudes that influence a pupil's approach to learning.

## ❖ Reflective task

There are a set of characteristics – such as paying attention (sit facing the front, not doodling) – that you expect to see adopted when your pupils are working. Take a moment to write down your own expectations for how pupils behave when both working and playing.

Working behaviours are:

Play behaviours are:

There is no doubt that your list of working behaviours will reflect your expectations as a teacher as well as your own education. What worked for you, helped you to learn, should work for others, right? Wrong! Now look again mindfully at the lists you made: are any behaviours mindless, do they support learning?

There is much to be gained by learning through play, turning work into play. For example, play can engage pupils, help them remember, allow them to make mistakes without consequence, help them draw distinctions, learn collaboratively and reduce anxiety. On the other hand, the concept of work carries a value; we get paid to work. You can take advantage of the benefits of play by being mindful of your language when engaging with pupils.

Here is my list of work and play definitions put together from pupils, teachers and parents. It sets out expectations that you need to be mindful of when planning and delivering your lessons.

Work is:

- hard;
- where you go to;
- what you get paid for;
- what you do as a job for somebody;

- often long hours and has rules and regulations you have to follow;
- where you wear a uniform;
- serious;
- full of challenges, of doing difficult things;
- where you have to be quiet and focused;
- stressful.

Play is:

- relaxing;
- something that clears your mind;
- activities undertaken with others;
- taking a break from work;
- relief from stress;
- fun;
- chatting and sharing things;
- pleasure;
- games you play;
- being happy.

# Learning myths

Having looked at play and work language and behaviours, it is appropriate that you mindfully explore some of the facts or myths about learning and learning behaviours. Langer (1997, p 2) writes about seven pervasive myths that she believes *'stifle our creativity, silence our questions and diminish our self esteem'.*

1. The basics must be learnt so well that they become second nature.
2. Paying attention means staying focused on one thing at a time.
3. Delaying gratification is important.
4. Rote memorisation is necessary in education.
5. Forgetting is a problem.
6. Intelligence is knowing what is out there.
7. There are right and wrong answers.

For learners I am sure adhering to these myths does have an impact on their achievements and their view of self as a learner. For you to prove if there is a positive or negative impact would require you to have built effective learning relationships with your pupils and of finding a way of tracking learning behaviours and outcomes over time. For you to decide the nature of the impact of these myths you will need to think in terms of PBCF, mindful learning and teaching, and your learning relationships with your pupils. If you accept Langer's myths then you need to ask why such myths prevail in learning and teaching, why mindless approaches are still part of the learning landscape.

A lot of what you do in teaching is driven by the measure of pupil achievement. In your teaching you follow practices that are aimed at raising standards. You need to be mindful of these practices and challenge them where they do not support PBCF, for if they do you will struggle in the long term to raise standards.

Schools are judged through pupil assessments and by pupil outcomes against national norms. The pupil is seen as the end product of a system of education – not unlike any other system that has an input, process and output. In education an accurate assessment of the end product is not easily achieved and this makes it difficult to determine the effectiveness of the process. For example:

- What pupils know or learn in schools may not have a demonstrable outcome for many years after leaving school.
- A terminal examination may not be the best tool to measure understanding or competence.
- In teaching there are a significant number of variables when it comes to learning and teaching and it may not be possible to allocate responsibility for an outcome to a single circumstance or group of circumstances or actions. Variables include prior learning, home support, social and economic factors, resources and pupil to teacher ratio.

It is important not to look at the structures or proxies in teaching and their claimed association on learning outcomes in isolation; you need to be mindful about what you can claim as behaviours that support or promote learning. Consider, for example, whether the reputation of a school is a product of the quality of the teaching and potential of the pupils or is the quality of the teaching and achievement of the pupils a product of the reputation of the school?

I have seen the highest standard of teaching in what may be regarded as the most challenging of schools (those regarded as needing improvement). I have also seen excellent pupil achievement measured against prior attainment in the same schools. Unfortunately, if such schools are measured against norms or benchmarks and fall short they are still regarded as needing improvement: a mindless action that ignores a major achievement and can result in more mindless actions to raise standards without effect.

I have also seen schools regarded as good or excellent with poor teaching but with a high achieving intake (based on a combination of known influencing factors on performance/outcomes) and instances of relatively low pupil achievement measured against potential. Where such schools don't fall below norms or benchmarks little or no action is taken in terms of requiring improvement, mindlessly ignoring potential.

A school can be seen to make significant improvements or slide down the performance tables as a result of a change in intake and from one year to the next. Much depends on the catchment and intake of a school in terms of outcome and consequences. For the school it not always a level playing field or a simple matter of structure and systems. You would think if it were simply a case of 'do this and this will happen' then the answer would have been found by now. Perhaps the myths prevail, and this prevents an objective (and mindful) look at the problem of pupil attainment, learning and teaching and therefore school performance.

If the continued call for raising standards, work readiness, what is often referred to as 'the basics' (a term never fully defined or agreed) and the continued struggle between academic and vocational education are anything to go by, we are far from coming to an answer. Without tackling the big debate about the purpose of education and who should direct the focus, it always comes back to a discussion about standards. The standard of education is judged by more than one consumer and each has their own agenda. This creates a certain climate in schools, a blame culture and you cannot avoid it, but I believe you can work around it in your teaching by mindfully building effective learning relationships with your pupils.

A way of raising standards in such a blame culture has always been to focus on the measures of outcome and not so much the process, especially if it this does not deviate from the myths listed by Ellen Langer. This is a typical product manufacturing model, an industrial way of thinking that seeks standardisation and performance indicators. The primary means of judging teacher effectiveness is the achievement of their pupils. In their report the Sutton Trust concluded '*Gains in pupil test scores are the best available metric to measure teacher performance*' (Sutton Trust, 2013, p 4). They do accept, however, that it may not be a perfect means of measuring teacher performance. This has echoes of the manufacturing process where it was always concluded that, as long as the raw material was the same, a poorly made item must be the result of a poorly trained or skilled craftsman. You know that not all pupils are the same and that at times you can find that the same pupil is not always the same from one lesson to the next. Pupil behaviour is not always consistent and we know this because pupil PBCF needs change, and learning relationships affect behaviour.

Teacher performance may not the key factor in pupil achievement, or indeed the only one. When you are mindful of PBCF, what you do, your focus, is directed at the pupil and this will have the effect of improving learning outcomes.

In being mindful we must be careful not to focus on novelty to bring about improvements in learning and teaching but on the underlying needs that are being addressed. Whenever you encounter a structural change, a new strategy or approach that improves learning and teaching, I challenge you to see how each of the four learning needs are being impacted. Does what is happening improve pupil voice, enhance a sense of belonging, offer an element of choice and is there a fun element within or associated with what is happening? Remember it may only require one of these needs to be met in an enhanced way for us to see an overall improvement in both engagement and achievement. This is where we need to be mindful, especially if we are to be able to dismiss the myths about how we learn best.

## The case for mindful teaching

Remember the alternative to mindful is mindless, a state of auto response or action without thought for options or consequences. It is hard to imagine teaching in such a way, it is hard to imagine driving in such a way, yet both do happen.

Getting to work each day can be a chore: the same route, the same traffic problems, the same delays and sometimes you may not even recall driving to work at all. What would your journey be like if you left at a different time and took a different route? What if you took a different route each day and mixed them up? Each day's journey would be less predictable, it may be more or less eventful, and you may make new discoveries including possibly better routes at different times of the day. Instead of operating in a mindless manner you would be functioning mindfully. What if we applied this analogy to teaching?

Are your lessons delivered in the same way each time; are you walking the same steps to discovery and understanding as the day or week or year before? If you are then you may be teaching in a mindless way and should not be surprised if you encounter mindless responses from your pupils.

In addition to Langer's seven myths, Prashnig has suggested a number of false beliefs, which include the following.

- Pupils learn best when seated upright at a desk or table.
- Pupils learn best in well-illuminated areas.
- Pupils learn more and perform better in an absolutely quiet environment.
- Whole-group instruction is the best way to teach.
- Effective teaching requires clearly stated objectives followed by detailed, step-by-step, logical, sequential explanations until all pupils understand what is being taught.

**(adapted from Prashnig, 1994, pp 1-2)**

If you are dismissive of what Langer and Prashnig have labelled as myths, ask yourself are you being mindful? It is not that any of these are true or false; it is that there are different opinions or views. If you are guilty of mindlessness then you must be wary of the effects on your teaching and pupils' learning. Remember the list at the start of this chapter and the possible lesson descriptions offered by disengaged pupils!

Langer says a mindful approach has three characteristics:

- *the continuous creation of new categories;*
- *openness to new information;*
- *an implicit awareness of more than one perspective.*

**(Langer, 1997, p 4)**

Here are some more mindful approaches that form part of my strategies in learning and teaching. Mindful approaches:

- consider the learning relationship as an essential foundation for learning and teaching;
- incorporate PBCF in learning and teaching (this includes planning and evaluation too);
- look at behaviour as a symptom of need and find ways to address that need;
- share your own learning journey and acknowledge the emotions associated with learning challenges;

- associate achievement with fun and promote the attitudes and practices of play within learning;
- avoid referring to learning as work;
- recognise the impact on relationships of even a casual teacher–pupil encounter and employ strategies to negate any impact that may result from any such encounters that may limit learning or learning relationships;
- use a range of pupil learning motivational strategies based on meeting PBCF needs;
- challenge myths and beliefs about learning;
- consider other views and opinions.

Ask yourself if any of these characterise your approach to learning and teaching. If they do then you are on your way to a mindful approach.

I know there will be those that doubt the impact of a mindful approach and I know that there will be those who will cite the practicalities of school and its structures, demands and external responsibilities as reasons why it will never work. What I am suggesting by being mindful requires no changes to structures, no special arrangements and no deviating from external responsibilities. There is, however, no instant fix either; it takes time for both you and your pupils to adjust to a mindful approach to teaching and learning. My belief and experience is that it does work and, like a focus on learning relationships and PBCF, a mindful approach can be scaled up across an entire school and even education system if we desire it.

I hope by now you can see that teaching can evolve, that there may be more than one way to teach and that there is no right or wrong way, but that you should always focus on PBCF. Sitting behind whatever you do in teaching are the four learning needs. The next chapter looks at how, through your mindful approach to teaching and learning, you can support independent learners.

## References and further reading

Budd Rowe, M (1986) Wait Time: Slowing Down May Be A Way of Speeding Up! *Journal of Teacher Education*. [online] Available at: www.scoe.org/blog_files/Budd%20Rowe.pdf (accessed 1 November 2020).

Mary Budd Rowe explains why learning to wait for answers to questions is an important part of learning and teaching.

Curran, A (2008) *The Little Book of Big Stuff about the Brain: The True Story of Your Amazing Brain*. Carmarthen, Wales: Crown House Publishing Ltd.

Langer, E (1997) *The Power of Mindful Learning*. Boston, MA: Da Capo Press.

Prashnig, B M (1994) *10 False Beliefs About Learning Causing High Stress and Burnout in Teachers*. [online] Available at: www.creativelearningcentre.com/downloads/10%20False%20 Beliefs.pdf (accessed 1 November 2020).

Sutton Trust (2013) *Testing Teachers*. [online] Available at: www.suttontrust.com/our-research/ testing-teachers/ (accessed 1 November 2020).

Teachers Toolbox (nd) *John Hattie's Table of Effect Sizes*. [online] Available at: www.teacherstoolbox.co.uk/effect-sizes/ (accessed 1 November 2020).

Visible Learning (nd) *Visible Learning Research*. [online] Available at: www.visiblelearning.com/content/visible-learning-research (accessed 1 November 2020).

These two sites will introduce you to Hattie's work and give you access to his effects tables.

QR link

Your notes

IF YOU CAN'T REACH THEM YOU CAN'T TEACH THEM

# 7. THE INDEPENDENT LEARNER

## What are independent learners and do you want them in your classes?

You may fear that the independent learner offers nothing more than another challenge and possible disruption to your planned learning. You may also worry about not being in control or of delegating too much responsibility for the learning to your pupils. Not all occasions call for the learner to be fully independent of you, nor can it be assumed that any pupil can be an independent learner. You have to consider the independent learner within the context of your learning relationship with them. You have to take into account the learning environment you have created through PBCF and your mindful approach as well as the skills, attributes and behaviours of the pupil and their past experiences of learning.

It may not be easy to get the conditions right to promote independent learning but consider the benefits of a productive learning relationship, one where the outcome is the result of more than one energy in the learning equation: a learning relationship where your efforts plus those of your pupils is greater than the sum. Where 1 plus 1 makes 11 and not 2!

As a teacher I can clearly recall the times where I have left a lesson feeling more energised than when I started, where the learning was a rhythmic dance of challenge, inspiration and insight. Where there was an interdependent relationship rather than a dependent one between teacher and pupil. If you have felt as though you were losing control or that the learning was too chaotic then you need to explore your relationship with the pupils and their readiness to undertake an independent learning role.

## WHAT IS AN INDEPENDENT LEARNER?

We need a common understanding of the term if we are to explore the learning landscape within which independent learners can thrive. Independent learning is not a new term and there are several associated or similar terms:

- self-directed learning;
- independent study;
- autonomous learning;
- flipped learning/flipped classrooms;
- learning to learn.

There are common characteristics of each as well as learning and teaching needs that arise from adapting or supporting such approaches to learning. These come about because the role of the teacher changes from the '*sage on the stage*' to the '*guide at your side*'; phrases used by Philosophy for Children (P4C) to describe their approach to developing independent learners.

## ❖ Reflective task

Take a moment to think about what it means to be either an independent learner or one that is dependent and how you would describe or recognise each.

IF YOU CAN'T REACH THEM YOU CAN'T TEACH THEM

- Mind map typical behaviours and attitudes of what you would consider dependent learners.

- Now do the same for independent learners. What behaviours and attitudes do they display?

## THE SCHOOL ENVIRONMENT

Before challenging your list of behaviours and attitudes you need to consider the school environment.

To some extent in schools all learners are dependent. Pupils are dependent on the teacher to provide:

- aims and objectives of the lesson;
- content;
- planning;
- learning resources;
- monitoring of learning;
- assessment;
- evaluation of learning outcomes for future planning;
- motivation and encouragement to learn.

It is your responsibility to teach each of the pupils in your class and to meet their needs, to actively seek engagement and to provide the reasons for learning; essentially, as you saw in Chapter 2, to build effective learning relationships and ensure learning takes place. You also know through your experience that one size does not fit all and that you will need to adjust your teaching and resources to reach all of the pupils in your class.

Notice how the onus here is on you to adapt and adopt strategies to meet the learner's needs. You can all too easily become solely accountable for the learning outcomes, forming a learning relationship where the pupil is totally dependent. This relationship is unbalanced and does nothing to foster mindful learning or PBCF.

Consider your descriptions of dependent and independent learners. I would claim that an independent learner is able to adapt to whatever learning environment they find themselves in, allowing them to satisfy their learning needs and maintain their learning focus. This is very much a characteristic of all successful learning journeys and is a key element of my concept of learning intelligence (LQ) introduced in Chapter 12.

## ❖ Reflective task

Tick all those that you think apply to your definition of the independent learner.

- ☐ Accepts their responsibilities within a learning relationship.
- ☐ Can adapt their approach to meet their learning needs.
- ☐ Engages mindfully in learning.
- ☐ Questions, reasons and evaluates.

- [ ] Explores independently.
- [ ] Understands about validity and value when investigating.
- [ ] Applies and transfers knowledge and understanding.
- [ ] Synthesises understanding.
- [ ] Curates knowledge.
- [ ] Develops lines of enquiry.
- [ ] Is able to discuss their learning journey.
- [ ] Understands their emotional response to learning and the influence of PBCF.

Can you add any more to the list?

## ❖ Reflective task review

This definition of the independent learner will help you recognise and promote them in your classes. Just remember that independent does not mean without guidance and support; it just means that occasionally the active responsibility for learning lies with the learner. This is evident in the LRRG in Figure 2.1.

My experience as a teacher showed me that some students are more successful in some subjects and with some teachers than they are with others. In fact, a change of learning environment could produce some unexpected outcomes. This might be explained by the notion of strengths or aptitudes; but what if this was not the case?

I believe as learners we develop a set of skills and behaviours built around early learning and social successes and these become our toolkit for dealing with future situations. Where we have the right tool for the job we are equipped and successful (given other influences are either neutral or supportive).

Albert Bandura says:

*Given the same environmental conditions, persons who have developed skills for accomplishing many options and are adept at regulating their own motivation and behaviour are more successful in their pursuits than those who have limited means of personal agency.*

(Bandura, 1989, p 1182)

A supportive environment, that meets learning needs and in which pupils have the appropriate skills and behaviours, is likely to encourage success. The reverse is also true; when the environment is toxic and pupils are ill-equipped they will struggle to be successful. The term 'success' means meeting personal potential and not an externally set target, grade or level of performance.

## Revisiting the learning relationship

I have mentioned the learning relationship as part of what characterises the independent learner. I also used the term when discussing the role of the teacher. Look back at Figure 2.11 that shows the ideal planned learning relationship. It is clear where the pupil independent learning aspects fit within the relationship as the pupil takes greater responsibility for the learning over time.

I want to emphasise how important it is that this relationship is a managed one between the teacher and learner if you are to create a supportive environment that will foster independent learners. I would recommend sharing the nature of this diagram with learners. Without seeing it in this form it is difficult to see the context in which teachers make decisions and take actions in supporting them. Learners need to understand how the relationship changes over time towards joint learning challenges.

Remember the diagram shows the ideal situation, a clear and well-managed process with each understanding their responsibilities and roles. This responsibility also implies the learner needs to be equipped to take on this role successfully. The learner should be aware of this transition and what it is they are working towards. This is more than just learning a subject; it is taking ownership of the learning. The characteristics of learners who have not understood or taken this path include having a limited set of skills on which to draw when faced with learning challenges and an overdependence on the teacher to direct the learning.

## Pedagogy and compliance

There are two issues related to the dependent learner I want to touch on here: changes in teaching pedagogy and the issue of compliance. The nature of teaching in schools is changing due in part to technology and to our growing understanding of how we learn and how the brain works. My view is the dependent learner is at a significant disadvantage if we use anything other than the didactic model that has characterised much of education in the past. In such a model the teacher is the authority and source of knowledge and organises all aspects of learning. The learner is a passenger, seen as a vessel to be filled. While there may be claims of efficiency and rigour for this model, I believe it promotes little more than compliance from the learner.

You may ask how being a compliant learner is anything other than a good thing. Surely we don't want non-compliant learners in our lessons? But that is only if we associate non-compliance with disruption or a challenge to authority. If you move away from this view, non-compliance can be seen as an attribute underpinned by questioning and challenging, not of authority but of knowledge and ideas. It is difficult to develop these if you have a curriculum purely focused on subjects and assessment of knowledge.

## The knowledge-based curriculum versus a learning-focused curriculum

Having a knowledge-based education system is like a man collecting bricks. There is a library to study the bricks and a museum to show the bricks but no one builds anything with the bricks.

In a learning-focused education system, bricks are explored for what they can create, new bricks are developed as new challenges are explored and there is a still a library of bricks to study and a museum to show the bricks.

It may be difficult to avoid the focus on knowledge in terms of the outcome of learning; indeed, knowing certain things is a distinct advantage, but that does not mean you cannot do something about the process. The key is to recognise what you are doing, why you are doing it and how you are going about it. With the right approach, a mindful approach, you can balance the two and develop independent learners at the same time

Table 7.1 shows the key characteristics of each type of curriculum under various headings. It is interesting to reflect on the four learning needs we have looked at and to see where they are promoted or subdued in each model.

It is clear that any developments in pedagogy will also require developments in the learner's efficacy and agency. Not to do so will make change very difficult if not impossible to sustain since teachers are only one half of the learning equation.

## Learning styles

Over the past decade we have seen the emergence of neuroscience and the implications for learning. One aspect has been the proposal of learning styles. Simple models consider visual, auditory and kinaesthetic (VAK) and others go further to consider a range of learning modalities There is a debate as to whether learning styles actually exist or not. To dismiss the concept that people learn differently, or more accurately have different learning preferences, would be wrong

Table 7.1 Knowledge-based and learning-focused curriculum comparison

| | KNOWLEDGE-BASED CURRICULUM | LEARNING-FOCUSED CURRICULUM |
|---|---|---|
| SUBJECTS | · SUBJECTS ARE BROKEN DOWN INTO FACTS AND THESE ARE TAUGHT OFTEN WITHOUT CONSIDERATION FOR THE APPLICATION OF SUCH. IT IS ENOUGH TO JUST KNOW, TO ACQUIRE KNOWLEDGE, AND NOT TO HAVE TO UNDERSTAND HOW TO USE THIS KNOWLEDGE.<br>· THERE IS A DEFINED SET OF BASICS THAT HAVE TO BE TAUGHT BEFORE STUDENTS CAN PROGRESS. | · SUBJECTS ARE TREATED IN A WAY THAT RECOGNISES THEIR VALUE IN LEARNING. APPLICATION IS IMPORTANT AND SUBJECT MATERIAL IS GIVEN A CONTEXT WITH A FOCUS ON HOW TO USE THE KNOWLEDGE.<br>· PBL (PROJECT-BASED LEARNING) IS AN EXAMPLE. |
| ASSESSMENT | · REQUIRES THE CONFIRMATION OF KNOWLEDGE BY TESTING AND THE GIVING OF ANSWERS WHICH MEET PRESCRIBED CRITERIA. THE TERMS *PROGRESS*, *BASELINE ASSESSMENTS* AND *TARGETS* CHARACTERISE THE LANGUAGE USED. | · IT IS EXPECTED THAT UNDERSTANDING WILL BE DEMONSTRATED, OFTEN BY THE APPLICATION OF KNOWLEDGE TO SOLVE PROBLEMS. THE DEMONSTRATION OF AN ABILITY TO TRANSFER KNOWLEDGE (FROM ONE SUBJECT TO ANOTHER) IS EXPECTED. THE TERMS *UNDERSTANDING*, *SYNTHESIS*, *EVALUATION* AND *APPLICATION* CHARACTERISE THE LANGUAGE USED IN ASSESSMENT.<br>· OPEN BOOK TECHNIQUES. MINDFUL LEARNING TECHNIQUES USED TO ASSESS. |
| DELIVERY | · THE CURRICULUM IS DIVIDED UP INTO INDIVIDUAL SUBJECTS TAUGHT IN ISOLATION FROM EACH OTHER AND OFTEN WITHOUT REGARD FOR CONTENT OR OVERLAP. THERE IS A HIERARCHY OF SUBJECTS BASED ON ACADEMIC HISTORICAL VALUES. BOOK-BASED DELIVERY. | · PROJECT-BASED, STRUCTURED TO DRAW ON KNOWLEDGE. COACHING MODEL. COLLABORATIVE LEARNING. LEARNING TEAMS (WILLIAM GLASSER). FLIPPED CLASSROOM. |

IF YOU CAN'T REACH THEM YOU CAN'T TEACH THEM

| | KNOWLEDGE-BASED CURRICULUM | LEARNING-FOCUSED CURRICULUM |
|---|---|---|
| TIMING AND ORDER | · A CHRONOLOGICAL ORDER IS ESTABLISHED AND SUBJECT KNOWLEDGE DELIVERED ACCORDING TO THIS PLAN. WHAT IS TAUGHT IN ONE YEAR IS DISTINGUISHED FROM THAT TAUGHT IN ANOTHER YEAR. INDIVIDUAL AGES ARE NOT ACCOMMODATED, ALLOWING FOR ALMOST A WHOLE YEAR IN AGE DIFFERENCE BETWEEN THE YOUNGEST AND OLDEST IN A SCHOOL YEAR. CHRONOLOGICAL AGE AND PROGRESS. DISPLAYED AS A PRODUCT (GRADE). | · FOUNDATION AND CHALLENGE. INDIVIDUALISED LEARNING. PROGRESSION BASED ON INDIVIDUAL LEVEL OF UNDERSTANDING. <br> · COMPETENCY-BASED. <br> · DISPLAYED AS A PROCESS. |
| LEARNING | · DEFINED AS KNOWING RATHER THAN UNDERSTANDING. LEARNING IS SEEN AS DEMONSTRATING KNOWING. <br> · COMPETITIVE LEARNING. EXTERNAL MOTIVATION. <br> · MEMORISATION OF FACTS. | · DEFINED AS A PROCESS THAT INVOLVES APPLICATION AND UNDERSTANDING NOT JUST KNOWING. LEARNING IS SEEN AS THE PATH THAT LEADS TO UNDERSTANDING (WISDOM). <br> · CO-OPERATIVE LEARNING. <br> · INTERNALISED MOTIVATION. |
| TEACHING | · THE TEACHER IS THE HOLDER OF KNOWLEDGE AND IS SOLELY RESPONSIBLE (HELD ACCOUNTABLE) FOR DELIVERY AND THE PROGRESS MADE BY STUDENTS. <br> · EXCLUDES OR SUBDUES EMOTIONS. TRANSMITTING KNOWLEDGE UNCHANGED. 'SAGE ON THE STAGE' STYLE OF TEACHING. | · SHARES AND EXPLAINS EMOTIONS LINKED TO LEARNING. <br> · FACILITATING LEARNING, SUPPORTING INDIVIDUALS. <br> · 'GUIDE AT YOUR SIDE' STYLE OF TEACHING. |
| STUDENT ATTITUDE | · FEAR OF FAILURE. <br> · LUCK IS SEEN AS PART OF SUCCESS. <br> · LEARNS TO FOLLOW. <br> · FIXED MINDSET. | · FAILURE IS SEEN AS PART OF THE LEARNING PROCESS. <br> · EFFORT AND HARD WORK ARE RECOGNISED FOR UNDERPINNING SUCCESS. <br> · LEARNS TO MAKE CHOICES. <br> · GROWTH MINDSET. |

→

| | KNOWLEDGE-BASED CURRICULUM | LEARNING-FOCUSED CURRICULUM |
|---|---|---|
| REPORTING/ FEEDBACK | · FORMAL AND KNOWLEDGE FOCUSED BASED ON WHAT HAS BEEN LEARNT. FOCUS ON FEEDBACK. | · FEEDFORWARD RATHER THAN FEEDBACK AND AN EMPHASIS ON DEMONSTRATING UNDERSTANDING. |
| STUDENT VOICE | · SUBDUED | · ENCOURAGED |

for it is part of the observed catalogue of teaching and learning. Some learners find diagrams more accessible than words or enjoy discussion more than reading. These I would describe as learning preferences; learners feel most confident and comfortable learning in the way that they prefer.

To dismiss exploring learning styles and not even try to establish an understanding of learning preferences would be to ignore one of the greatest benefits: having a dialogue about learning with the learner. It is also a fundamental step in the teacher letting go within the learning responsibility partnership.

However, I do not think it necessary, or possible, for you to plan for and adopt several ways of teaching at once or over the period of a lesson in order to satisfy the notion of learning styles. If you consider a teacher trying to satisfy three different learning styles in one lesson then there is three times the planning, possibly three times the resources and three times the number of explanations. What is more, a school-wide approach would require each teacher to do the same and deliver in the same way with the possibility of limiting their own unique way of teaching, almost tying their professional hands behind their backs. I have seen the impact this has on teachers and the outcome is twofold. First it creates a great deal of stress for the teacher and second it disturbs the pupils.

I am not ignoring individual learning preferences and I am not suggesting you ignore differentiation but I think it far better to equip the learner with the knowledge and understanding to deal with whatever learning environment they are in. My own experience is that learning about learning, not just the process but the emotions, is as important as any other aspect of our development as learners.

## DO LEARNING STYLES HAVE A VALUE?

Learning brings with it a host of emotions varying between embarrassment to elation. Left to our own devices we will adopt a way to learn that best suits us, in harmony with our feelings and past experiences. Environmentally some may prefer a quiet place, a formal desk and good light and others may prefer music, an informal position and somewhere cool to learn. Watching a video or listening to a recording may be preferred to reading or discussion when developing an understanding of a concept.

No teacher or classroom could be asked to provide such a variety of environments or learning strategies in a single lesson yet there may be 30 individual learners, all with their own preferences. Lesson planning, differentiated resources, seating arrangements and limited environmental changes can help but once again that is the responsibility of the teacher and not the learner.

## ❖ Reflective task

Consider for a moment what it is like to learn in an environment that is not your preferred one. You may find this difficult because you have probably learnt to adapt. Focus on any emotions you may have. Remember the pennies task and think again about your feelings before, during and after the task. Record your environmental reaction feelings below.

How I feel learning outside of my preferred environment:

## ❖ Reflective task review

If you mentioned feelings such an anxiety, discomfort or difficulty concentrating then you are experiencing what many pupils may feel in a lesson where they are unable to satisfy their learning preferences.

The value of learning styles or any other teaching and learning strategy is in understanding how you feel when learning and linking these emotions to learning preferences and the four learning needs, PBCF. A discussion can help re-map the associations you have made during earlier learning experiences. A successful re-map can change your emotional state when faced with certain subject material or challenges.

There are therapies that help us deal with anxiety and stress in the same way as re-mapping our learning experiences and emotions does. In such approaches you learn to acknowledge how you feel and to separate it from your behaviour or response to a situation. You begin to take control of your emotions in a managed way. An example that comes to mind is an irrational fear of spiders. Often the approach taken in overcoming such fears is to be exposed to the stimulus but in a controlled way and in a supportive environment. As you become more confident, your proximity to the stimulus may be changed so that eventually you experience that which earlier had caused you to feel fearful. In understanding your emotions you can behave in a measured way, maintaining control.

Knowing and learning about the way you feel when you are in an environment that does not meet your learning preferences or that triggers anxiety is immensely powerful in overcoming learning limitations. It also reinforces that fact that how you feel when learning has nothing to do with how clever you are, only how well your environment does or does not match your learning preferences. It also reinforces the idea of resilience, of persisting until challenges are overcome, of seeing learning as a problem-solving activity. It also acknowledges and legitimises as part of the learning process the feelings of embarrassment, of being unsure and the fear of being wrong or failing.

## Pupils adapting to their learning environment

Being able to adapt to the learning environment to meet learning needs is a mark of the independent learner. I can best describe this through the following contrasting scenarios.

### Case Study

#### THE DEPENDENT LEARNER

John finds it difficult to stay focused in the lesson; his thoughts wander to other alternative pathways, he wonders *'what if?'* and imagines other possibilities. When he tunes back into the lesson, two or three minutes has passed and he is now no longer at the same stage as the teacher or the rest of the group. He faces two options: own up to mentally wandering or disguise his current position. How he responds will depend on his emotional map of both the teacher and the subject as well as how his learning needs (PBCF) are fulfilled. He may hold a degree of anxiety about owning up if he has been openly admonished in the past and so a part of the lesson goes unlearnt. At a later date, when that understanding is called on to make further progress, he will find he is struggling. The mental emotional map will be added to, this time a feeling of worthlessness or stupidity may be added and associated with the subject. It is not unrealistic to see a pattern develop that leads to a dislike of the subject and a decline in achievement.

IF YOU CAN'T REACH THEM YOU CAN'T TEACH THEM

## THE INDEPENDENT LEARNER

John knows that he can zone out when he goes exploring a train of thought and so does the teacher. He is encouraged to mind map his thoughts as a way of recording them for thinking about later; this reduces the time missed. When John asks what he missed it is not treated as a misdemeanour and he is encouraged back into the lesson flow. John is aware of how he can research and explore information himself and so can find videos posted by the school on YouTube or an intranet or read lesson notes posted in a similar way. Knowing John likes to explore, the teacher can use John's ideas to review the topic in a mindful way with the class later. Acknowledging John's preferences for the way of learning provides positive feedback, helping him build a mental emotional map which favours the subject and his ability to learn.

I have only considered one aspect of learning needs but I hope I have shown how the scenario can change dramatically for the learner and teacher by adopting an approach that considers supporting the independent learner and is mindful. The challenge you face is dealing with more than one John and you may find yourself overwhelmed. If this is the case, you are not thinking mindfully! Co-operative (not the same as compliant) learners make mindful teaching much easier. If you have uncooperative learners it is more often than not a case of you not meeting their learning needs.

# Develop independent learners

When you introduce something different, it is useful to find a way of signalling this to your pupils. As with any situation where you are considering change, you need to consider your learning relationship first and decide if it is a) an appropriate time for the change to be introduced and b) if your pupils are in a position to accept a challenge. Finding an introductory approach is the best way to do this; it gives you an opportunity to assess before committing time and resources. It also means you can easily return to your current approach without risking progress.

## PHILOSOPHY FOR CHILDREN

One approach is the Philosophy for Children programme, P4C. I have found this a great tool for introducing pupils to the idea of independent thought and action and in assessing their readiness to take on a learning challenge. A fundamental aspect of P4C is the idea that the teacher is a guide and not a sage.

The idea that a teacher can know everything and is up to date with every aspect of their subject and pedagogy, that they are never wrong or make a mistake, is a hard one to implement these days. The true role of a teacher has always been somebody who is always willing to learn and to explore. It is a far harder path or approach to take than many realise.

## THE TEACHER AS A GUIDE

Being a guide does not mean absolving yourself of responsibility for pupil learning. There is a different set of responsibilities and a different learning relationship when becoming a guide. The teacher guide must take their charges from point A to point B on the learning pathway but in a way that allows the learner to experience things for themselves, to explore within boundaries and to experience risk and failure in a managed way.

It is clear to many that we need to make it a priority to develop independent learners, those who can make sense of the ever-expanding knowledge base for themselves. They must be shown how to access, interpret, determine value, record and apply knowledge and understanding to more than a limited set of situations. It is this emerging, more important role the teacher needs to adopt in preparing students for entering the world. A secondary issue is the world no longer waits outside of the school gates; it has breached that barrier and presents itself in vivid form to the youngest of learners. Technology is a bridge to a world that education has no control of. You must therefore adopt this new role as soon as possible if you are to avoid conflict and challenge the more traditional teacher role within your classroom.

## References and further reading

Bandura, A (1989) *Human Agency in Social Cognitive Theory.* [online] Available at: www.uky.edu/~eushe2/Bandura/Bandura1989AP.pdf (accessed 1 November 2020).

Lonsdale, M (2020) *What is Self-Directed Learning - and Is It Important?* [online] Available at: https://mentoreducation.co.uk/learning-tips/what-is-self-directed-learning-and-is-it-important/ (accessed 1 November 2020).

O'Doherty, M (2006) *Definitions of Independent Learning: Initial Overview.* [online] Available at: http://archive.learnhigher.ac.uk/resources/files/Independant%20Learning/Independent_Learning%5b1%5d.pdf (accessed 1 November 2020).

### LEARNING STYLES

Dexter, P (2018) *One Response to the 'Learning Styles' Debate.* [online] Available at: www.britishcouncil.org/voices-magazine/response-learning-styles-debate (accessed 1 November 2020).

Prashnig Style Solutions (nd) [online] Available at: www.creativelearningcentre.com/ (accessed 1 November 2020).

Topp, G (2019) *'Neuromyth' or Helpful Model?* [online] Available at: www.insidehighered.com/news/2019/01/09/learning-styles-debate-its-instructors-vs-psychologists (accessed 1 November 2020).

IF YOU CAN'T REACH THEM YOU CAN'T TEACH THEM

## NEUROSCIENCE

Royal Society (2011) *Brain Waves 2: Neuroscience: Implications for Education and Lifelong Learning*. [online] Available at: https://royalsociety.org/topics-policy/projects/brain-waves/education-lifelong-learning/ (accessed 1 November 2020). The full report is available for download from this link.

## FLIPPED LEARNING AND FLIPPED CLASSROOMS

Bergmann J (nd) *Flipped Learning Simplified*. [online] Available at: www.jonbergmann.com/ (accessed 1 November 2020).

The two people credited with being pioneers in this concept of turning learning on its head are Jon Bergmann and Aaron Sams. Jon Bergmann has a website that helps define what flipped learning is and is not.

## GAMIFICATION

Learning Theories (nd) *Gamification in Education*. [online] Available at: www.learning-theories.com/gamification-in-education.html (accessed 1 November 2020).

Your notes

IF YOU CAN'T REACH THEM YOU CAN'T TEACH THEM

# 8. THE DANGERS OF LABELLING LEARNERS

## Why label?

In education labels are everywhere and they are seductive. Whereas we know people change, they mature, they learn from experience and develop new skills and abilities, the labels that get applied have a tendency to stick and are very difficult to remove once applied.

Labelling makes the world of learning and teaching much easier to manage and in some cases safer. Labels appear in all aspects of life and education. Among the many labels you may use in teaching are labels for rooms, subjects, books, storage, along with pupils' needs, achievements, efforts and behaviours. You can get carried away labelling; there are benefits to being organised that encourage you to do so. When working with pupils, labels can be useful. For example, being identified as belonging to a house system or tutor group will help create a sense of belonging or knowing a pupil is dyslexic can help in securing additional time when sitting examinations. But without being mindful they can become an end in themselves rather than an aid in the process of improving learning and teaching. In this chapter I want to make the practical association between labelling and PBCF (building effective learning relationships) rather than discuss the many labels and their use in education. In the *Further reading* section there are links to Howard Becker's labelling theory as well as specific education-related articles on labelling. These will enable you to achieve an overview of the wider impact, concerns and issues related to labelling in education.

## learning labels

As professionals, teachers want to know how and why pupils learn best. Being a teacher means you want to know the best way you can help your pupils to learn. You want to identify and discuss ways to improve learning, so it is natural you should look for ways of discussing your observations and ideas. Labels provide a shorthand description but often lack the detail necessary to understand the individual. The concept of general intelligence or IQ is one such example. In Chapter 12 I discuss a range of learning labels associated with ability including IQ and Howard Gardner's multiple intelligences.

You will use learning labels in your reporting. Some will be positive labels and others more cautionary as you try to convey your praise or concern in an abbreviated form. Adjectives such as *independent, eager, motivated, hardworking, easily distracted, disruptive*, etc might be used.

## Personal reflection

Around 1982 I moved school and took over a classroom from a retiring teacher. Looking through the desk drawers I found copies of reports he had written going back many years. The standard comments did not deviate a great deal: '*Good lad*', '*Satisfactory progress*' or '*Works well*'. As I looked through the years there was no noticeable change, one report looked very much like another, until suddenly '*Good lass*' appeared. This change must have been when girls started doing metalwork! I wonder at the value of these reports and the interpretations of the labels used, for they are very personal to the teacher who used them.

## ❖ Reflective task

What reporting label-forming adjectives have you used or come across and were they appropriate or fair?

IF YOU CAN'T REACH THEM YOU CAN'T TEACH THEM

# Consequences of labelling

When considering applying a label you should think about accountability and morality. Labels set expectations on the part of those who apply them, encounter them and receive them. When involved in any form of assessment you have to ensure the accuracy and validity of that assessment and the appropriateness of the label. If you do not fully understand the criteria or mismanage the assessment, pupils may become falsely labelled. The application, meaning and the interpretation of a label needs to be consistent; where they are not confusion and damage to the learning relationship can be done. The hasty determination of a label applied to a pupil might appear to solve an immediate or pressing problem for the school but can have much longer-term implications for the pupil.

Adding or removing a label can have consequences for a pupil in terms of their self-image and their sense of belonging. For example, a pupil recognised as gifted by one school could raise their self-image. Should the pupil join another school where they are no longer recognised as gifted they are likely to face a degree of uncertainty and self-doubt. A pupil who early on in their school career gets labelled as having behaviour problems can find it difficult to shed this label as they mature. They may even give up trying to show they have changed and live up to the behaviour expected of them.

Labels can have the effect of raising or lowering expectations, of pupils living up to – or down to – the label they have received. A certain status can result from having a label applied to you. For example, being labelled as talented at sport could give a pupil certain privileges or status. The form of status or privilege is group dependent; being labelled clever may give benefits in one group and disadvantages in another.

At the start of my teaching career I was told of the 'D stream complex', an example of a self-fulfilling label. The term set a ceiling on expectations and this was evident in the negative behaviour and limited aspirations of some pupils. This is something that can stay with people for life. On giving feedback, a university tutor said this of her mature student's response:

---

*Her words to me at the time were: 'I've always been a C person.' My overwhelming reaction was one of shock and surprise, because Sam seemed content, happy even. Sam thought she had achieved as she was expected to achieve, while I knew that she could do so much more. I sensed from Sam evidence of an impoverished attitude to learning, a lack of resilience and resourcefulness in terms of independent learning, and the barriers of self-limiting learning capacity – all because she was labelled early in her school career.*

---

(Taylor, 2015, np)

Allowing pupils to self-label has its consequences. A pupil facing a learning challenge and failing may tell themselves that they are stupid. Unless you intervene quickly this can be a lifelong belief, a disadvantaging label. A pupil who has not been challenged may think they are more able to take on a learning challenge than they are and, should they fail, be emotionally ill-prepared to deal with it.

Without appropriate support, lifelong self-beliefs can be established that hinder future learning. Using labels to make comparisons risks losing sight of the details involved in determining a label in the first place. Any definition can be open to interpretation and not all definitions fit 100 per cent of the criteria; it is more a general fit in many cases. Sub-labels can be grouped together to form an overarching or composite label, which has the effect of further diluting contact with the original behaviours and allows for an element of corruption in the application.

## The learner perspective

Labels are especially important to individuals for they can provide reassurance, even safety. Labels become part of a view of self, how you identify to others. Labels can offer pupils a sense of belonging but if they are unfairly applied, they can result in harm. Labels can also impose on the pupil a set of responsibilities or expected behaviours that, unless they are prepared for, can also cause harm

### ❖ Reflective task

What labels were applied to you during your school career and what effect did they have on you?

## Permanent and temporary labels

The labels of family and friend are two very important labels. They are helpful, they meet your needs and give you a sense of identity but they differ in one important respect and that is permanency. The family label is something that is permanent; whatever happens to our relationship with those in our family circle, family will always be family. In schools it is not unusual for a family name to become synonymous with a set of behaviours and you need to be mindful of any preconceptions you may hold when you encounter a pupil with the same family name. You also need to be mindful of the pressures that a family name may apply to a pupil. This is particularly important where there are siblings or relatives in the same school.

Friend, on the other hand, is a non-permanent or temporary label. Friends can become ex-friends. Friend is an example of a label that could stay with you after it is no longer relevant or possibly appropriate. The label of friend can demand allegiances and behaviours that identify you as being part of a group or as holding a role within a group and can either challenge or support behaviour in line with social and moral norms.

# Challenging labels

You may be familiar with the phrase 'The exception proves the rule.' But is this true in learning and teaching? Learning is about making mistakes and so if you mislabel then you must work at correcting the situation and this involves challenging the rule. Have you heard teachers, or indeed parents, say something like '*He's a boy, what do you expect?*' or '*Girls are always much neater and tidier than boys.*' If you have then you should recognise the use of labels to perpetuate myths. Myths need to be challenged.

## LABELS AND PBCF

As a teacher you will use labels in your relationship with pupils. How labels impact that relationship can be seen through the four learning needs. Table 8.1 shows examples of both the positive and negative impact of labels on relationships through each learning need.

**Table 8.1 Labels and PBCF**

| LEARNING NEED AND LABEL TYPE | POSITIVE ATTRIBUTE OF LABELLING | NEGATIVE ATTRIBUTE OF LABELLING |
|---|---|---|
| POWER RESPONSIBILITY LABEL | OFFERS A PLATFORM FOR EXPRESSION AND PUPIL VOICE. | CAN LIMIT PUPIL VOICE. A RESPONSIBILITY LABEL MAY INFER POWER OVER OTHERS. |
| BELONGING IDENTITY LABEL | STRENGTHENS SENSE OF BELONGING, PROVIDES SECURITY AND IDENTITY. | CAN SET EXPECTATIONS OF BEHAVIOUR AND ATTITUDES AT ODDS WITH THE INDIVIDUAL'S NATURE OR ABILITIES. |
| CHOICE ACHIEVEMENT LABEL MEMBERSHIP LABEL | ACCESS TO FURTHER LEARNING OPPORTUNITY. SENSE OF BELONGING. | CAN LIMIT ACCESS TO LEARNING OPPORTUNITIES. OSTRACISED IF ASSOCIATION IS NOT HELD IN REGARD BY MAJORITY OF PUPILS. |
| FUN PERSONALITY LABEL | CAN SUGGEST A BALANCED APPROACH TO LEARNING; BEING ABLE TO CELEBRATE AS WELL AS REACT POSITIVELY TO CHALLENGES. | CAN SET LIMITING EXPECTATIONS IF ACCEPTED BEFORE MEETING PUPIL. |

This is a limited number of example of labels and their impact on pupils and the learning relationship. Some labels, such as achievement, could sit within more than one element of PBCF; choice and fun both involve achievement labels. The need under which each label appears can determine different positive and negative label attributes. When considering labels I would encourage you to use Table 8.1 to assess the value of the label and what aspect of the learning relationship it impacts.

## Can you avoid labels?

Resisting labelling learners is much harder than you think. It is also difficult not to fall into the trap of accepting them at face value. When you have a good learning relationship with your pupils you will find it easier to describe them without using labels and instead by describing their character, their learning needs, their successes and on occasion their failures. When reporting on pupils is required, try to talk of individual pupil learning behaviours. If you can achieve this your pupils will be appreciative, and the learning relationships will benefit.

### ❖ Reflective task

Make a list of labels you find useful and those that are unhelpful in learning and teaching

· Useful labels

· Unhelpful labels

Alternatively using Table 8.1, identify a number of labels associated with each element of PBCF and give a positive and negative attribute of each.

IF YOU CAN'T REACH THEM YOU CAN'T TEACH THEM

# References and further reading

Advocating Creativity (2012) *Why Must Little Boys Be Like Little Girls?* [online] Available at: https://4c3d.wordpress.com/2012/10/21/why-must-little-boys-be-like-little-girls/ (accessed 1 November 2020).

This blog article asks is it of any use to compare boys with girls and points to the issue of labels setting gender expectations.

Markman, A (2014) *The Danger of Labelling Others (or Yourself).* [online] Available at: www.psychologytoday.com/us/blog/ulterior-motives/201406/the-danger-labeling-others-or-yourself (accessed 1 November 2020).

A report on a study about personalities and success at school explored in the June issue of the *Journal of Personality and Social Psychology*. Notably this study involved Carol Dweck. '*This result raises the possibility that if people were trained to think that personality characteristics can change, then they might do better in school*' (Markman, 2014).

Owen, C (2018) *Labelling In Education: Supportive or Stigmatising?* [online] Available at: www.huffingtonpost.co.uk/entry/labelling-in-education-supportive-or-stigmatising_uk_5a6ca38fe4b006be66080f17?guccounter=1&guce_referrer=aHR0cHM6Ly9kdWNkZHVja2dvLmNvbVS8&guce_referrer_sig=AQAAAHE2eoj4WwYdHPPmiW7YNXzVB6nuRRN2La5Ix5FcInZZDm75Zla7VzoB9wfrHhIRs4LbkElkrtuLMjTAXgu9XLThMjy16qp--YmZLgoKcipcAIOmeCAyYsUrUeHK5GDtxtAKvquAjpiRbDh0Xag2Bylvw3Jk7_0n3WGIfqTPsK8P (accessed 1 November 2020).

This short blog article lists the many labels we use with the pupils we teach and reminds you that adolescent brains are work in progress.

jezselle.weebly.com (nd) *How Labelling Theory Affects Attainment.* [online] https://jezselle.weebly.com/ (accessed 12 September 2020).

A UK-focused website that discusses '*how labels can effect a child's learning, development and behaviour during school and the attainment gap*' and looks at the correlation between working class families and academic achievement. The site also describes Howard Becker's labelling theory.

Taylor, C (2015) *When We Label Students by Ability, We Limit their Potential to Learn.* [online] Available at: www.timeshighereducation.com/blog/when-we-label-students-ability-we-limit-their-potential-learn (accessed 1 November 2020).

QR link

Your notes

IF YOU CAN'T REACH THEM YOU CAN'T TEACH THEM

# 9. THE LEARNING MAP

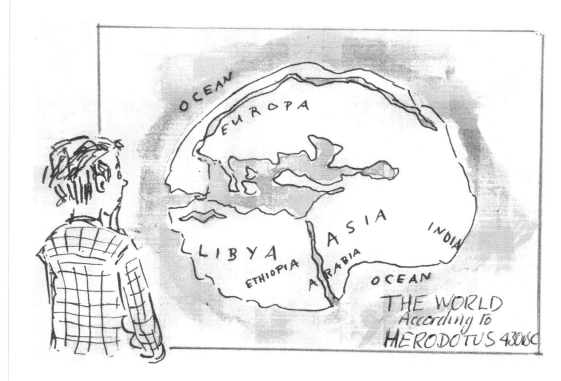

## Introduction

When working with learners I am aware of their self-belief about what they can and cannot learn. This is more than the ideas of a growth or limiting mindset from Carol Dweck; at times it is almost a physical manifestation.

## Personal reflection

In conversation pupils will point to examples from their past experiences of learning and what they were and were not able to achieve. I began to think of these as road blocks to learning and the analogy with a learning map became my way of discussing learning challenges and beliefs with pupils. I discovered that lots of features you will find on a map are analogous to learning. These provided a narrative for talking about learning in a practical and almost physical way. Together the pupils and I were able to discuss learning barriers and opportunities in the same way as you would the physical topography of a map. The concept of the learning map had developed.

## The map analogy explored

The idea of a learning map is a very useful tool when talking to pupils about learning for it gives you a language that is non-limiting and non-threatening. The language you can use supports seeing learning as a problem-solving activity. You can ask '*How do you get from point A to point B?*' or '*How do you get around an obstacle?*'

The learning map is best defined as what we believe we are good at and not good at, what we can learn, and what we cannot learn. I like the symbolic nature of a map because it is something that can be drawn and redrawn, extended and refined. Talking to pupils I was able to point out that at times people believed the world was flat or that there was nothing at either pole. Being able to refine and redefine your view of what you are capable of is how learning should be. Unfortunately some pupils have a map that consists mainly of barriers or have large areas marked 'Do Not Enter' and in their view the map cannot be redrawn. Understanding a pupil's learning map is essential if you are to help them develop as learners. Building effective learning relationships helps you to see the learning landscape as your pupils do.

## Born to learn

*Seeing comes before words. The child looks and recognises before it can speak.*

**(Berger, 1972, p 7)**

Before developing a spoken language and attending school we are not aware of what we can or cannot learn; we only experience learning. There is a lot we learn in the first 12 months before we develop our language skills and have an understanding of vocabulary. By the time we learn to talk and understand what is said to us we have achieved a great deal. It is unlikely we have ever thought any of these things are beyond us. It is not until later that children begin to develop a view of themselves as learners; a view that is influenced by what is said to them at home and at school.

We do not have learning experiences in isolation. It is impossible that your learning experiences are not influenced by your environment and those within it. Your behaviours are moderated by the social norms you live in. Your attitudes are influenced by how those around you approach their challenges. You develop skills, attributes and attitudes that are encouraged by your peers and mentors. The skills you acquire help you to navigate this environment and in part adopt a role within it. You become socialised and in doing so begin to draw your learning map.

# Drawing the learning map

You may be blind to the influences I have mentioned. You could accept your 'ability' as a simple truth because it easier than challenging that notion. As a teacher you may also be unaware of previous influences on prior performance of your pupils and this could result in a prediction of future progress in a way that limits rather than promotes it. Just something to be mindful of!

Our learning map is closely linked to what Carol Dweck refers to a '*growth mindset*' (Dweck, 2014), that as a result of a challenge, of working hard, our abilities can grow. You form an opinion about how good a learner you are, or how intelligent you are, and the things you can achieve. Your beliefs in this regard can be glimpsed by what Dweck refers to as '*fixed-mindset triggers*'. Table 9.1 lists the triggers and responses Dweck gave in her 2015 talk at the Festival of Education.

**Table 9.1 Fixed-mindset triggers**

| TRIGGERS | RESPONSES |
|---|---|
| FACING CHALLENGE | ANXIOUS |
| STRUGGLING | FRUSTRATED AND WORRIED |
| HAVING SETBACKS | DISCOURAGED, DEFENSIVE |
| BEING CRITICISED | ANGRY, DEFENSIVE, ASHAMED |

If you reflect on how your pupils respond to these triggers it will give you an insight into the topography of their learning maps.

# The school environment

The school is just one environment that impacts the learning map but it is a significant one. School is advertised as a learning environment; it is where we go to learn and to study. Since it is so significant you need to be aware of the impact it has on learning and the formation of the learning map.

Those learners that are successful in schools have often developed a detailed learning map and have learning preferences that match the school environment. They have the skills, attributes, attitudes and behaviours that allow them to access the learning and they feel comfortable in navigating within the school environment. While many go on to achieve within life, there are some who find learning outside of the school environment difficult. Perhaps this is because they have failed to develop broader learning strategies through a lack of challenge at school. In terms of the learning map, they have stayed within the paths and not gone exploring on their own or got lost.

There are pupils who don't do well at learning in school. These pupils are either seen as being unable to learn, perhaps labelled 'less able', or who have emotional or other behavioural challenges that cause them to respond poorly to the school environment. This can be dealt with successfully if you look at the symptoms rather than the outcome (often the behaviour) and develop the pupil's learning strategies as well as meeting their four learning needs. I find using educational vocabulary in my dealings with pupils who struggle at school puts me at a disadvantage; they do not listen. Changing to terms and analogies in using a map improves their engagement, breaking earlier developed attitudes to learning.

# Linking topology to learning

Pupils may find themselves in a learning landscape that is mountainous. Mountains can be seen by some pupils as barriers to learning. You can encourage pupils to conquer them and then to see them as vantage points from which to see other learning opportunities. A subject may be represented by a mountain (I have found this is often maths!). By talking about how mountains are conquered through working in teams, by accepting help and having staging posts you can show how a subject can be conquered too. A rolling landscape may represent minor challenges that are easily overcome or an opportunity to celebrate achievement. Bridges and tunnels can be symbols of improving a learning journey and of overcoming learning challenges. A stream that needs to be crossed can represent pupils building a bridge between what they know and what they need to understand. Roads become learning routes; you find your way along and see landmarks you recognise.

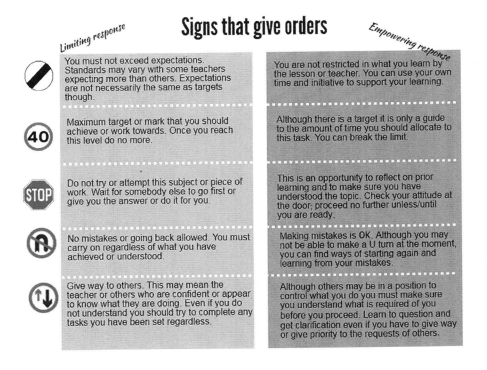

**Figure 9.1 Learning responses to road signs**

IF YOU CAN'T REACH THEM YOU CAN'T TEACH THEM

Visualising the learning map and finding analogies in our everyday lives can help in managing learning needs too. Motorways could get you there quicker, but minor roads may be more interesting or offer greater challenges. There can be favourite places to visit. No-go areas can represent past learning experiences and forks in the road can represent opportunities and choices.

In terms of roads, I have worked on using the Highway Code as a metaphor for learning. The signs and symbols are most appropriate and can form learning symbols for use in the classroom. This is a great way to change mindsets too. Figure 9.1 provides examples of limiting responses or empowering responses to a situation as represented by the signs. This approach also helps separate the subject content from the learning strategies or experience through visualisation and promoting the idea of strategies to overcome barriers.

## Summary

My aim in writing this chapter was to introduce a creative element into the way we can approach meeting learning needs and help pupils see the challenges of learning objectively. Each time I visit the learning map analogy I find new opportunities to express learning and teaching situations.

## Personal reflection

In discussing the impact of target grades on learning with a colleague I was reminded of the learning map and a recent driving experience. On my way to a meeting I had been held up and decided to save a little time by taking the motorway and not stopping for petrol. I had estimated I had enough fuel to get me there. The journey up the motorway was stressful, not because of traffic but because I became less sure of having enough petrol. All through the journey I kept looking at the gauge, the motorway signs that told me how far to go and back at the fuel gauge. I remembered little of the journey and would have struggled to describe any of it to anyone who asked, and I certainly did not enjoy it. I got to my meeting on time but mentally stressed and not really ready for the meeting. Does aiming for a target grade have the same effect on our learning journey? Do we seek shortcuts, and do we actually take the opportunity to enjoy the learning experience?

Taking time to explore your own learning map is a worthwhile exercise. It will help you recognise those things you share with your pupils and give you an opportunity to be creative in the way you see learning and the challenges your pupils face. All of this helps build learning relationships and supports PBCF.

## ❖ Reflective task

Draw your own learning map in the space below. What learning challenges have you visited, how did you get there, what was the journey like, what were any barriers or obstacles, what did you find on the way?

---

## References and further reading

Berger, J (1972) *Ways of Seeing*. London: Penguin Books Ltd.

Dweck, C (2014) *Developing a Growth Mindset with Carol Dweck*. [online] Available at: www.youtube.com/watch?v=hiiEeMN7vbQ&ab_channel=StanfordAlumni (accessed 1 November 2020).

If you are looking for inspiration regarding maps and road signs, *The Official Highway Code* is full of useful learning tips if read with a creative mindset! Also, Ordnance Survey map symbols are something pupils will be familiar with as part of their geography studies:

IF YOU CAN'T REACH THEM YOU CAN'T TEACH THEM

BBC Bitesize (nd) *OS Map Skills.* [online] Available at: www.bbc.co.uk/bitesize/guides/z6j6fg8/revision/2 (accessed 1 November 2020).

Hawgood, D (2010) *OS 25k Map Symbols.* [online] Available at: www.geograph.org.uk/article/OS-25K-map-symbols (accessed 1 November 2020).

QR link

Your notes

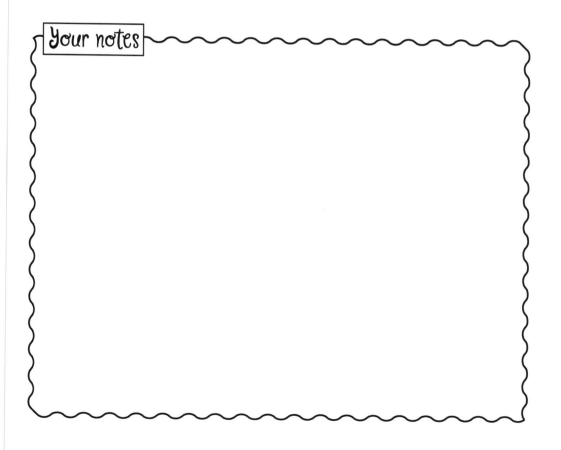

# 10. TIME MANAGEMENT

## Time management and the NET equation

### Introduction

Teaching is a full-on job; there is no doubt that it is demanding both physically and mentally. Teaching can be draining and leave us without the energy or motivation never mind the capacity to change our approach. It is only fair then if I am suggesting change – although much of building learning relationships and PBCF is about approach and attitude – that I consider how you can best manage this often scarce resource: time.

# Urgent/important matrix

You may be familiar with the urgent/important matrix in Figure 10.1. It is also referred to as Eisenhower's principle.

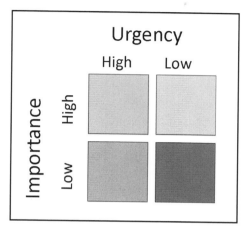

**Figure 10.1 Urgent/important matrix**

For a three-minute explanation you can access a short video *Introducing the Eisenhower Matrix* (Eisenhower.me, nd). You can also find more detail in *The 7 Habits of Highly Effective People* by Stephen Covey (2004).

The urgent/important matrix is one of the tools for managing time and although useful it suggests an acceptance of the tasks, a compliant attitude on the part of the individual. Sometimes in teaching it can be better not to do something, not to make time for it, than to try to do it or fit it in somehow. Often the high-urgency and high-importance tasks are the most demanding and involved and can get left to last. I have noted on several occasions that people are apt to favour the low-urgency and low-importance tasks over them. The result is we are busy, but on the wrong things. This is where the 'not enough time' (NET) equation comes in; it makes us look carefully at the things we do and why we do them. It ensures you make best use of the time you allocate to teaching and checks if you are doing too much.

I want to reassure you that everything in this book requires no more time to implement than what you are doing now. What is required is a change in the way you think about teaching and learning, what you see as priorities and where you put your effort in making the changes that are needed.

I am not ignoring the fact that any change initially needs a little more time and that capacity is key to adopting any change. I have known teachers who have no more capacity for change but have been pushed into change – and the stress and pain that this causes. Rarely does it result in the change adopted becoming effective nor does it become embedded in the habits of the individual or the culture of the school. When it fails, as it does more often than not, a new change or initiative is proposed in an effort to get the desired outcomes. The result is more change and even less capacity for change. Doing more of what does not work, for whatever reason, is not going to move you forward. You need to think and do something differently. Taking an approach that seeks to understand and manage learning needs I believe is that 'something'.

While there has been a great deal of study regarding time management, teaching is different. In teaching, time management is more than just dates, times, meetings or tasks and many of the things that take up your time often feel beyond your control. As you have seen in the early part of this book, teaching requires the building of effective learning relationships and getting to know your pupils; this all takes time. In teaching you need the flexibility to use time where it is most needed and to do this you must have reserve capacity. Working flat out, responding to every need, taking on additional tasks, all deplete your reserves and give you little flexibility. My response to managing time more effectively in teaching is the 'not enough time' (NET) equation. Balancing the equation is what it is all about if you want to build your reserves and be more flexible in your teaching.

# The problem of not having enough time

Not having enough time leads to a whole host of problems for teachers both at school and at home. Manifestations of not enough time include:

- being late;
- not finishing tasks;
- missing out on social or family occasions;
- being tired all the time;
- losing your sense of humour;
- going into work early;
- experiencing a lack of capacity for change or for learning anything new.

This is not an exhaustive list and you may be wondering if there is anything you can do about it. The short answer is yes, but you have some questions to answer first.

## ARE YOU REALLY SHORT OF TIME OR ARE YOU JUST SPENDING IT UNWISELY?

Before you declare that you have too much to do or that there are not enough hours in the day, think what you would say to somebody who does not have enough money or if you ran out of money yourself. This analogy with money and time is not as daft as it sounds; people say 'time is money'. You need to spend your money wisely if you want to buy everything you need. In a similar way, if you want to accomplish everything you want to do, you need to spend your time wisely.

Taking the money analogy a little further, here is what most people would do about not having enough money.

1. Borrow, hoping to pay it off later, but there may be interest to be paid.
2. Economise by finding cheaper alternatives, cutting some things out or by being creative.
3. Look for ways to earn more money.

IF YOU CAN'T REACH THEM YOU CAN'T TEACH THEM

Which would you regard as the best long-term solution or which one would you advise your best friend to do? My guess is that you would choose the most sensible, that of economising and being creative. Number 1 is just storing up trouble for later and number 3 will need more time!

## WHAT DO YOU DO IF YOU DO NOT HAVE ENOUGH TIME?

Here is what people do when they are short of time.

1. Find more hours in the day. You could cut back on sleep since you were not sleeping that well anyway! Perhaps work during lunch to make more time available for work.
2. Multi-task; do more than one thing at once. But how well and how much stress does this involve just keeping track of everything?
3. Stop doing something; plan better or share the task to make time savings.
4. Work quicker but this may involve lowering standards or cutting corners.

So which would you recommend doing? Options 1, 2 and 4 all lead down the same path. They are a little like 1 and 3 in the previous list, and do not actually tackle the root cause or problem. Being stressed, not sleeping, dashing and rushing is not good for you or the quality of your work.

You know you should be doing number 3 in the list above: stop doing something or share the task. I would add that you need to be honest with yourself too; just like with money, acknowledge when you have not got enough. If the solution to managing your time was as easy as being told what to do and then doing it, you would have done it by now.

The question is how can you move from knowing what you should be doing to actually doing it? Many people who seek this answer turn to life coaches or look outside of themselves. Many have such a profound experience that it changes them forever and others just do it, just make the change as if it were as easy as flicking on a switch. There is a realisation that must occur for there to be the will, the motivation or energy to change. I think we would all agree that if we do not have enough time then we should stop doing something, plan better or share the task in order to save time.

## Is 'not enough time' a universal standard?

An important question: is your 'not enough time' the same as mine, or anyone else's? I know people who take all day to do something that others can do in half the time yet they complain of not having enough time. I would suggest 'not enough time' is a variable. There are three variables in the NET equation:

1. the task;
2. the resources at hand;
3. the person.

To see how these three affect the equation, consider preparing, planting and harvesting a field. Bear in mind this is much like teachers who build learning relationships, teach and then celebrate learning.

## 1. THE TASK

The task is fixed; there are no obvious shortcuts. You cannot plant until you have prepared the field and you cannot harvest until the crop has reached maturity. This should be a fixed aspect of the equation (I am focusing on the task and not how long each aspect takes). If, however, the task includes unnecessary activities then savings can be made. If you have not decided what crop will be planted before starting then time can be wasted while the decision is made. You may also be too early or late in preparing the field.

## 2. THE RESOURCES AT HAND

The resources at hand is a double variable because it also depends on the person carrying out the task. One person may need something another does not. Having a tractor to prepare the land, plant and harvest the crop would save time. A tractor would be an excellent resource to have to help in the NET equation. What if the person who you have asked to carry out the task cannot drive a tractor or the tractor needs repair? Now the resource is no longer of such value. You may invest in training and maintenance but this could be a long-term payback strategy.

## 3. THE PERSON

The person who will undertake the task is most certainly a variable. We know people who are more diligent, more creative or more industrious than others. Being the right person for the job is essential if you are going to balance the NET equation.

# It's not all your fault

The NET outcome is not just a factor of the individual. Because there are three factors involved in the NET equation you are not entirely responsible for not having enough time. You have the same amount of time in a day as everyone else and the same number of days in a year. How many years you have can be affected by how well you look after yourself and that includes managing your time correctly to avoid unnecessary stress.

Sometimes a resource may let you down or become unavailable or a 'deadline' may move forward. These are examples of influences that may be out of your control. What you can control, however, is how you respond to them to ensure the NET equation remains balanced.

## EXPLORING THE THREE NET FACTORS

By exploring the three NET factors you will begin to see how you can make decisions to balance the equation.

1. **The task.** How interesting, urgent or important you consider the task influences the time you spend on it. It is the pauses, the distractions or time off-task that prolong completing the task. Your level of engagement will affect the time it takes to complete and it works both ways: too engrossed and you may put in more time than necessary; little interest may mean you spend too little time on the task. A poorly completed task may have to be done again. We can write this as:

$$\text{Task} \times \text{engagement factor} = \text{Task time (Tt)}$$

2. **The resources at hand.** Along with those resources that are physical or technological in nature you are also a resource implication of the NET equation. A resource can also be a team of people, their level of enthusiasm or a sum of money. The level of resource you need may not be available and this can unbalance the equation. You know about training and skill requirements and that time needs to be allocated to these areas. The problem is that often they are not and you may be expected to learn on the job. The level of resources available has an influence on how motivated you are. The level of motivation to achieve something is also influenced by how challenging something is. Learning a new skill can be motivating and help in engagement; doing something too often and without challenge can demotivate people. Getting the balance right is important in NET calculations. We can write this as:

$$\text{Resource} \times \text{training time} = \text{Resource time (Rt)}$$

3. **The person.** It should be obvious now that *you* are involved in all three aspects of NET. This gives you considerable scope for balancing the equation. You should be able to see that there are some decisions you should make before allowing the NET equation to get out of hand. This is the secret of time management. You must take a series of decisions and make reasoned compromises with others in order to manage time effectively and avoid you experiencing NET. Stephen Covey says that time management *'is really a misnomer – the challenge is not to manage time, but to manage ourselves'* (Covey, 2004, p 150).

$$\text{NET} = \text{Task} \times \text{Person} \times \text{Resources}$$

which can be written as

$$\text{NET} = \text{T} \times \text{P} \times \text{R}$$

We have developed this further into:

$$\text{NET} = (\text{Task and engagement}) \times \text{Person} \times (\text{Resources and training time})$$

$$\textbf{NET} = \textbf{Tt} \times \textbf{P} \times \textbf{Rt}$$

Your engagement level, your personal circumstances and what experience/training you have and need are all involved in balancing the NET equation. This gives you a number of options other than finding more time.

## DECISIONS AND COMPROMISES

I have explained we all have the same number of hours in a day and that to do more you have to make a few decisions. Here are the key decisions in the secret to time management.

- Find more working hours in the day.
- Multi-task; do more than one thing at once.
- Stop doing something.
- Work quicker, be more efficient in what you do and how you do it – this could mean better resources or more resources and this includes other people and their time.

A piece of good advice is to avoid procrastination. Making decisions and taking action in a timely manner is important. Time is of no lesser or greater value according to how close it is to the deadline. An hour spent on the task on day one is of the same length as one on the penultimate day. You may do more on the penultimate day but that is only because you are running out of time! If you understand this then you are well on the way to avoiding NET. If you change behaviours you have every chance of solving the NET equation; it should be reassuring that the solution is in your hands. This brings us back to the questions you have to ask yourself and the decisions you have to make in order to manage your time wisely and balance the NET equation.

## NET BALANCING QUESTIONS

The following questions will help guide you in balancing the NET equation. They should be your go-to list whenever you are feeling that you do not have enough time. Ask yourself regularly:

- Do I have to do this task?
- Should I delegate this task?
- Is this a task I am qualified in doing?
- Will I be fully engaged in accomplishing this task?
- Have I the resources at my disposal to accomplish this task?
- Could anyone else accomplish this task better than I could?
- What am I avoiding doing by attempting this task?
- What percentage of my working time will this task require and is it proportionally acceptable given the returns expected?
- What should I stop doing in order to accommodate the new task?
- Is it time to ask for help?

- Do others really know how much I have on at the moment and who do I need to keep informed of my workload?
- Is this a realistic expectation/situation?
- Are there any resources available to me that could save time and help accomplish the task sooner and to the expected standard?
- Do my expectations exceed the expected standards or outcomes (am I trying to do too much)?
- Does this task need to be done now or at all?
- What tasks will soon come to completion and what time will this release?
- Is this a task I am suited to?
- How much time will I allocate to the task?
- How will I monitor or record the time spent on the task so I am alerted to possible problems?
- Where is this task in my hierarchy of urgent/important?

You may develop a simple flowchart to help you to ask the questions most relevant to you in a suitable order. For example, you may not be able to delegate tasks and so asking this question is irrelevant. In such a case it may be more appropriate to ask: *'Do others really know how much I have on at the moment?'* It is common to assume they do and often they do not. This may lead to the important question: *'What should I stop doing in order to accommodate the new task?'*

## WHY TRY TO BALANCE NET?

Balancing the NET equation is important for a number of reasons.

First, you work best when you are refreshed, when not under stress or in a conflict situation, just like learning! Borrowing time from family can cause you conflict and borrowing it from social or leisure time can cause you stress and anxiety. Being tired can mean you make mistakes. Rectifying mistakes takes more of your time.

Second, being at your best means working more objectively and making better decisions, which ultimately leads to improved efficiency and a better outcome all round. When you are at your best you are more objective and less prone to irrational actions or behaviours.

Finally, a measure of how well you are doing at balancing the NET equation is your degree of happiness, the type of happiness which is reflected in how content you are and the quality of your life. When you believe you have a good quality of life you are meeting some of your basic needs and, guess what, our learning needs are the same as our working needs, the only change is the context and therefore the specific working-related requirements. In asking *'Do you have a quality life?'* Barbara Prashnig says, *'It is important to understanding that maintaining the quality of our lives is so vital that for many of us it can become a matter of life and death'* (Prashnig, 2008, p 247). Dramatic you may think but it underlines why we need to understand and manage our own needs and why as teachers we need to be mindful about the needs of those we teach.

# NET and learning needs

Not unexpectedly you will ultimately return to learning needs in the context of time management. Here are the four needs and how they relate to time management.

- **Power** – having a voice and being able to influence decisions about the things that affect you including the tasks you are asked to be involved in, your responsibilities and the expectations placed on you.
- **Belonging** – having a sense of purpose, being part of a team, trusted, given responsibility, acknowledged for what you achieve and the efforts you are making.
- **Choice** – being able to have control over your work–life balance. Being without guilt over the choices and decisions you make.
- **Fun** – being engaged, having positive relationships, having objectivity, achieving balance, ability to maintain a perspective.

The learning needs acronym 'please be child friendly' can easily be adapted in NET terms to be 'please be *colleague* friendly'. If you are in a leadership role, perhaps even part of a small team, try using PBCF in your interactions with those you are involved with. It works.

## ❖ Reflective task

This is an opportunity for you to review your NET equation experiences. Remember to be honest with yourself. Marking or writing reports while watching TV takes longer than just writing reports or marking. Doing two contrasting things at the same time can detract from the pleasure and sense of achievement you gain from doing them individually.

- Think of an occasion when you felt you did not have enough time.

- Reflect on how you felt using PBCF to identify key emotions.

- Describe your response to the situation and the outcome. Did you suffer stress or anxiety, were you motivated? Was the outcome what you had hoped for?

- Consider each of the NET balancing questions and ask yourself if any would have balanced the equation had you taken note of the answers and actioned them.

Note: Write in a personal journal or in the notes section at the end of the chapter.

IF YOU CAN'T REACH THEM YOU CAN'T TEACH THEM

# Closing comment

For you to be able to balance the NET equation will be a developmental process. Not every occurrence will have the same unbalancing factors nor will you be able to balance every occurrence. When NET remains unbalanced you will have to acknowledge the impact on you and take remedial action when you can. Look after yourself so you can look after your pupils.

## References and further reading

**Covey, S R (2004)** *The 7 Habits of Highly Effective People*. **London: Simon & Schuster.**

Stephen Covey's book is a well-respected book on management. The chapter 'Principles of Personal Management' covers what he refers to as **habit 3** that looks at time management. He also covers Eisenhower's principle, referred to as *'the time management matrix'*.

**Eisenhower.me (nd)** *Introducing the Eisenhower Matrix*. **[online] Available at: www.eisenhower. me/eisenhower-matrix/ (accessed 1 November 2020).**

**Halford, S G (2009)** *Be a Shortcut: The Secret Fast Track to Business Success*. **Hoboken, New Jersey: John Wiley & Sons Inc.**

A really useful read on building your support team is by Scott G Halford. Although it is promoted as the secret to business success it covers a lot of aspects relevant to teaching.

**Prashnig, B (2008)** *The Power of Diversity*. **3rd ed. Stafford: Network Educational Press Ltd.**

## QR link

IF YOU CAN'T REACH THEM YOU CAN'T TEACH THEM

# 11. JOHN'S 12 RULES

## Teachers are learners

My teacher training course involved both my subject specialism and the theoretical and practical aspects of teaching and lasted three years plus a probationary year. It was a good grounding, but I have said that to be a teacher you must remain a lifelong learner and in doing so you should be open to advice and ideas. Sometimes you learn without really knowing it; that was the case with me and John's 12 rules.

When I started teaching I made a friend in the department who became my mentor, and he took me under his wing. This chapter is about what I learnt from my friend John about teaching and life that made a significant impact on me as a teacher and a person. I hope you get as much from his sage advice as I did.

First, something my dad used to say to me: '*Anyone can get it right the first time; it takes a craftsman to put it right when it goes wrong.*' I think that when we can do something, when we have no need to struggle, we don't really dig deep in terms of developing our understanding. It is only when things go wrong that we gain both insight and a deeper understanding. The caveat is that you must be willing and able to make the effort.

As a young teacher I was both organised and relaxed in the classroom and had a natural affinity with the students I was teaching. I faced no real challenges in terms of behaviour from my pupils. The love of my subject and my enthusiasm, two essential elements in teaching, carried me through any challenges – and my pupils with me.

It was not until some 12 years later when I had moved from my first school to a rural comprehensive and then to a town-centre school that I was professionally challenged. I had to dig deep, I had to find strategies and approaches that worked with pupils who had different experiences and challenges in their lives from those I had taught previously. That is when John's guidance and advice came to the fore. I recognised in my approach the things John had taught me and their value in understanding and managing learning needs: I refer to these as 'John's 12 rules'.

## John's 12 rules

First, there are actually 13; but more of that later! Here are John's 12 rules presented to you as they were often said by John and without interpretation.

1. Set your stall out and be ready before you make a start.
2. If you are going to pick something up, know where you are going to put it down.
3. There is no point in struggling; don't make things difficult for yourself.
4. A blunt tool is dangerous.
5. Always ask questions to elicit the least number of responses.
6. Always work out what you want to know before you ask the question.
7. Just because it's broken doesn't mean it cannot be mended.
8. Using or having something is not the same as owning it; you are just looking after it.
9. A lesson has a beginning, middle and an end when you are leading it; at other times let the students get on with it.
10. When you have got it organised, somebody else will use it.
11. Get it home first and then decide what you are going to do with it.
12. Always have a project on the go.

If you think about them and relate them to your experiences as a teacher, some are common sense. However, if you think about them in terms of the context of this book and what I have said about building learning relationships, PBCF and mindful learning and teaching, you will begin to see the depth to these rules and their value for your teaching.

## THE RULES EXPLAINED

### Rule 1: Set your stall out and be ready before you make a start

Rule 1 is a planning rule and it can apply to any aspect of teaching from resources to the environment in which you teach. Pre-empting problems and having things at hand for when they are needed makes for good lessons. In lesson planning, Rule 1 involves planning the beginning, middle and end of a lesson (see Rule 9) in a way that recognises learning needs.

- At the beginning – belonging and choice (and fun).
- In the middle – power and choice (and fun).
- At the end – power and fun by recognising and celebrating achievement.

### Rule 2: If you are going to pick something up, know where you are going to put it down

This is a rule about making a commitment, about doing what you say you are going to do and ensuring consistency; an essential element of building learning relationships and building trust with your pupils. This is one of the practical steps of building a sense of belonging as well as learning about the consequences of the choices you make.

### Rule 3: There is no point in struggling: don't make things difficult for yourself

If something is not working then change it or do it differently. Sometimes you need to step back and look at learning from the learner's perspective once again. If you are struggling to teach a group then you must stop and ask why. If the class or individual pupil behaviour is not as it was then are you no longer meeting their learning needs?

### Rule 4: A blunt tool is dangerous

It's true you have to put far more effort into cutting with a blunt tool than sharp ones. You stand a greater chance of hurting yourself than in cutting cleanly. You need to look after and sharpen your tools to make them effective. In teaching this involves creating a sense of belonging as well as being organised.

The process of being organised means listening to people and considering options or choices that can or need to be made. You are giving people a voice, meeting their need for power.

A learner who does not know what they are doing or the consequences of their choices makes teaching very difficult. In my experience they take up a great deal of your time and energy and make little progress. It important that you create an inclusive learning environment and recognise individuals' needs by allowing them to express themselves in a constructive way. Like a blunt tool that needs time spent on it to sharpen it, you may have to spend time helping pupils find the right way to express themselves.

## Rule 5: Always ask questions to elicit the least number of responses

The level of energy in a class is important; get it wrong and you have chaos. You can control the energy level by what you say and how you act. Lots of students shouting 'yes' or putting up their hands can mean you miss a great deal of important information on which to base your teaching and relationships. Asking a question that has multiple responses such as '*Who needs pens, paper or textbooks?*' will not help you easily work out exactly what is needed and will only add to the confusion and delay in getting pupils on task. See Rule 6.

## Rule 6: Always work out what you want to know before you ask the question

An obvious one you may think, but be careful. For example, when checking who has what, asking who has not got a pencil rather than who has a pencil produces far fewer responses and is more manageable (see also Rule 5). More to the point, through your phrasing you can emphasise what you want to know in order to include pupils rather than underlining their exclusion (mindful teaching). There is that sense of belonging again.

I have known teachers be surprised by the answers to questions on examination papers. Instead of mocking the student or laughing at their answer, you should look carefully at the question. When preparing tests or exploring pupil understanding, it is always best to start with the answer you want and work out a question that will show you if the student understands or not.

## Rule 7: Just because it's broken doesn't mean it cannot be mended

This is as much about relationships and reputations as it is about anything else. Labelling students is seductive but labels stick and can be determining (see Chapter 8). They can influence how you approach or deal with people before you get to know them. There is also a link to achievement, especially if you consider that many of the algorithms used to predict future performance or targets are based on prior performance or attainment. Always be willing to offer a fresh start, a new beginning and keep an open mind.

## Rule 8: Using or having something is not the same as owning it: you are just looking after it

Ownership versus stewardship is an interesting concept: can we really ever own something or are we just looking after it? If we are looking after it then there is a sense of responsibility that comes with ownership, especially when it comes to handing things over or relinquishing an idea in favour of something else. Ownership tugs at our beliefs and our values, both things we should often visit and re-evaluate. Borrowing something has a different set of responsibilities attached to it. If you borrow an idea you should be careful not to corrupt it for your own purpose. If you borrow a resource you should ensure it is returned when agreed and in the same condition. There is a lot of conflict that can erupt from borrowing in education if the rules are not clear, especially among pupils. Borrowing also helps develop a sense of responsibility in your pupils.

In terms of teaching you play only a temporary part in the development and the learning of your pupils so you have a responsibility to do no harm, to not put them off learning.

## Rule 9: A lesson has a beginning, middle and an end when you are leading it: at other times let the students get on with it

In learning and teaching, observing pupils is as important as your explanations, prompts or feedforward. The temptation is to be always leading a lesson from the front, to be beating some mythical drum in time with your lesson plan. Pupils benefit from being given time to practise or explore something that is new to them.

Standing back, observing and judging what mistakes are made by your pupils in order to support and encourage learning is both important and at times difficult. I was once told, '*It's not how hard you work that counts; it's how hard your pupils work*'. Walking around the class and observing is as important as asking questions or directing the lesson. Learn to watch body language and you will get to see who understands and who needs help. Remember too that we learn from our mistakes so let your students make a few. If you are meeting their learning needs they will feel comfortable enough to make a few; if not they will be reluctant and will hide what they can.

## Rule 10: When you have got it organised, somebody else will use it

Sometimes you wait for others to initiate a change or introduce an idea and sometimes if you ask to do something you get given all sorts of reasons why you cannot do it. This can be limiting in a number of ways. How do you learn if you do not try something new now and then? Showing initiative is no bad thing and if there is an environment that encourages it, so much the better. PBCF is so important in implementing this rule. Creating the right learning environment will encourage your pupils to engage in learning and helps build learning relationships. In teaching, ideas soon become adopted once they are introduced; it just needs somebody to get the ball rolling. If you are passionate about something get on and do it and if somebody else makes use of it then take it as a compliment.

## Personal reflection

I remember spending part of my holiday fitting out my school workshop; I had been suggesting it needed doing but received little encouragement or help. Things sort of worked, but there was no system that the students could easily use to access resources. Over a holiday I got on with sorting it out. On returning to school I took John into the workshop to show him the results of my efforts, proudly opening up a cupboard I had built for all the silversmith tools. These had been scattered about and I had polished and mounted each one in a cupboard ready for use. When I opened it there was one missing. I could not believe it, but then we heard the tap, tap, tapping of a planishing hammer on metal. Looking around the corner we saw another teacher using it to make a copper bracelet. I felt rather peeved but then Rule 8 and Rule 10 both came to mind!

## Rule 11: Get it home first and then decide what you are going to do with it

It's easy to think about this rule if we talk about being offered something but think of it instead as accepting a challenge. Be objective when deciding what to do, take time to listen and to cogitate before making a decision or taking an action. The challenge could be teaching a difficult class, learning something new or helping a colleague. There are plenty of challenges in education; you do not have to go looking for them.

There is a caveat, however, about your capacity to take on something new (see Chapter 10). You have to realise you cannot do everything nor can you give everything you do 100 per cent of your time, energy or effort. It just does not add up! Remember you can take something home and make a decision to do nothing with it, not ignore it but make a firm decision on a suitable course of action.

Another interpretation of this rule is don't turn your back on somebody who needs help. This includes pupils and colleagues and occasionally parents too.

## Rule 12: Always have a project on the go

This is a very important rule in teaching. I have mentioned the importance of projects earlier on in terms of always being a learner. What projects can you as a teacher take on? When I started teaching, John had an old 1930s motorcar chassis at the back of his workshop; it was one of his 'projects'. It got the attention of many of his pupils and in part that is the aim of having a project; it is something to talk about and brings people into your sphere of influence. This is something you can respond to or not, build a relationship based on a common interest or shun people away and keep it to yourself. As a teacher or leader you need to find ways of drawing students into your sphere of influence.

Unfortunately, John died before this particular project got finished; he was at it for at least 35 years. Over that time it progressed from more than just a chassis of a 1936 Triumph Gloria to something resembling a collection of parts. Not all the parts, you understand, but more than he started with. I can recall numerous adventures as we went looking for bits and pieces. I could not let Gloria go when John died and so now she is one of my projects and I am fully implementing rules 7, 8 and 11! (See Figure 11. 1.)

**Figure 11.1 Gloria in her present state with me, still a work in progress. As John would say, 'All will be achieved in the fullness of time' but he never said by who**!

## MORE ABOUT PROJECTS

A project does not have to be a physical item; it can be a skill or indeed anything that keeps you in the mindset of a learner and gives you an opportunity to meet and work with other people. Remember the poster on how to learn anything and the seven steps (Figure 5.4)? Each step is also part of taking on a project.

- Get real.
- Make a lifestyle change.
- Use technology.
- Dive in and get involved.
- See learning as a gateway.
- Make new friends.
- Don't worry about mistakes.

## The update: Rule 13

There was a thirteenth rule too, one I was initially sure John did not know about but was used by others who knew John: If you don't know what to do with something, give it to John.

When John died he had four lawnmowers and no grass to mow and a shed full of other people's projects as well as his own. John also had some very good close friends including past pupils, teachers and fellow project devotees. I like to think that this was down to Rule 13.

The more I visit these rules I have begun to believe John knew of Rule 13. Perhaps it should be written as: Always be approachable, turn nobody away and always help if and when you can. There is a significant responsibility in being a teacher and it is expressed in no better way than in Rule 13.

Rule 13 is also about listening; that is why it is part of PBCF. Listening in teaching is also about paying attention because you never know when and how the request for help is going to be made. It may be the student who lingers at the end of a lesson or the one that gives you a hard time throughout the lesson. It may be the one who says '*Hi*' in the playground or in a lunch queue, or the one that constantly forgets their pen, tie, books, PE kit or whatever. Remember, actions can speak louder than words.

Rule 13 can be demonstrated by how you end the conversation as well as the fact that you accepted the approach in the first place. The conversation can end with a reassurance that you are also responsible for the learning and that you will do your part in the next lesson so long as they come along prepared to have a go and not give up. Saying '*Thank you for helping me in understanding what it is you have learnt today and the challenges and what I need to plan for in our next lesson*' certainly applies Rule 13, and '*I look forward to seeing how well you do tod*' goes a long way in PBCF terms because you have listened and not rejected your pupil's approach.

People often expose themselves to a greater degree when they need help and acknowledge that help than at any other time. We are vulnerable at this stage and need to feel safe with those we turn to for help.

PBCF is a critical part of creating both the environment and the relationships that allow you to help others, to be a teacher in the best sense of the word. A teacher not just of subjects, but of people, and willing to learn yourself.

There you have them, John's 12 rules; I hope you find time to reflect on them and ways of building them into your teaching if you are not already doing so.

**❖ Reflective task**

Take one or more rules over the course of a term and make a note of how they have applied to your teaching. If you don't have any projects on the go then I would recommend you start with Rule 12.

**QR link**

IF YOU CAN'T REACH THEM YOU CAN'T TEACH THEM

# 12. LEARNING INTELLIGENCE

## Introduction

This chapter is really where my current learning journey started after leaving the classroom. I have had the opportunity to go exploring the education landscape and to find an answer to a question that had been with me since I started teaching: Why do some pupils struggle to learn in one subject or with one teacher and not with another?

Up to this point, through PBCF, I have provided a narrative that covers part of the answer. In Chapter 6 on mindful learning I showed that teacher approach can influence pupil engagement. In Chapter 8 on the dangers of labelling pupils I explained how labels can set up self-beliefs and can limit pupil effort and engagement. The learning map in Chapter 9 showed how past experiences can influence future efforts and self-beliefs about learning. The underlying issue, building effective learning relationships, brings all these elements together. After all, if you can't reach them you can't teach them – but I believe there is something else involved in successful learning too. There is a second narrative needed in order to complete the answer to my question.

# What makes successful learners?

The teacher has a key role in creating a supportive and inclusive learning environment by building effective learning relationships. The reason for this is that where the learning environment meets the needs of the pupil then they are more likely to be successful learners and reach their potential. Not all pupils experience such environments while at school. Some pupils do not begin to realise their potential until leaving school or until something changes that affects their learning environment or them as learners.

My observations as a teacher, as a coach and mentor as well as a parent, have shown me that there are also learners who are able to learn successfully no matter what environment they find themselves in. What if anything is it that is different about these learners, what marks them out as a successful learning hero able to learn in any environment or under any challenge? I have found that they all exhibit one ability and that is an ability to manage their learning environment.

Successful learners recognise when learning needs are not being met and the impact this has on their learning. This recognition is not always formally recognised; it can be more an instinct that they follow. Unlike some learners who lack such agency, they can adapt their learning strategies to make up for things missing in their learning environment without self-labelling or losing motivation. My belief is that such learners approach learning as a problem-solving activity. In doing so they learn certain skills, adopt certain behaviours, have an identifiable attitude to learning and possess a set of attributes that allows them to overcome environmental learning limitations.

# Developing the learning intelligence concept

In looking for a way of describing this I looked for similar terms that are used to define learning abilities or how clever pupils are (intelligence). The traditional IQ and, more recently, EQ, are two terms I have explored along with Howard Gardner's theory of multiple intelligences.

## INTELLIGENCE QUOTIENT

My starting point for finding a suitable term for an ability to manage the learning environment was IQ, also known as general intelligence (G). Used as a measure of intelligence and achieved by testing, IQ is the most recognised measure of intelligence. IQ has been held up as a measure of a person's ability to learn for a long time, although history suggests this was not the intended use. Today IQ is not seen as the predictor of success in life it was once thought to be. An extract from the *History of IQ Tests* (123test.com, nd) tells the story:

---

*The first modern intelligence test in IQ history was developed in 1904, by Alfred Binet (1857-1911) and Theodore Simon (1873-1961). The French Ministry of Education asked these researchers to develop a test that would allow for distinguishing mentally retarded children from normally intelligent, but lazy children. The result was the Simon-Binet IQ test. This IQ test consists of several components such as logical reasoning, finding rhyming words and naming objects.*

*The score for the IQ test in combination with a child's age, provides information on the intellectual development of the child: is the child ahead of or lagging other children? The IQ was calculated as (mental age/chronological age) × 100.*

Binet thought the test limited and could not truly quantify intelligence, believing that intelligence was influenced by a number of factors. He also thought that it changes over time and that a child's background needs to be taken into account when making comparisons. Binet developed his questions based on areas not directly taught in schools and included problem-solving skills, an aspect of learning that I recognise as very much managing your learning environment.

Like many theories and ideas about learning and intelligence they can be put to use for purposes they were never intended for. When the test was adapted by Lewis Terman at Stanford University in the United States to produce a single score (IQ) it became the Stanford-Binet Intelligence Test. An IQ score has since been seen as a measure of intelligence and used in a variety of selection processes. The term intelligence can be applied to the process of learning as in Binet's original brief and therefore is relevant in defining the ability to manage your learning environment.

## EMOTIONAL INTELLIGENCE

Emotions are a key part of learning, something building effective learning relationships is based on as well as your understanding of the impact of PBCF on how pupils feel about learning. Emotional intelligence (EQ) is seen as the ability to recognise and manage your own emotions as well as those of others. It has been suggested by Daniel Goleman that it is a better predictor of an individual's future success than IQ.

*The abilities that set stars apart from average at work cover the emotional intelligence spectrum: self-awareness, self-management, empathy, and social effectiveness.*

**(Goleman, 2004, np)**

This is understandable because few people become successful without the help of others and being able to recognise and support the emotional condition of others helps in building strong and effective teams.

Unlike IQ there is no scale for emotional intelligence, but three skills are often recognised as being part of EQ and are observable through behaviour. These skills are:

- an ability to identify and describe or name your own emotions at any given time;
- an ability to understand and apply emotional influences to your thinking and actions;
- an ability to manage your emotions and where necessary help others to do the same.

People often form part of the learning environment, be it teachers or peers, so being emotionally aware is an attribute that can be used to manage the learning environment.

IF YOU CAN'T REACH THEM YOU CAN'T TEACH THEM

Although his writing focuses on work and career-based explanations and examples, Daniel Goleman believes that emotional skills can be taught and developed. Emotions are a key part of learning and being able to develop and apply them to situations gives some weight to the idea that you can also develop your learning intelligence.

## MULTIPLE INTELLIGENCES

In his theory of multiple intelligences (MI), Howard Gardner claims intelligence is more than one thing and does not define your fate nor can you assess intelligence through a pencil and paper test. His theory is based on a range of research including his definition of intelligence:

*An intelligence is the biopsychological potential to process information in certain ways, in order to solve problems or fashion products that are valued in a culture or community.*

(Gardner, 2016, np)

Howard Gardner lists eight intelligences that meet his definition:

1. linguistic;
2. logical-mathematical;
3. spatial;
4. body-kinaesthetic;
5. musical;
6. interpersonal;
7. intrapersonal;
8. naturalistic.

Although he cannot provide any evidence, Gardner is open to the idea of other possible intelligences such as the following:

- existential, asking the big questions, such as why are some people evil or why do we die?
- pedagogical, the teaching of things to others.

As for assessing MI, Gardner's suggestion is to create a rich environment and observe pupils interacting within that environment. Through observation you should be able to determine which intelligences a pupil exhibits. Gardner created a 'spectrum classroom', rich in multiple learning opportunities, for this purpose. Observing pupils in the learning environment is part of being a teacher. What assessments you make because of your observation is based on your focus, what you are looking for. Looking only for compliant behaviour will limit what you discover about a pupil's ability to manage their learning environment.

In terms of education, Gardner is careful to stress that you do not set out to teach to achieve MI; rather you develop a pluralised MI approach to achieve whatever your educational goal or values are. To teach to pass a test only tells you how well you pass a test and does not raise your IQ, improve your EQ or your mindset. This is something you should also be mindful of with learning intelligence (LQ).

I see the idea of LQ sitting comfortably alongside Gardner's list of intelligences and meeting his definition of an intelligence. LQ is both focused on solving problems and about learning.

## LEARNING THEORIES AND LQ

Learning theories are numerous and fall into three main camps.

1. Behaviourism – new behaviours or changes in the way we behave because of an association between stimulus and response.
2. Cognitivism – by thinking about, processing, information we develop understanding and can retain it.
3. Constructivism – your experience of the world allows you to construct your knowledge and understanding.

Learning theories are important because they provide a language to explore learning and a context in which to analyse behaviour. Each type of theory suggests an approach to teaching, a set of behaviours to be encouraged in the pupil and strategies for the teacher. The fact that there are multiple theories suggests we have not yet found the answer or that people learn in different ways. The learning environment that is created as a result of applying any theory to a learning experience has an impact on a pupil's ability to learn. How prepared or able that pupil is in managing that environment affects the outcome.

# A learning narrative

An important aspect in your teaching is about having a story to tell pupils that draws them in. Your personality, your experiences and your passion and enthusiasm for learning are all part of that story.

You need a narrative, a story that brings all the elements together in a way that makes sense and can be related to learning experiences. Early on that narrative was influenced by experience, both from my own learning journey and that of my pupils. Later the narrative was added to by exploring theories of learning styles and of learning preferences. More recently, researching theories of EQ and MI have provided me with more pieces of the jigsaw but not a complete narrative. Cognitive science suggests that there are many pieces, that the narrative is composed of interdisciplinary elements.

Our ability to learn is not just defined by a single general intelligence (IQ) nor through our emotional awareness (EQ) or what learning abilities or intelligences we demonstrate (MI) and the learning preferences we have. It is defined by all of these things as well as the yet-to-be-fully-defined working of the brain, which we are only beginning to understand.

Providing a narrative that will allow you to embrace all these elements and understand how they fit into the learning jigsaw has been my breakthrough. The name I have given this narrative is learning intelligence (LQ) – the ability of the learner to understand and manage their learning environment to meet their learning needs.

# The learning environment

The managed learning environment for you and your pupils is the school. It is not only the location, grounds, buildings, classrooms, facilities, specialised areas and corridors, but also the people who work in and contribute to that environment, the practices, policies, behaviours and social aspects. The movement, noise and energy that comes from pupils, teachers and other staff give the buildings a life and a character. Some revel in such an environment and some feel overwhelmed. Perhaps the fall back in achievement you see in a pupil's performance as they change school or phase in their education can be attributed to their struggle to become familiar with their new surroundings.

LQ is about how a pupil can manage their learning environment or at least understand it and the impact it can have on them as a learner.

Preferences in the way a pupil learns can evolve from early learning experiences and influences. Exposure to any learning environment that is supportive and rewarding can develop in individuals a preference for learning. If learners experience such environments at an early age, then preferences are soon established and will have a significant impact on future learning. In effect as a result of a preference, learners develop learning approaches that favour their progress within that particular environment. Learners can become good at subjects such as music, art or sports because of their earlier success and support within environments that are rich in particular factors.

If you accept that a pupil's approach to learning is affected by their ability to manage their learning environment to meet their learning needs then you are moving away from the idea that you can evaluate pupil ability based only on observed performance. Where observation takes place in a non-supportive environment without evaluating pupils as learners, any assessment will be prone to error. This explains why when you assess a pupil under different conditions, essentially a different environment, you will record different outcomes. Some pupils will excel in coursework and do less well in an examination environment. The idea of ability and that it can be represented on a scale derived from a series of written tests conducted in an environment that some pupils may not be able to manage effectively is brought into question.

## THE SCHOOL ENVIRONMENT

The school buildings play a significant part in pupil learning experience and poor school design can have a negative impact on learning. Factors include crowding, difficult pupil flow, noise, light and temperature. Other than a few fundamental concerns, design in education has for the most part disregarded the impact the learning environment has on a pupil's ability to learn.

In the UK the Department for Education (DfE) has published school design standards that state:

*The School Building Handbooks (Nursery, Primary and Secondary) provide advice and guidance on the planning and design of new school buildings and the standard to which they should conform.*

*They deal with the site, the building, circulation space and playing facilities – all matters which influence the learning environment within which the curriculum is delivered.*

**(DfE, 2020, np)**

Despite the second paragraph of this statement, learning environments often fail to consider anything other than ergonomics and cost. It is left to you the teacher to make the best of what is provided, to turn a space into a rich learning environment.

Pupils have to find a way of dealing with their learning environment if they are to avoid feeling anxious or stressed. A pupil being able to leave one lesson and to arrive at another in the right frame of mind to learn is as important as a good learning relationship and well-planned lessons and resources.

## THE HOME ENVIRONMENT

As a teacher you cannot ignore the impact of the home environment on a pupil's learning experiences. As soon as you set homework you are influencing that pupil's learning outcomes due to the impact of the home environment on their learning opportunities.

Some pupils have better home resources than others, including support for learning. Where the home environment is not conducive to learning, the school environment becomes critically important and so does the ability to manage it effectively to meet learning needs. Where a pupil is not able to manage the school environment but has a supportive home environment, they may benefit from having homework. The home environment may allow them to focus on their learning without the anxiety or stress of school.

## Describing learning intelligence

Research and experience suggest that there are a number of elements that influence how you manage your learning environment and how effective you are in doing so; it is a considered decision based on personal agency, experience and current influences. Ideally you would approach learning as a problem-solving activity and seek a satisfactory learning strategy based on your needs and the learning environment you are in.

Strategies that I have experienced pupils adopt offer a suggestion of the different levels of LQ and the key elements involved.

# STRATEGY 1

· Withdrawing from the learning environment to mitigate any toxic impact on you or your learning.

This would be the case only where a pupil has not been able to regulate their behaviour or is limited in some way in finding a workable solution. For example, a pupil arranges it so they exit (or are asked to leave) the classroom or they withdraw into themselves.

If this is the only strategy adopted and there is no secondary action then this indicates a low level of LQ ability. Adopting a secondary action such as finding an alternative way to learn either with the help of others at a different time or in a different environment or develop personal agency would indicate a higher level of LQ ability.

# STRATEGY 2

· A pupil openly expresses which of their learning needs are not being met.

A pupil recognises what is happening and wants either reassurance or help in identifying a way of mitigating any circumstances that are impacting on their learning. They are expressing a degree of tolerance to the environment. Pupils who opt for this strategy could either be very vocal and needy of you and your time or just require reassurance and a little guidance.

This indicates a developmental level of LQ ability, where a pupil is able to regulate their behaviour, even if for a short period of time, and articulate their needs.

# STRATEGY 3

· A pupil is able to find a way of independently learning even if the environment does not immediately meet their learning needs.

They express their needs and negotiate a way of satisfying them in any situation. Where this is not possible they are able to delay learning and seek an alternative opportunity. Pupils who behave in this way are often referred to as 'independent learners' because they are in control of their learning.

This indicates the highest level of LQ behaviour. A pupil can self-regulate, express their needs, draw on several possible strategies or even defer learning. They do not associate the limitations of the learning environment with their ability to learn.

## Elements in managing the learning environment

I have found four key elements that promote the ability to manage the learning environment:

- skills;
- attributes;
- attitudes;
- behaviours.

For each of the four elements (SAAB) there is a subset of aspects associated with learning which enable you to develop LQ through your teaching (see Figure 12.1). LQ is not a subject to be taught or assessed. LQ is a way of thinking, a state of mind to be developed within an effective learning relationship you have built through PBCF.

# Elements for managing the learning environment

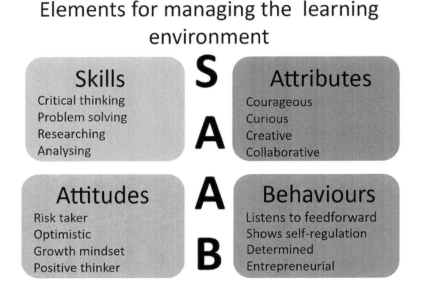

**Figure 12.1 SAAB**

## Learning intelligence and teaching

The importance of LQ for teaching is that it is a narrative for learning theories and ideas and not a fixed or pre-determined premise. For example, in Figure 12.1 you will recognise elements from different ideas and theories about intelligence and learning. In attitudes there is growth mindset, a focus for Dweck's approach which involves 'grit', something mentioned by Goleman as to why EQ is a predictor of success.

In design terms, LQ is a well-written specification for learning, it is not exclusive, and it is not resource-, time- or knowledge-bound. As new theories and ideas appear, they can be set beside LQ to see where they fit, if at all, in the learning narrative. This will give you a sense of scale or importance for the theory or idea and help you determine how much time, energy and resources should be given to it.

IF YOU CAN'T REACH THEM YOU CAN'T TEACH THEM

Teachers have experienced a range of pressures to raise standards and to improve learning and teaching and will continue to face others. LQ prevents you from adopting or falling for the one-size-fits-all approach. You will see examples of this problem from past theories and ideas that have been adopted in education. Such examples include using IQ as the single measure of intelligence, labelling learners according to learning styles, insisting every pupil can achieve anything if they set their mind to it and teaching to develop intelligences.

In the same way as EQ has shown a capacity to predict success in business and relationships, in my own teaching LQ has shown a capacity to provide success in learning. The nature of LQ as a narrative for learning gives a meaningful home to what works in learning and teaching.

I am still working on refining LQ as a narrative; it is after all a learning journey.

## References and further reading

123test.com (nd) *History of IQ Test*. [online] Available at: www.123test.com/history-of-IQ-test/ (accessed 1 November 2020).

Department of Education (DfE) (nd) *School Design Standards*. [online] Available at: www.education-ni.gov.uk/articles/school-design-standards (accessed 1 November 2020).

Gardner, H (2016) *BbWorld Live 2016, Las Vegas, NV*. [online] Available at: https://howardgardner.com/videos/ (accessed 1 November 2020).

Gardner, H (2006) *Multiple Intelligence New Horizons*. New York: Basic Books.

A good introduction to the idea of intelligence going back to Binet and detailing the research and conclusions about the concept of intelligence. Chapter 13, 'The Future', starts with what Howard Gardner describes as the eight phases in the study of intelligence, giving a historical perspective encouraging us to see the many sides or views of intelligence.

Goleman, D (1999) *Working with Emotional Intelligence*. London: Bloomsbury Publishing Ltd.

The observations by Daniel Goleman that led him to declare a **'new yard-stick'** in being able to predict success in a post-education world of work and career echo my observations about success in learning that led to the concept of LQ.

Goleman, D (2014) *Emotional Intelligence*. [online] Available at: www.danielgoleman.info/daniel-goleman-what-predicts-success-its-not-your-iq/ (accessed 1 November 2020).

## USEFUL WEBSITES

Marenus, M (2020) Gardner's Theory of Multiple Intelligences. *Simply Psychology*. [online] Available at: www.simplypsychology.org/multiple-intelligences.html (accessed 1 November 2020).

This is a succinct description of Gardner's Theory of MI written by Michele Marenus.

**Advocating Creativity in Education (2014)** *LQ and the Link to Homework.* **[online] Available at: https://4c3d.wordpress.com/2014/06/08/learning-intelligence-lq-and-the-link-to-homework/ (accessed 1 November 2020).**

This article explores the value of homework in relation to learning and LQ. It discusses how important homework is and whether it could be the antidote to a limiting school environment.

Your notes

IF YOU CAN'T REACH THEM YOU CAN'T TEACH THEM

# INDEX

analytical thinking, 121
anxiety, 8, 11, 13, 15, 54, 91, 126, 138, 195
Aparta, Krystian, 116
approachability, 205–7
attribution theory, 123

Bandura, Albert, 121, 123, 162
behaviourism, 212
behaviours, 29
   and mindful learning and teaching, 148–9
   and Monday mornings, 12
   reflecting on, 6
   self-understanding of, 10
   and Sundays, 10–12
belonging, 55, 59, 64, 67–71, 83, 87, 112, 201–2
   benefits of, 70–1
   educational context, 65
   and emotions, 115
   and friendship, 57
   and fun, 87
   and groups, 124
   and labelling, 173, 176
   and not enough time, 196
   peer groups, 148
   in planning, 101, 102, 107
   and reassurance, 106
Berger, J, 182
Binet, Alfred, 210
boredom, 78, 86, 87, 109, 140
borrowing, and responsibilities, 203

Campbell, Joseph, 104
challenges, 25
   Monday mornings, 12
   relationships, 5–6
   responding to, 14
   Sundays, 10–12
   surviving versus thriving, 6–8
   teaching dynamics, 8–9
   teaching improvement, 16–17
   time management. *See* time management
challenging group, 89–90

change prompts, 20
choice (freedom), 59, 60, 64, 76, 80–1, 109
   benefits of, 84
   broadening approach to learning through, 81–3
   case study, 79–80
   in classroom, 76–8
   decision making, 78–9
   educational context, 65
   importance in assessment, 83–4
   and not enough time, 196
   offers, 79–80, 105
   poor choices, 78
choice theory, 59
class management, 25
co-dependence, 26–7
cognitivism, 212
coin challenge, 135–8
comfort zone, moving out of, 15, 83
commitment, 201
communication, 127
compliance, 16
   and dependent learners, 162–3
   as motivation to learn, 53–4
compliant learners, 147, 163
confident learners, 146–7
consistency, 30
constructivism, 113, 212
continuity, 30
co-operative learners, 169
coping strategies, 6
Covey, Stephen, 193
creative capacity, 41
curriculum, knowledge-based versus
      learning-focused, 163, 164

Davies, Charlotte, 58
defensive triggers, 2
dependent learners
   adaptation to learning environment, 168
   definition of, 118
   disadvantages, 162
   issues related to, 162–3

design process, 110–11, 113–14
  evaluation, 112
  ideas, 112
  learner's perspective, 113
  problem, 111
  questioning, 111–12
  realisation, 112
  solution, 112
  teacher's perspective, 112–13
Dewey, John, 110
differentiation, 118
discipline, and fun, 89–90
disengaged learners, 30, 55, 140, 147, 154
distorted learning transition, 39, 40, 43
Dweck, Carol, 50, 123–4, 181, 183

effort, 124–5
Eisenhower's principle, 189–90
emotional experience, 116
emotional intelligence (EQ), 99–100, 210–11,
    216, 217
emotional needs, 83
emotional state, 126
emotions, 114–15
encouragement, 54
environment. *See* learning environment
'even better if' approach, 3
experience
  experiencing learning, 182
  learning from others' experience, 49
  past experiences, and reluctance, 55–6
external relationship pressures, 38–9

failure, fear of, 48
false beliefs, 54, 154
family label, 176
fear, 48, 114–15
feedback, 2–3
  and defensive triggers, 2
  and relationships, 3
feedforward, 2
  concept of, 3
  thinking process, 3–4
feelings
  exploration of, 9
  and relationships, 14

fixed mindset, 50, 123, 183
flight or fight response, 78–9
freedom. *See* choice (freedom)
friend label, 176
friendship, 106
fun, 59, 61, 64, 85–6, 112
  benefits of, 91
  and discipline, 89–90
  educational context, 65
  forgoing, 86–90
  linking with achievement, 88–9
  and not enough time, 196
  and rewards, 90
  and stress, 90–1
  target-driven culture, impact of, 87–8
  teacher's impact on, 88

Gardner, Howard, 174, 209, 211
Glasser, William, 10, 59, 61, 72, 76
Goldman, Daniel, 99, 211
Goldsmith, Marshall, 2
Goleman, Daniel, 100, 210, 216
government policy, 28–9
growth mindset, 50, 123, 183, 216

Helmstetter, Shad, 126
Hero's Journey. *See* learning journey
hierarchy of needs, 57
*History of IQ Tests*, 209–10
home environment
  and engagement in learning, 56
  and learning intelligence, 214
homework, 82–3
Hughes, David, 41, 56, 74

ideas, experimenting with, 112
independent learners, 35–6, 40, 79,
    157–8, 215
  adaptation to learning environment, 168–9
  definition of, 158
  development of, 169
    Philosophy for Children (P4C),
      169
    teacher guide, 170
  and school environment, 160–2
instinctive response, 49

intelligence quotient (IQ), 209–10, 217
intelligence, definition of, 211

John's 12 rules, 199, 200
   being objective, 204
   belonging and being organised, 201–2
   commitment, 201
   initiatives, 203–4
   labelling, 202
   ownership versus stewardship, 202–3
   preparedness, 202
   projects, 204–5
   questioning strategy, 202
   readiness, 201
   standing back, observing and judging, 203
   struggles, overcoming, 201

Kell, Emma, 8
knowledge-based curriculum, 163, 164

labelling learners, 202
   challenging labels, 177–8
   consequences of, 175–6
   learner perspective, 176
   learning labels, 174
   and PBCF, 177–8
   permanent and temporary labels, 176–7
   reasons for, 173–4
   resistance to, 178
   self-labelling, 175
Langer, Ellen, 143, 151, 153, 154
language, and mindful learning, 149–51
leadership, 8
   leadership teams, 28, 42
   responsibility of, 40–2
learn anything, guide to, 116
learner self-image, 119–20
   focusing points, 121–2
   and labelling, 175
   learner feeling, 126
   learners' influencing factors, 120–1
   view of self, 123–5
learners, successful, 209
learning environment, 14, 115, 166, 203
   artificiality of, 60, 76
   choice in, 76–8

home environment, 56, 214
inclusive, 201, 209
and intelligence quotient (IQ), 209, 210
and learning intelligence (LQ), 213–14
and learning map, 113, 183
and learning needs. *See* learning needs
management elements, 215
as motivation to learn, 50, 52
and multiple intelligence, 211
positive, 10
pupils adaptation, 168–9
and relationship, 24
school environment, 24, 76, 160–2, 183–4
suitability, 118
toxic, 78
learning experiences, 182
learning groups
   compliant learners, 147, 163
   confident learners, 146–7
   disengaged learners, 30, 55, 140, 147, 154
learning heroes, 104–5
learning intelligence
   strategies, 214–16
   and teaching, 6–8
learning intelligence (LQ), 79, 160, 208, 212
   and learning environment, 213
      home environment, 214
      school environment, 213–14
   and learning theories, 212
learning journey, 124, 125
   challenges and possible failures, 107–9
   deciding to try, 106
   demonstration, 110
   embedding learning and resilience, 109
   learning strategy, 107
   making ready, 106
   new learning challenge, 105
   prior knowledge, use of, 105
   reassurance and support from teacher, 106
   reluctance and nervousness, 105
   seeking help, 106–7
   sharing of, 114, 115
   success and rewards of new skill or knowledge, 109
learning labels, 174
learning map, 122, 181–2, 185–6
   analogy, 182

learning map (Cont.)
    drawing, 183
    impact of school environment on, 183–4
    linking topology to learning, 184–5
learning myths, 151–3
learning narrative, 212–13
learning needs, 43, 45–6, 124, 206
    addressing, 61
    belonging, 67–71, *See* belonging
    choice. *See* choice (freedom)
    communication, 127
    consequences of ignoring, 148
    consequences of not being met, 92
    context, 60–1, 65–6
    design process, 110–14
    and engagement in learning. *See* learning,
        engagement in; motivation to learn
    fun. *See* fun
    impacts of being mindful of, 143–6
    influence of, 56–7
    and labels, 177–8
    learner self-image. *See* learner self-image
    learning heroes, 104–5
    learning issues, 114
    learning journey, 105–10, 114
    and learning zone, 58–60
    lesson planning, 99–103
    modelling, 116
    physical and sensory needs, 56–7
    in planning, 131–4
    power. *See* power (voice)
    problem-based learning, 110–11
    strengthening of, 96
learning passports, 97
learning preferences, 81, 183, *See also* choice
learning relationship responsibility ratio graph
    (LRRRG), 31–2, 161
    examples, 32–5
    explanation, 37–8
    impact on, 39–40
    independent learners, 35–6
    realistic and planned, 37
learning relationships, 14–16, 162, 209, *See also*
    learning needs
    balance in, 25

co-dependence, 26–7
context of, 24–5
external pressures, 38–9
and feelings, 14
government responsibility, 28–9
importance of, 5–6, 42–3
learner teacher, 24–5
and lesson planning, 106
and motivation to learn, 53–4
as motivation to learn, 50
parents/carers' responsibility, 28–9
policy, 149
pupil responsibility, 27
school responsibility, 28
teacher responsibility, 27
learning styles, 81, 163–8
learning theories, 212
learning zone, 58–60
learning, engagement in, 46–7, 84, *See also*
    motivation to learn
    and effort, 47
    and experience, 48–50
    and home, 56
learning-focused curriculum, 163, 164
lesson planning, 99–100
    considerations and approaches, 100
    consistency, 99–100
    environment description, 115
    example lesson planning headings
        considerations, 103
        pupils' status, 102
        pupils' previous knowledge and new
            learning, 102–3
        teaching approach, 103
        teaching resources, 103
        unit content, 102
    learning needs management, 101
listening skill, 9

Maslow, Abraham, 57, 58, 61
Mayer, John D, 99
MIC model, 1, 22, 41
mindful learning, 83, 112–13, 141–2
    and behaviours, 148–9
    and language, 149–51

mindful teaching, 83, 112–13, 141, 142–3
    and behaviours, 148–9
    case for, 153–5
mindfulness, 139–40
    approaches, 154–5
    characteristics, 154
mindless learning, 113, 140
mindless teaching, 140–1
mindset theory, 50, 123–4, 183
Monday mornings, 12, 14–16
motivation to learn, 45, 46–7, 50, 121
    compliance, 53–4
    push and pull motivations, 53
    and relationship, 53–4
    reluctance, 55
        past experiences, 55–6
        peer pressure, 55
    rewards, 53–4
    through needs, 51–2
multiple intelligences (MI), 211–12

narrative approach, 212–13
needs, motivation to learn through, 51–2,
        See also learning needs
negative self-talk, 121
NET. See not enough time (NET); not enough
        time (NET) equation
new courses, popularity of, 38
non-compliance, 78, 122, 163
not enough time (NET), 190, 197
    and learning needs, 196
    reasons for, 190–1
    response to, 191
    as universal standard, 191–2
not enough time (NET) equation, 189, 190, 191–2
    balancing, 194–5
        reasons for, 195
    person, 192, 193
    resource, 192, 193
    task, 192, 193

Ofsted, 11, 28
open translation project, 116
organised, being, 201–2
ownership versus stewardship, 202–3

parents/carers' responsibility, 28–9
passion, 121
past experiences, and reluctance, 55–6
pastoral systems, 68
PBCF approach. See learning needs
pedagogy, and dependent learners, 162–3
peer groups, 148
peer pressure, 55
permanent labels, 176–7
Philosophy for Children (P4C), 158, 169
physical needs, 56–7
planning, 131–4, 201
play, and learning, 150–1
poor choices, 78
power (voice), 59, 64, 72, 106
    educational context, 65
    exploration of, 73
    and not enough time, 196
    pupil empowerment, 75
    school context, 73–4
    in teaching and learning, 74
Prashnig, Barbara, 50, 54, 154, 195
preparedness, 202
problem-based learning, 110–11, See also
        design process
problem-solving capabilities, 121
process-oriented praise, 124
procrastination, 194
project-based learning approaches, 106
projects, 204–5
pull motivation, 53
pupil empowerment, 75
pupil learning passports, 97
pupil responsibility, 27
push motivation, 53

questioning, 143–5, 202
questions, asking, 75

Rath, Tom, 124
readiness, 201
reflection, 1, 6, 48–50, 102
    reflection prompts, 20
    template for, 21
relationships. See learning relationships

reluctance, 55, 78
  and learning preference, 82
  past experiences, 55-6
  peer pressure, 55
resilience, 109, 121
responsibility, 205-7
  abdication of, 38
  external relationship pressures, 38-9
  government responsibility, 28-9
  of leadership, 40-2
  for learning relationship, 27, 30-1
  learning relationship responsibility ratio
       graph (LRRRG), 31-2
    examples, 32-5
    explanation, 37-8
    independent learners, 35-6
    realistic and planned, 37
  parents/carers' responsibility, 28-9
  pupil responsibility, 27
  school responsibility, 28
  teachers' responsibility, 27
rewards, 47, 52, 74, 109
  and fun, 90
  as motivation to learn, 53-4
Robinson, Sir Ken, 16, 86
Rowe, Mary, 143

Salovey, Peter, 99
sarcasm, 91
school design standards, 214
school environment, 24, 160-2
  artificiality of, 76
  impact on learning map, 183-4
  and learning intelligence, 213-14
school responsibility, 28
school rules, consistency in application of, 73-4
self-actualisation, 57
self-beliefs, 48-9, 50, 113, 120, 121, 122, 123, 124, 125, 208
self-defeating action, 59
self-esteem, 48
self-image. *See* learner self-image
self-labelling, 175
self-motivated learner, 54
self-talk, 126
sensory needs, 56-7

silences, listening to, 9
spectrum classroom, 211
standards, and learning myths, 152-3
Stanford-Binet Intelligence Test, 210
Stevenson, April, 121
stewardship versus ownership, 202-3
strength, 124-5
stress, 54, 90-1, 126
struggles, overcoming, 201
sub-labels, 176
successful learners, 209
Sundays, 10-12
supportive, being, 205-7
surviving teachers, 6, 8
Sutton Trust, 153

talent, 124-5
target-driven culture, impact on fun, 87-8
Taylor, C, 175
teachers
  beingness, 5
  burnout, 8
  challenges, 13-14
  feelings, exploration of, 9
  as guide, 170
  knowing their pupils, 67-70, 79, 96
  as learners, 199-200
  responsibilities, 27, 160
  surviving category, 6, 8
  taking responsibility, 205-7
  thriving category, 6, 7, 8
  understanding their behaviours, 10
Teachers' Standards, England, 27
teaching
  dynamics of, 8-9
  improvement of, 16-17, 146
  learning groups, 146-7
    complaint learners, 146-7
    confident learners, 146-7
    disengaged learners, 147
  and learning intelligence, 6-8
temporary labels, 176-7
Terman, Lewis, 210
thriving teachers, 6, 7, 8
time management, 17, 188

decisions and compromises, 194
influencing factors, 192–5
and NET. *See* not enough time (NET); not enough
    time (NET) equation
urgent/important matrix, 189–90
Toffler, Alvin, 43
traditional way of target-achieving, 88

urgent/important matrix, 189–90

vocational drive, 13, 17

Weiner, Bernard, 123
well-being, 11
work readiness, 153
work–life balance, 8

Zanshin, 6, 139